FareStart is a non-profit, social entrepreneurial organization in Seattle, Washington, USA.

Through our job placement and training program we provide real solutions to some of our society's most pressing challenges - homelessness, joblessness, poverty and hunger.

Our work is based on three beliefs:

Food is central to our emotional, physical, and economic well-being.

Solutions that provide real value to a community have the best hope of lasting.

People have incredible capacity to change their lives with the right support.

THIS BOOK IS A CELEBRATION OF OUR 25 YEAR JOURNEY.

MEGAN KARCH, CEO

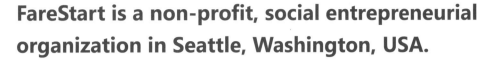

FARESTART

Great Food. Better Lives.

Author: Colin McCaig

Designer: Erica McCaig

Editor: Liberty Munson

© 2016 FareStart

www.farestart.org

Print and color management by iocolor, Seattle

Printed in China by Shenzhen Artron Color Printing LTD

ISBN 978-0-692-61691-8

MEGAN KARCH

Until poverty, hunger, and homelessness are eliminated, we have a responsibility to do more. FareStart alone won't end homelessness, but we are one of the solutions.

FARESTART IS A SPECIAL PLACE.
IT ATTRACTS SPECIAL PEOPLE.

Whether it's the staff and volunteers committing their time, the financial supporters committing their treasures, or the students committing to their lives...
FareStart attracts really special people.

We are fortunate to have so many people drawn to our mission. They are the safeguards that help us not lose our way.

I arrived at FareStart from a different part of the country, and the organization was totally new to me. I was living in the Baltimore area when a search firm called asking if I'd be interested in interviewing with FareStart.

I came to Seattle and met with the staff and volunteers. I could feel their passion and commitment to the mission. On the plane ride home, I decided I'd like to work with them. Barbara Hill became my mentor, and she brought the soul of the organization alive for me. Just by being around her, I knew our number one priority would be culture - keeping the spirit of FareStart alive.

I also knew I had to bring foundation and structure to what we were doing, that we'd need to find a balance between culture and growth. The challenge with bringing structure to growth is figuring out how maintain the essence of who you are.

We are fortunate to have so many people drawn to our mission. They are the safeguards that help us not lose our way.

I look back over my life now, and I see tipping points that shaped who I am.

My mother taught me compassion. She helped me see me that people are complex, that you don't throw anyone away.

I grew up on a farm where school was 45 minutes away. There were no close neighboring houses.

I remember a man called Charlie.

He would stop by our house and help our family - planting peas in our garden, fixing my bike, giving us kids a few of his pennies.

One day, I said to my mother that I wanted to bake cookies and take them to Charlie. When I told her I didn't know where Charlie lived, she explained he was homeless. I didn't even know what "homeless" was. She said some neighbors were allowing him to live on their property but that I could not go visit Charlie. He was allowed to visit us, but I was not allowed to visit him.

I was 10 years old and, with a friend and an indomitable spirit, went searching for Charlie. We found the shack he'd built. But, Charlie was really angry we were there. He told us to go away. I went home upset and talked with my mother about my experience. She explained that Charlie was dealing with challenges and demons in his life - ones I didn't yet understand.

My mother taught me compassion. She helped me see that people are complex, that you don't throw anyone away.

She helped me see that he was still the Charlie I knew even as he struggled with his demons.

Our community cared for Charlie; he ate dinner at our or a neighbor's house, and he was allowed to live in his shack for over 20 years. As I got older, I wanted to understand what the bigger community, our society, was doing about the issue of homelessness.

My family gave me my first sense of belonging and connection.

Over time, I came to understand how to build it for myself. Some of the people walking through the FareStart doors have never had this sense of belonging and community. Some have had it but have lost it along the way. Others had a community they'd built that wasn't leading them in the right direction.

I help others build their new community, their safety net, their connections, and their sense of belonging. We teach our students that they have the ability to rewrite their own stories...to create what they want their lives to be. We help them see that the past informs, but does not dictate, their future.

Some people think of us as solely as a culinary school. That's not who we are. We create a context that helps individuals have a chance to be transformed - to author their own story.

Food and culinary training is a tool to do that. But, we do a lot more than create chefs. We're in the business of creating that right type of support that builds the right type of community. It's amazing to listen to our students when they speak at a graduation.

They say this is more than a training program.
They say this is family.

We all teach each other in different ways. And, I learn so much by what I do here at FareStart. The impact I have on other people helps me see myself in new ways. It helps me remember that I, too, am empowered to write my own story.

This book celebrates 25 years of transformation.

Megan K—

I wanted the opportunity to change who I am for my daughter. To be able to hear her voice every day, and to know that my family is proud of me, makes me proud too.

—Kimberly, 2013 FareStart Graduate

I came to FareStart feeling defeated. I left with courage, confidence, hope. And, a future. Things that I hadn't had in a long time.

—Dan, 2012 FareStart Graduate

  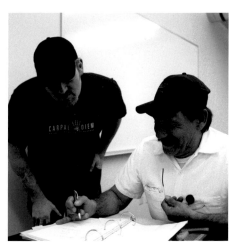

FARESTART JOURNEY

18

FARESTART LOGO

38

FARESTART ORIGIN

66

LEADERSHIP

100

COMMUNITY

128

HOMELESSNESS

172

TRANSFORMING LIVES

214

GUEST CHEF NIGHT

282

POWER OF MANY

352

TIME, TREASURE, & TALENT

414

Recipes

FARESTART JOURNEY

37   Crab Cakes, *FareStart Restaurant*

29   Oregon Bay Shrimp Louie Salad, *FareStart Restaurant*

34   Polenta, *FareStart Restaurant*

FARESTART LOGO

42   Apple Cider Vinaigrette, *FareStart Restaurant*

59   Chef Kim's Marinara Sauce, *Chef Kim Cosway*

55   Citrus, Carrot, Avocado Salad, *Barbara Grace Hill*

45   Lemongrass Chicken Meatballs, *FareStart Catering*

65   Pasta with Marinated Tomatoes, *David Linton*

FARESTART ORIGIN

89   Butterscotch Sauce, *Pastry Chef Nikol Nakamura*

75   Celebration Roast Pastry, *Chef David Lee*

94   Coffee Granita, *Pastry Chef Nikol Nakamura*

93   Coffee Whipped Cream, *Pastry Chef Nikol Nakamura*

72   Common Meal...Soup!, *Chef David Lee*

85   Pumpkin Brown Butter Soup, *FareStart Restaurant*

90   Toasted Coffee Walnuts, *Pastry Chef Nikol Nakamura*

LEADERSHIP

127 Cioppino, *Chef Matt Janke*

112 Flank Steak Küleua, *Cheryl Sesnon*

121 Lemon Caper Aioli, *FareStart Catering*

115 Pecan Chicken with Sour Cream Mustard Sauce, *Cheryl Sesnon*

124 Porcini Mushroom Soup with Truffle Crème, *Chef John Howie*

123 Southwestern Seasoning Mix, *Chef John Howie*

111 Tomato Marmalade, *Cheryl Sesnon*

COMMUNITY

161 Dow-Jay, Ngow-Yok-Soong (Chopped Beef and String Beans), *David Coffey*

166 Salmon Roasted in Butter, *Jennifer Teunon*

155 Striped Seabass, *Chef Joseph E. Jimenez de Jimenez*

149 Tomato Basil Soup, *FareStart Restaurant*

HOMELESSNESS

179 Chef Buck's Tarragon Chicken Salad, *FareStart Restaurant*

211 Fall Greens with Tomato Chervil Vinaigrette, *Chef Lisa Dupar*

212 Fennel Rubbed Steamed Salmon, *Chef Tom Douglas*

190 Simple Vegetarian Corn Chowder, *David Wertheimer*

201 Thai Curry Sea Scallops, *Chef Chris Keff*

TRANSFORMING LIVES

252 Braised Beef, *Chef Robert Spaulding*

224 Chef Gary's Pumpkin Muffins, *FareStart Restaurant*

272 Chef's Special Bing Cherry Salsa, *Chef Don Curtiss*

244 Chocolate Espresso Torte with Cinnamon Hazelnut Crust, *FareStart Restaurant*

223 Corn and Bacon Chowder, *Chef Gary Holler*

265 Fennel, Apple, and Celery Salad, *Chef Matt Janke*

227 Focaccia Bread, *FareStart Restaurant*

266 Hollandaise Sauce, *Chef John Howie*

271 Kaspar's Healthy No Oil Avocado Green Goddess Dressing, *Chef Kaspar Donier*

TRANSFORMING LIVES, *continued*

237 Lemon Couscous, *Chef Thierry Rautureau*

243 Pan Seared Polenta, *Chef Ericka Burke*

247 Peanut Sauce, *FareStart Restaurant*

256 Radicchio-Belgian Endive Mix, *Chef John Howie*

255 Sherry Vinaigrette, *Chef Wayne Johnson*

231 Veal Broth, *Chef Mauro Golmarvi*

280 Veal Sweetbread and Maine Lobster, *Chef Thierry Rautureau*

GUEST CHEF NIGHT

318 Ancho-Chili Rubbed Salmon with Sweet Chili Hollandaise, *Chef John Howie*

333 Baked Gnocchi, *Chef Brendan McGill*

294 Baked Washington Halibut, *Chef Thierry Rautureau*

309 Beef Tenderloin with Corn and Chanterelle Mushrooms, *Chef Ethan Stowell*

339 Butternut Squash Puree, *Chef Robert Spaulding*

335 Creamed Nettles, *Chef Brendan McGill*

302 Fresh Chevre & Pecan Flaxseed Crostini, *Chef Tom Douglas*

290 Grilled Leg of Lamb Moroccan Style, *Chef Thierry Rautureau*

342 Kale, White Bean, and Linguiça Soup, *Chef Amy McCray*

350 Kaspar's Apple Cider Vinaigrette, *Chef Kaspar Donier*

348 Kaspar's Indian Duck Curry, *Chef Kaspar Donier*

317 Lime Cream, *Chef John Howie*

345 Linguiça Sausage, *Chef Amy McCray*

324 Porchetta con Portobello, *Chef Mauro Golmarvi*

301 Roasted Brussels Sprouts, *Chef Tom Douglas*

298 Roasted Cipollini Onions, *Chef Tom Douglas*

314 Roasted Corn Recipe, *Chef John Howie*

315 Southwestern Roasted Corn Mashed Potatoes, *Chef John Howie*

293 Washington Green Asparagus Soup, *Chef Thierry Rautureau*

POWER OF MANY

380   BBQ Base, *Chef John Howie*

358   Blue Cheese Dressing, *Chef John Howie*

371   Blue Cheese, Shrimp and Pear Salad, *Chef John Howie*

404   Chevre Cheese, *Rory Farrow*

384   Kaspar's Northwest Berry Meringue Cake, *Chef Kaspar Donier*

372   Pickled Onion, *Chef Robert Spaulding*

383   Saffron Risotto with Pacific Northwest Fruits De Mar, *Chef Jeff O'Brien*

361   South of the Border Surf and Turf, *Chef Robert Spaulding*

394   Veggie Napoleons, *FareStart Catering*

TIME. TREASURE. & TALENT

450   Aceitunas Andaluces (Marinated Olives), *Jerry Meyer and Nina Zingale*

444   Baked Alaska, *Chef Dimitri Ponomarchuk*

495   Buttermilk Pie, *Gregg Johnson*

477   Christmas Swedish Meatballs, *Andrew and Angela Dodd*

487   Grandma Glotzbach's Oatmeal Cake, *Mary Snapp*

457   Grilled Asparagus with Truffle oil and Grana Parmesan, *Stuart Holmes*

504   Grilled Chipotle Corn, *Craig Russell*

483   Jambalaya, *Mary Snapp*

458   Jicama, Orange and Avocado Salad, *Stuart Holmes*

443   Nuts and Berries Chocolate Martini, *Chef Dimitri Ponomarchuk*

484   Rhubarb and Blueberry Crisp, *Mary Snapp*

437   Roasted Red Pepper Sauce, *FareStart Catering*

435   Salmon and Peas Pasta, *Bill Adamucci*

503   Tangy Asian Noodle Salad, *Craig Russell*

466   The Canlis Salad, *Chris Canlis*

496   Zita's Meat Marinade (Flank Steak), *Gregg Johnson*

"We come to you broken, from all
walks of life... You take us in, and you
nurture us and give us new skills,
confidence, and then, send us out into
the world as these beautiful creatures.

And, I thank you from the
bottom of my heart."

- Devona, Farestart 2010 Graduate

TOMATILLO

Since its inception, FareStart
has produced over 9 million
meals through the
community meals program.

FARES

JOURNE

TART
Y

EVERY PERSON DESERVES THE CHANCE TO CHANGE HIS OR HER LIFE STORY.

Each person's life story is valid. Every path, no matter the turns and hardships, demands respect and compassion. Yet, not everyone has a place where his or her life's journey is welcomed, not everyone has a community where they can learn to honor and shape their own story.

This is especially true for people who have lost their way. Those who are traveling down paths where they risk losing everything they hold as important, including themselves. Whether this starts by a person's choices or forces beyond one's control, these are paths that can lead to invisibility, where finding true north becomes almost impossible.

FARESTART IS ONE OF THE FEW PLACES IN OUR COMMUNITY POISED TO WELCOME AND EMBRACE THE STORIES AND LIVES OF PEOPLE IN NEED, TO HELP THEM TAKE THAT STEP.

At FareStart, each of us is deeply committed to the same ultimate goal - to empower individuals to transform their lives.

This goal has long rallied us, calling a committed group of citizens together to help at-risk individuals. Since our founding, we have always kept our mission in sight, even as we mature beyond what anyone could have imagined or hoped.

"Compassion through food...it's as alive today as it was 25 yea

Our Story

In 1988, David Lee, chef and entrepreneur, recognized a need to serve Seattle's homeless and disadvantaged populations with nutritious and culturally appropriate food. To that end, Lee founded Common Meals (later renamed FareStart), a for-profit business.

1988, David Lee, chef and entrepreneur, recognized a need to serve Seattle's homeless and disadvantaged populations with nutritious and culturally appropriate food.

Lee recognized in those early days that food was an extraordinarily powerful and uniting tool through which individuals could transform their lives. There have been many special moments and milestones since those early days. Over the past 25 years, FareStart has provided opportunities for 8,000 people to transform their lives, while also serving 9 million meals to disadvantaged men, women, and children. **Thank you for helping to make those transformations possible!**

Annual Students Served: 10

Annual Students Served: 75

Young author helps the homeless

Eleven-year-old Nicholas Walker wrote a book about a homeless boy and gave the profits from its sales to Common Meals.

COMMON MEALS
LUNCH BUFFET
MON - FRI 11:00AM - 2:00PM
ONLY $5.95

- Common Meals officially became a non-profit
- Job training began at 1902 2nd Ave
- First Guest Chef Night

- Second ca
  opened: B

Timeline

1987 — **1992** — **1998** — **2000**

- Common Meals founded by Chef David Lee

- Name is changed from Common Meals to FareStart
- Opened first café: Antioch
- Life skills added to training program

DowntownSeattleFORUM

Food Industry Fights Common Enemy

Common Meals: A Joint Effort to Feed the Hungry

The main cours

Annual Meals Produced: 60,000

Annual Meals Produced: 150,000

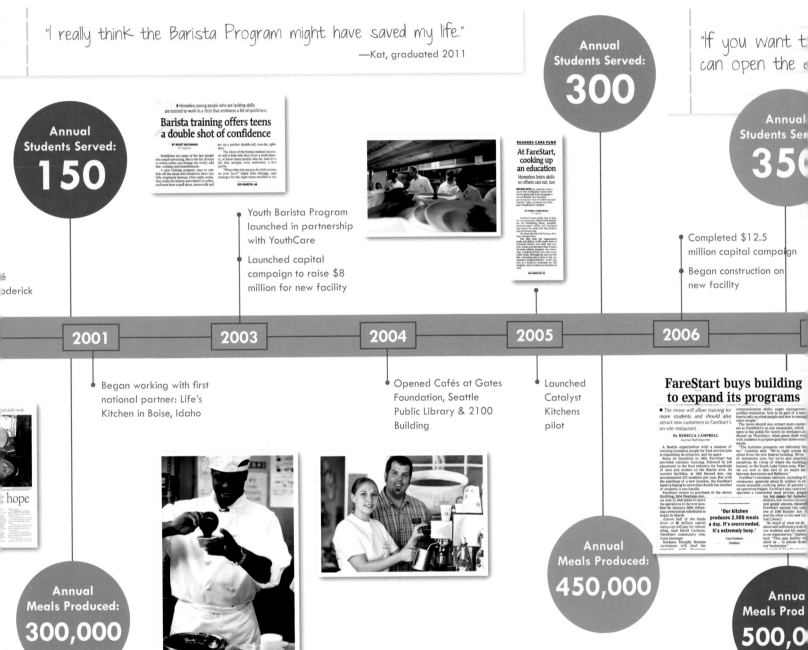

ago. FareStart has stood the test of time. Congratulations to the st

"I really think the Barista Program might have saved my life."

—Kat, graduated 2011

"If you want t
can open the

Annual Students Served: 300

Annual Students Served: 150

Annual Students Ser 350

▶ Homeless young people who are lacking skills
are trained to work in a field that embraces a bit of quirkiness

Barista training offers teens a double shot of confidence

BY WYATT BUCHANAN

Youth Barista Program launched in partnership with YouthCare

Launched capital campaign to raise $8 million for new facility

READERS CARE FUND

At FareStart, cooking up an education

Homeless learn skills so others can eat, too

Completed $12.5 million capital campaign

Began construction on new facility

é
oderick

| 2001 | 2003 | 2004 | 2005 | 2006 |

Began working with first national partner: Life's Kitchen in Boise, Idaho

Opened Cafés at Gates Foundation, Seattle Public Library & 2100 Building

Launched Catalyst Kitchens pilot

FareStart buys building to expand its programs

■ The move will allow training for more students and should also attract new customers to FareStart's on-site restaurant.

By REBECCA CAMPBELL
Journal Staff Reporter

'Our kitchen produces 2,500 meals a day. It's overcrowded. It's extremely busy.'

David Carleton
FareStart

hope

Annual Meals Produced: 300,000

Annual Meals Produced: 450,000

Annual Meals Prod 500,0

Ashley Cecil, Artist

and changing lives." —Chef David Lee, FareStart Founder

"I shine now. I couldn't have done it without FareStart. It's brought me out again."
—Elaina, graduated 2015

Focus on serving women and graduate wage progression

Record 203 Graduates

25 YEARS — FARESTART CELEBRATES OF TRANSFORMING LIVES

GACY RCLE

- 10th Anniversary of our Youth Barista Education and Training Program
- Catalyst Kitchen's network reaches 50 organizations in 3 countries
- 21st Annual Great Food, Better Lives Gala Auction raises over $1M!
- FareStart Legacy Circle Founded

- Opening of FareStart Café at Pacific Tower
- Catalyst Kitchens reaches 65 members

- Celebrate 25 years!

| 2013 | 2014 | 2015 | 2016 | 2017 |

years!
art Industries
eatured on *Top*
giving episode
ypse"
ct donor
ogram

Annual Meals Produced: 676,000

- FareStart expands to new location at Pacific Tower on Beacon Hill, moving School Meals and Catalyst Kitchens programs
- Added 2nd catering venue "Panoramic Room" at Pacific Tower

- Youth Culinary and Customer Service Training Program Launched
- Catayst Kitchens members train over 12,000 students since launch
- Opening second food location at Pacific Tower

P CHEF SEATTLE

826,000 meals provided to schools and shelters and other non-profits in the community

Enhanced transitional employment program

FARESTART
Great Food. Better Lives.

ff, students and supporters of FareStart for keeping the flame alive

"change your life, you need to decide to do it. Anyone or for you, but it's up to you to walk through it."
—Shon, graduated July 2011

CATALYST KITCHENS

Annual Students Served: 800

Annual Students Served: 700

- Completed 5-year strategic plan for local and national expansion

- Started Farm-to-School Program
- Improved curriculum for FareStart students
- 100 adults graduated

- Launched Catalyst Kitchens as a 20-member network
- James Beard Humanitarian Award
- Launched FareStart Industries pilot
- The first of four award-winning Microsoft Cookbooks, benefitting FareStart, is published

LE CI

07   2008   2009   2010   2011   2012

- Moved into new 33,000 sq. ft. building at 7th & Virginia

- Opened second café at Gates Foundation
- Launched Graduate Support Services

- Celebrate 20
- Launch FareS
- FareStart is f Chef's Thanks "Turkeypocal
- Circle of Imp recognition p is launched

The Washington Post

Teaching the homeless to feed the hungry: Seattle's FareStart spreads its mission nationally

By Associated Press, Thursday, September 1, 11:16 AM

SEATTLE — When he spent his days smoking crack and helping women sell themselves, Brandon Hicks had little occasion to ponder an herbed goat-cheese tartine.

But here he was in the kitchen of FareStart, a Seattle nonprofit that specializes in turning around lives like his, carefully weighing dollops of a savory cheese mixture onto small slabs of baked dough to be served with arugula and roasted cherry tomatoes. Before long, hundreds of diners would begin arriving at the restaurant

T O

Annual Meals Produced: 500,000

"FareStart is a real healing place. You come to FareStart broken down and beat up and you are met with such acceptance. I could not have put myself back together again. FareStart did that for me."
—Jayna, graduated April 2011

Annual Meals Produced: 600,000

"I have a job I love because of FareStart.

Not only a job, a career.

Life is beyond my wildest dreams!"

- Shannon, 2012 FareStart graduate

hange your life, you need to decide to do it. Anyone
r for you, but it's up to you to walk through it."

—Shon, graduated July 2011

**Annual
Students Served:**

800

**Annual
Students Served:**

700

Launched Catalyst
Kitchens as a 20-
member network

James Beard
Humanitarian Award

Launched FareStart
Industries pilot

The first of four
award-winning Microsoft
Cookbooks, benefitting
FareStart, is published

LE
CI

Started Farm-to-School
Program

Improved curriculum for
FareStart students

100 adults graduated

Completed 5-year
strategic plan for local
and national expansion

07	2008	2009	2010	2011	2012

Moved into new 33,000
sq. ft. building at 7th &
Virginia

Opened second café at
Gates Foundation

Launched Graduate
Support Services

Celebrate 20

Launch FareS

FareStart is
Chef's Thank
"Turkeypoca

Circle of Imp
recognition p
is launched

T O

**Annual
Meals Produced:**

500,000

"FareStart is a real healing place. You
come to FareStart broken down and beat
up and you are met with such acceptance.
I could not have put myself back together
again. FareStart did that for me."

—Jayna, graduated April 2011

**Annual
Meals Produced:**

600,000

THROUGHOUT THE YEARS, FARESTART HAS REMAINED COMMITTED TO FOOD'S POWER TO SUSTAIN LIFE AND BUILD CULTURES, FAMILIES, AND ECONOMIES.

With new abilities and a reframed life story, each graduate becomes part of the solution - working together with FareStart and other partners to bring an end to poverty, hunger, and homelessness in our region.

Twenty-five years since our founding, we have provided 8,000 people with the opportunity to transform their lives, while also serving over 9 million meals to disadvantaged men, women, and children in the community.

Over time, we have proudly accepted accolades for our pioneering work and innovation, understanding that with each recognition we assume the responsibility of continually expanding, challenging ourselves to take on more aggressive goals, and then, meeting them.

FareStart has expanded and is connecting with other community members to maximize the quest to end hunger, homelessness, and poverty both in our region and across North America.

"I have a job I love because of FareStart.

Not only a job, a career.

Life is beyond my wildest dreams!"

- Shannon, 2012 FareStart graduate

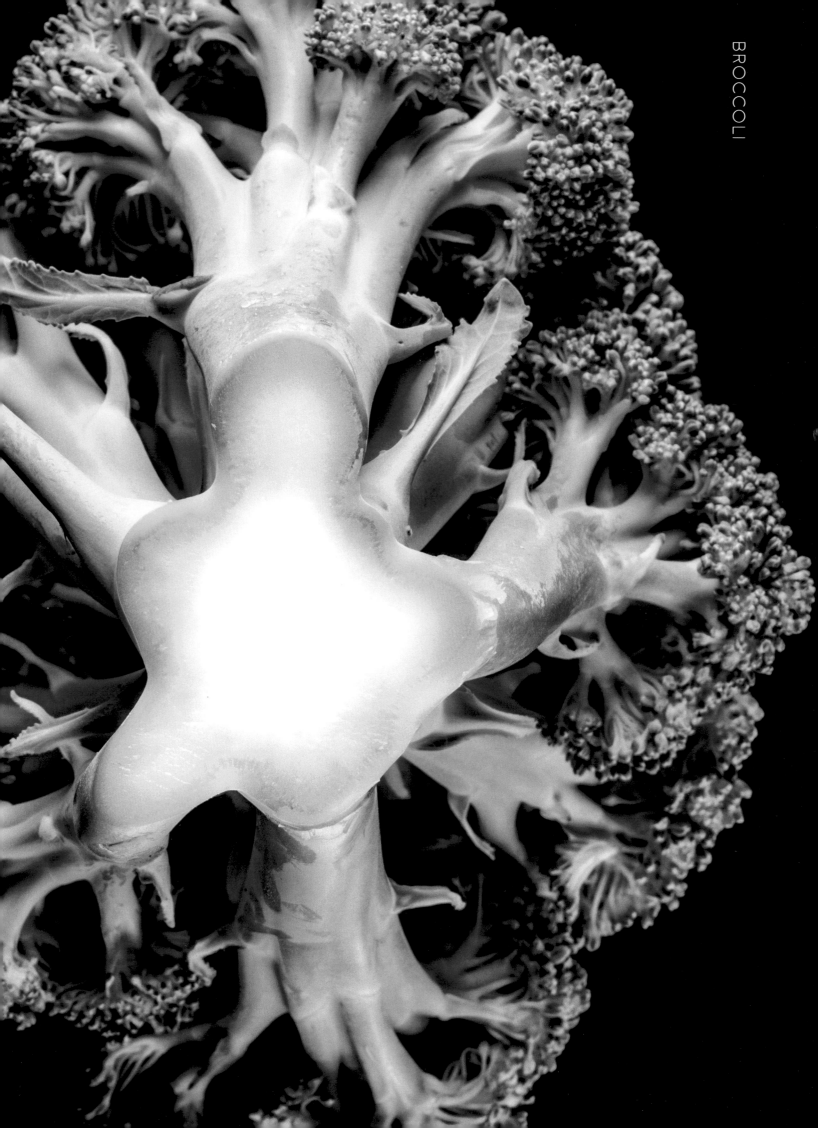

BROCCOLI

Shrimp

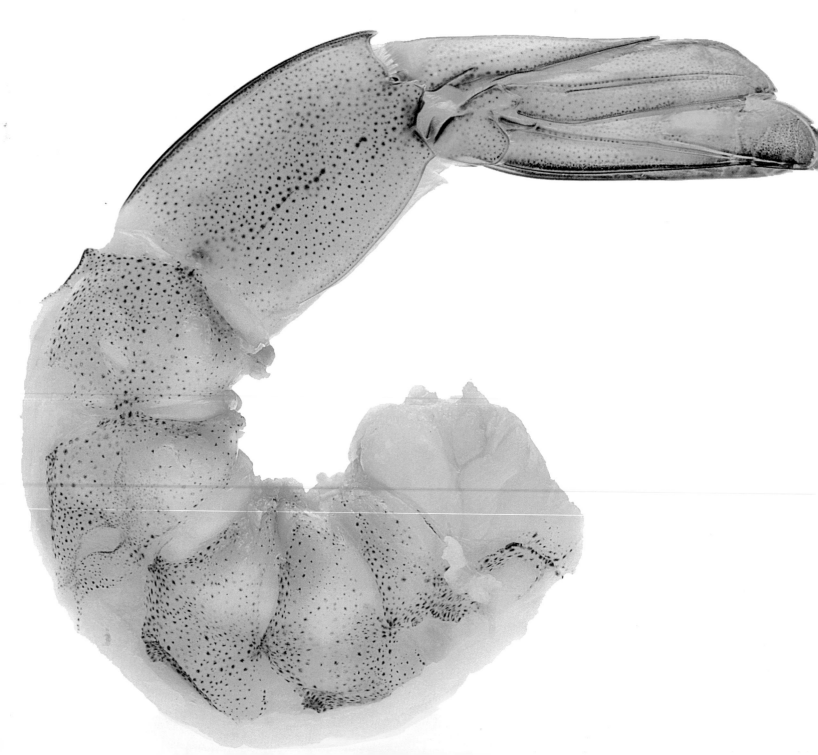

Oregon Bay Shrimp Louie Salad

FareStart Restaurant

INGREDIENTS

2 pounds Oregon Bay Shrimp (pink shrimp)

2 pounds asparagus

2 ripe avocados, sliced and fanned

1 pint grape tomatoes, cut in half

4 heads baby iceberg lettuce, cut into halves

2 lemons, cut into 8 wedges, seeds removed

1 English cucumber, cut into bite-sized pieces

1 cup Castelvetrano olives, pitted and halved

4 eggs

Louis Dressing:

2 cups mayonnaise

½ cup ketchup

2 tablespoons onion, grated

2 teaspoons horseradish

1 tablespoon lemon juice

1 tablespoon tarragon, finely chopped

2 tablespoons Tabasco™

Salt and pepper, to taste

INSTRUCTIONS

To prepare the asparagus, boil it in salted water for 2 minutes or until bright green. Plunge into ice water until chilled. Cut into bite-size pieces.

Place eggs in saucepan large enough to hold them in single layer. Add cold water to cover eggs by 1 inch. Heat over high heat just to boiling. Remove from burner, and cover pan. Let stand in hot water about 12 minutes. Shock in a bowl of ice water. Peel, and cut in half.

To make the dressing, combine all ingredients.

Place all salad ingredients on the plates you are using to serve your salads. Use your artistic discretion. I suggest placing the shrimp on top. Drizzle with Louie dressing. Serve immediately.

You know what's cool about this dish?!? Oregon Bay shrimp is a sustainable product. Oregon's pink shrimp fishery is recommended by Monterey Bay Aquarium's Seafood Watch program as a "Best Choice" for environmentally concerned seafood consumers!

JOAN CURVEY

LIFE SKILLS INSTRUCTOR

I have been in the nonprofit employment and training industry since 1997, working previously with **Temporary Assistance for Needy Families** recipients that were referred by the **Department of Social and Health Services** to the various agencies I worked for.

In 2004, I was conducting an intake with one of my clients, and she mentioned being interested in enrolling in the FareStart program, so she could learn how to be a prep cook.

> When I was at my worst and felt powerless and hopeless, a lot of people entered into my life and gave me the support and hope I needed to turn my life around.

AT THAT TIME, I HAD NOT HEARD OF THE FARESTART PROGRAM. SO I DID MY RESEARCH AND IMMEDIATELY BECAME INTRIGUED BY THEIR MISSION OF TRANSFORMING LIVES BY USING FOOD AS THE BRIDGE OF HEALING.

I knew at that moment that I wanted to be part of their team. It took ten years for my vision to become my reality, and on October 27, 2014, I joined the team as their Life Skills Instructor.

Some of my responsibilities to the students are to assist them with managing their emotions so that they can get and keep a job and to instill hope that they can create a new life for themselves and their families.

I have experienced some of the same challenges in my past that our students are going through or have been through. When I was at my worst and felt powerless and hopeless, a lot of people entered into my life and gave me the support and hope I needed to turn my life around. Now, I am prepared and able to give that support and hope back to our students. **Paying it forward!**

JC

Every Friday, the staff and student body have the privilege to celebrate our graduating students. To hear their stories of what it took for them to graduate and know that they have a hopeful future is always inspiring and emotional.

They all express their gratitude to the staff and their fellow students for their support and for not giving up on them during the process.

IT IS TRULY A WONDERFUL AND SPECIAL
WAY TO END EACH WEEK!

Every first Wednesday of the month, the staff and students get to invite their family and friends to our Community Dinner to share a meal and come together as a community. What makes it unique is our Phase 2 students *(students in weeks 6-10)* assist with prepping, cooking, and serving the meal. Sharing a meal with our student's family and friends is always so heartfelt.

Great food has a way of bringing people together and demonstrating love, support, and a sense of family.

JOAN CURVEY

LIFE SKILLS PROGRAM

Students in Life Skills classes are regularly asked to write down affirmations - who they are in the world and what FareStart has meant to them as they go through the process of rewriting their life stories.

HERE IS A SAMPLING...

If we build on a foundation of what is truthful, the things we build on can never be taken. – *Joseph*

I believe that everything that is not love is not hate but fear. I want to be free of fear of every kind. I want to BE love. I want to be the master of my life. – *Thomas*

Who I am in this world is someone who is always honest and full of integrity. Always being a good example to everyone I come in contact with. A quick learner who is always striving for growth, has many talents, and is good at teaching them to others. – *Matt*

Negativity is like rain, and I wear a raincoat. – *Louie*

Life is 10% what happens to me and 90% how I react to it. – *Sarah*

I'm not the same person I was in week one of the program or even yesterday... I believe in myself, and now, I trust myself and the decisions I'm making. – *Kimberly*

Polenta

FareStart Restaurant

INGREDIENTS

2 cups polenta

1 quart water

2 cups milk

4 ounces butter

4 ounces Parmesan cheese, grated

INSTRUCTIONS

Bring water and milk to a boil. Whisk in polenta. Lower heat to medium, and cook until mixture starts to thicken.

Add butter and cheese, and cook until cheese is completely melted and the polenta is soft.

Milk

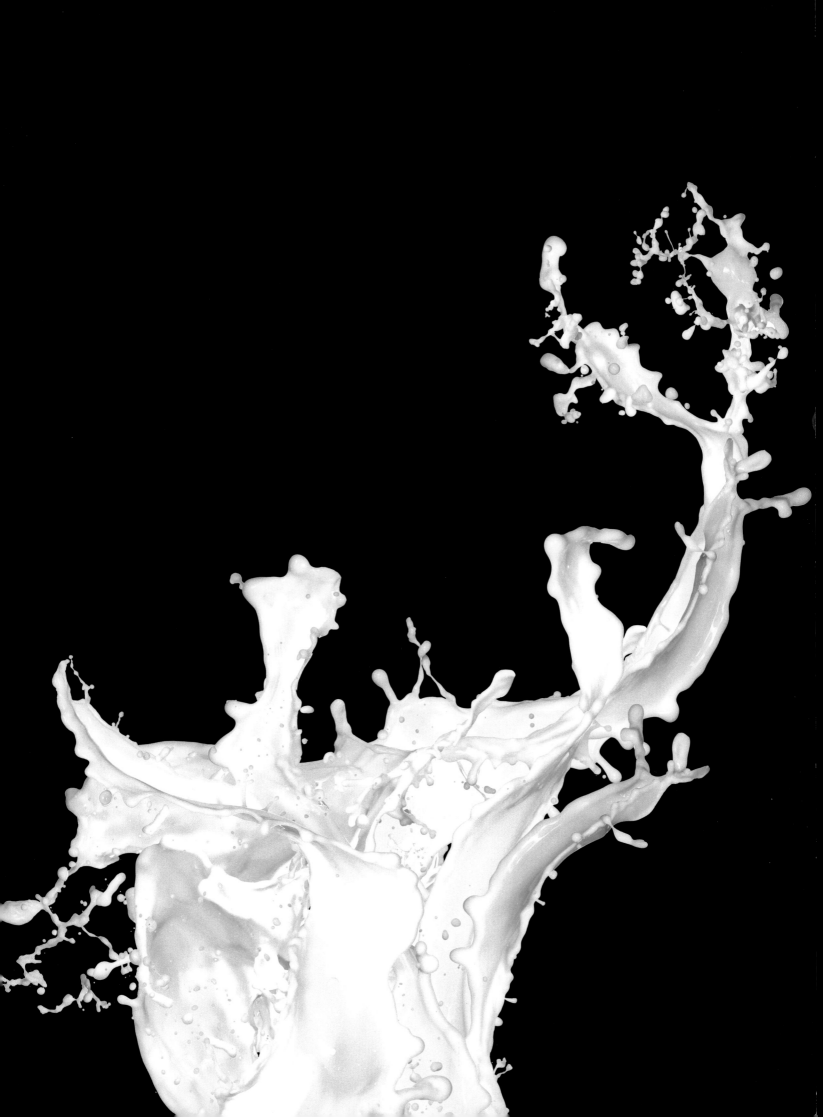

Crab

CRAB CAKES

FareStart Restaurant

INGREDIENTS

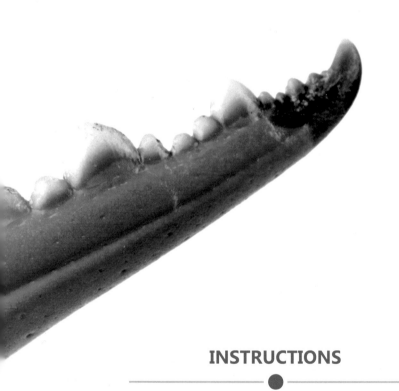

1 pound Dungeness crab, re-picked

½ cup mayonnaise

2 tablespoons sour cream

2½ teaspoons Dijon mustard

½ teaspoon paprika

2 tablespoons red pepper, small diced

2 tablespoons yellow onion, small diced

½ tablespoon apple cider vinegar

½ cup Panko, plus more for breading

4 tablespoons butter

Lemon caper aoili *(Recipe in book)*

Micro-greens or chives

INSTRUCTIONS

Preheat oven to 350 degrees F.

In a mixing bowl, mix everything, except the crab, panko, and butter. Gently fold crab into this mix, and then, fold in panko.

Portion using a ¼ cup measuring cup and a ring mold. Roll in panko. Melt butter in a nonstick pan over medium high heat. Sear cakes on both sides.

Finish by baking for 10 minutes. Serve with a little dot of lemon-caper aioli top and a little garnish of micro greens or chives.

An estimated 3,000 students in
the Seattle Public School
District are homeless – roughly
one in every classroom.

OUR L

OGO

...started in 1987, the organization was originally a for-profit company named "Common Meals."

In 1992, Common Meals officially became a nonprofit. Because there was nothing "common" about the work of the organization, the Board and staff decided to change the name.

You order the tomato basil soup John cooked.

John gets hands on training in our kitchen.

John lands his first full-time job in seven years!

FARESTART
Great Food. Better Lives.

The Rippling Effect of the FareStart Logo

FareStart's logo represents how our work and mission support our students and our surrounding community... transforming lives through job training and placement in the food service industry. The logo depicts a spoon dipped into a bowl of soup symbolizing the transformation of a student's life and the ripple effect of the positive impact on our community.

APPLE CIDER VINAIGRETTE

FareStart Restaurant

●

¼ cup shallots or red onion, roughly chopped

1 tablespoon Dijon mustard

¼ cup honey

¼ medium Granny Smith apple, peeled and rough chopped

½ cup apple cider vinegar

½ teaspoon black pepper, ground

1½ cups olive oil

1 teaspoon salt

●

Blend all ingredients together, except oil.
Slowly pour in oil while blending.

pple

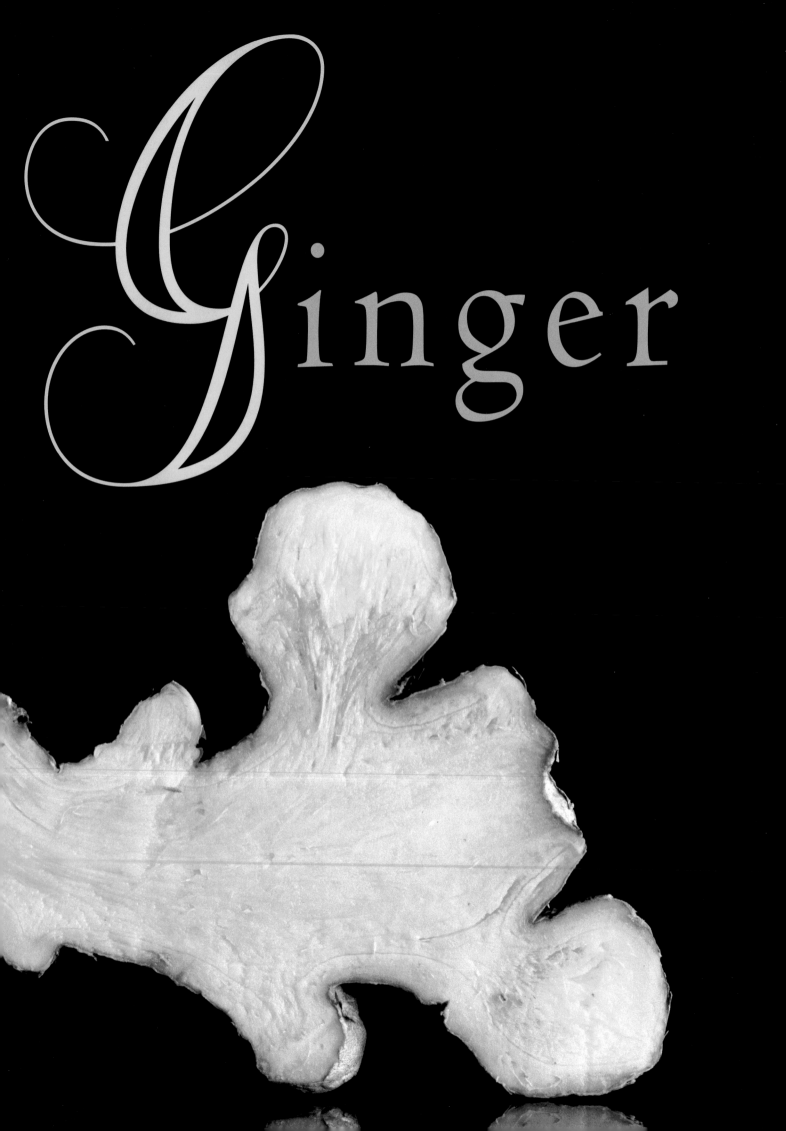

Ginger

Lemongrass Chicken Meatballs

FareStart Catering

INGREDIENTS

⅔ cup sweet chili sauce

3 tablespoons soy sauce

2 teaspoons Sriracha

2 tablespoons rice wine vinegar

2 tablespoons fresh ginger, minced

2 tablespoons garlic, minced

¼ cup fresh lemongrass, minced

2 tablespoons onion, minced

1 tablespoon salt

½ cup Panko, soaked in ¼ cup milk

2½ pounds ground chicken thighs

INSTRUCTIONS

Preheat oven to 350 degrees F.

In a stand mixer with the paddle attachment, mix the sweet chili sauce, soy sauce, Sriracha, vinegar, ginger, garlic, lemongrass, onion, and panko on medium speed until uniform in color and texture.

Add chicken and salt. Mix with paddle until the chicken is integrated and feels slightly tacky.

Portion into 1½ ounce balls. Bake until internal temperature is 165 degrees F.

Serve hot with spicy peanut sauce and cilantro.

BARBARA GRACE HILL

PAST FARESTART STAFF AND BOARD MEMBER

"

FARESTART BELIEVES
WE ARE ALL MORE
THE SAME THAN WE
ARE DIFFERENT.

I THINK WE ARE ALL BORN IN THE LIGHT.

For me, there were a few years of
sinking into the dark, but I found
my way back again.

I came back stronger, convinced that life is
beautiful, and that it's hard. That it's beautiful,
and that it's scary. And, along the way
I learned not to go it alone.

I had a really loving family and an amazing dad. My dad
introduced me to Common Meals, as it was known back then.

FareStart believes we are all more the same than we are different.
That's been shown to the many people who have come to its
doors. The students face a choice over and over, every day. Over
the entire 16 weeks of the program, every second of every day,
they must choose to make a change. And, that's not easy.

I know...*I faced a similar choice once.*

That café was the genesis for David, bringing in the homeless he was feeding and teaching them to cook in his kitchen and to make meals for the café.

_____

In the beginning, David Lee was cooking for shelters out of a church kitchen. My dad was interim minister at the church on Capitol Hill, and David was given permission to use the kitchen.

My dad became a mentor to David, and they became very close.

David wanted to expand and found the 2nd Avenue location. He originally wanted just the kitchen, but it came with the café. That café was the genesis for David, bringing in the homeless he was feeding and teaching them to cook in his kitchen and to make meals for the café.

My dad and two others were the original three Board members of Common Meals. They were charged with going out and getting three more Board members. I was working at Starbucks at the time but loved the work that Common Meals was doing, so I got involved with Common Meals and joined the Board.

We had some amazing individuals join at this time, including Judge Judith Hightower and Cheryl Sesnon.

David is a great entrepreneur and ultimately concluded he was better on the idea side of things. He brought in someone to do the day to day managing. It was not much longer after this that he decided to move on.

BUT, HE WAS THE ONE THAT BUILT THE FOUNDATION AND INTRODUCED THE IDEA OF THE SCHOOL.

At this stage, Cheryl stepped off the Board and into the Executive Director role. I was still at Starbucks, and they were tremendously supportive of my involvement.

I knew that FareStart was something that had to be, in a way, bigger than all of us. But, it needed some loving attention. Cheryl met with me one day and asked if I'd join FareStart. **I agreed on the spot.**

Shortly after, we realized that we didn't have enough money to pay the rent.

I remember getting down on my knees in front of the landlord and begging him to give us one month. He was so kind and generous and agreed.

When Cheryl and I learned that the rent hadn't been paid, we approached Thierry Rautureau and Tom Douglas and asked for help. We said we needed to put together an auction and to do it fast. We organized that first auction within the month!

Thierry created an amazing six course French meal with a glass of wine for each course. In preparation, he told the students how foie gras, one of the courses, was made.

He was describing how the grain is shoved down the throat of the geese when I walked into the kitchen and saw the students, street smart and tough people, with eyes as big as saucers.

We held the auction on 2nd Avenue with the guests all tucked up cozy in the restaurant. Thierry was cooking the foie gras in the kitchen with the students when the **fire alarm went off.**

The fire brigade came through the lobby and told us we needed to evacuate the building. I had just been on my knees a month ago, and here I was begging again.

I explained we had to have the auction to save the organization. I brought them into the kitchen, so they could see we were just cooking foie gras and that was what had caused the smoke.

The evening continued, and after the fourth glass of wine, people became very generous.

WE RAISED ENOUGH TO KEEP OUR DOORS OPEN!

Starbucks was so supportive. They asked me what we needed, and I think I said coffee. We were all working so hard and just needed the caffeine. So, they supplied the coffee and have supplied it ever since.

One of the people to come in to see what we were doing was Terry Heckler of Heckler and Associates. We were still called Common Meals at the time. Terry said, "I really understand why you're doing this; it's an amazing thing." Heckler Associates were the ones that had created the Starbucks brand name and logo.

Terry told us we needed to reconsider the name "Common Meals." He said that we were doing so much more than meals and that there was absolutely nothing common about what we were doing.

Terry donated his time and took us through the process of rebranding and that's how we became "FareStart." He was also responsible for creating the iconic spoon and ripple logo.

Howard Shultz, CEO of Starbucks, also came down to see what was going on. He's a beautiful man, and his family history and story is very poignant.

We went in to see the chef instructors and students in the kitchen, and he says,

"Which ones are the instructors,

and which ones are the students?"

And, I said, "You tell me."

His eyes filled with tears. He got it.

I let him know everything I'd learned at Starbucks was helping me at FareStart.

It was about service, building community, doing a few things well, and not taking on more until you do those first things well.

I've learned you can't make anyone change, but you can be there when they are ready to change. We had been teaching people to cook, as a vehicle, but introducing the life skills training allowed for moments when the students could come together and tell their story.

One of the things we tell the students is that where you have come from is not as important as where you are going.

OUT OF VULNERABILITY AND SHAME, IF YOU CAN GET TO THE OTHER SIDE, COMES STRENGTH AND COURAGE.

BARBARA GRACE HILL

INSTRUCTIONS

Preheat the oven to 400 degrees F.

Add the minced garlic, salt, pepper flakes, and ¼ cup olive oil to the cooled, toasted spices, and stir. Add the carrots to the mix, and toss well. Place the carrots and spice/oil mix on a baking sheet in one layer, and roast for 30 minutes or until lightly browned and al dente.

Meanwhile, supreme the grapefruit. To supreme fruit, cut off the top and bottom of the fruit, place fruit on cutting board, and cut off the peel and pith from the sides. Cut each section free from the membrane resulting in segments of fruit only with no peel, pith, or membrane. Set aside. Squeeze any juice remaining on the peel and membranes into a salad bowl. Set aside.

When the carrots are done, remove from oven, and allow to cool to warm.

Remove avocados from the fridge. Halve them lengthwise, remove the pits, and peel. Cut the flesh lengthwise into slices sturdy enough that they don't break when tossed. Put the avocado slices in the salad bowl with the reserved orange juice; add the lime juice and remaining 2 tablespoons olive oil. Toss gently with your hands. Push the avocado to one side of the bowl. Add the chopped onion and carrots mixture, and toss gently, being careful not to break the avocado slices.

Add the grapefruit segment, arranging them evenly throughout the avocado and carrot mélange. Top with the cilantro, and serve immediately.

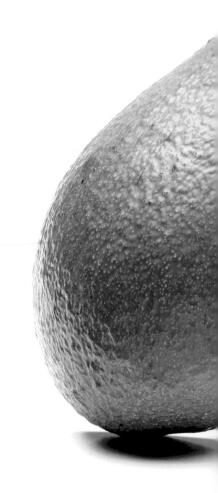

CITRUS, CARROT, AVOCADO SALAD

Barbara Grace Hill

cado

INGREDIENTS

¼ cup purple onion, chopped

4 medium garlic cloves, peeled and minced

1½ teaspoons cumin seeds, toasted and ground

1½ teaspoons mustard seeds, toasted and ground

1½ teaspoons coriander seeds, toasted and ground

¼ teaspoon sea salt

1 teaspoon red pepper flakes

¼ cup plus 2 tablespoons extra virgin olive oil

30 or so similarly sized peeled carrots *(each about the size of your pointer finger)*

1 large or 2 small grapefruits

2-3 ripe but firm Hass avocados, chilled

2 tablespoons freshly squeezed lime juice

A handful of cilantro sprigs

"FareStart trains anybody who is willing to do the work on how to be employed in any professional kitchen or restaurant in the food service industry.

But, you have to be determined, once and for all, to make that decision to change your life. Knowing that you are part of a family, they have your back, and they are always going to be there for you - that gives you balance.

It helps you take the shackles off."

- Johnny, FareStart graduate

SHALLOT

Tomato

Chef Kim's Marinara Sauce

Chef Kim Cosway

INGREDIENTS

24 ounces tomatoes, diced

24 ounces tomato sauce

1 ounce garlic, roughly chopped

1 ounce shallot, peeled and roughly chopped

½ large yellow onion, large diced

1 tablespoon fresh thyme

1 ounce brown sugar

2 tablespoons olive oil

½ tablespoon dried basil

½ tablespoon dried oregano

1 teaspoon chili flakes

Salt and pepper, to taste

INSTRUCTIONS

Heat oil in a large pot; add garlic, onion, and shallot. Sweat until slightly golden and partially broken down. Add diced tomatoes, tomato sauce, and all herbs. Bring to a simmer.

Add sugar, chili flakes, salt, and pepper. Cook for 30 minutes.

Remove from heat, and lightly puree sauce with emersion blender. There should still be some chunks in it.

Serve over polenta *(Recipe in book)* or your favorite pasta.

DAVID LINTON

When people connect with this organization, and its mission, they feel better for it; they learn from it, and they take away from it more than they can possibly give.

> I think what's unique with the FareStart philanthropic experience is that you really are giving people a gift when you introduce them to this program, and in my capacity as a FareStart Board member, I've learned how incredibly affirming it is to invite others to serve.

My first exposure to FareStart was when my wife and I came to a fundraising event. It was part of the capital campaign raising money to purchase the Virginia Street building we're now in. I listened to Megan and a student speak, and I was hooked. I thought Megan possessed something extraordinary, that she had tremendous capability. And, the way the student spoke was so authentic. It wasn't a pitch on why I should give money; it was just him telling his story.

I realized no one could tell that story without having found a place of redemption. This was incredibly powerful to me.

A friend of mine and prolific "connector of people," Ken Glass, was on the Board at the time, and he recruited me to serve. I did a year on the committee for strategic planning and from there, joined the Board. I've served on a number of boards, for-profit and not-for-profit, and this has been my most personally fulfilling experience. When people connect with this organization, and its mission, they feel better for it; they learn from it; and they take away from it more than they can possibly give.

I remember when we crossed the $1 million mark at the Gala Auction. It was a big moment for the organization and, as President of the Board at the time, it was a big moment for me, too. You could see the genuine enthusiasm of everyone there.

DL

Guest Chef Night is a pretty incredible experience. I don't know many other organizations that have a way to connect to their community emotionally in this way. It's genuine. I saw a student speak, and he had all his extended family and kids there. I saw how much joy the student had brought back in to their lives, not just his own but theirs as well.

When I originally saw the **FareStart logo,** I really didn't understand the underlying meaning. I'd heard what it was supposed to mean, but I didn't really understand it. Now, I see that every individual extends beyond themselves. If someone is lost, they are not just lost by themselves; it affects their family, friends, and co-workers.

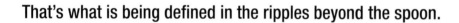

That's what is being defined in the ripples beyond the spoon.

When we help an individual resurrect their life, everybody else who is connected to that individual also gets resurrection. One of the most important messages we want to tell people is that they need to...

...come through the door - for when you leave, you'll leave with more than you ever dreamed of.

When you hear the FareStart graduate's stories, you realize there's not much difference between any of our lives. We're all only one or two degrees away from being homeless or disenfranchised…a couple of life events that could happen. That's all.

One of the things I learned firsthand is the notion that you can't help someone who doesn't want to help themselves. But, when they're ready to help themselves, WHOA! It's a magic moment. And, you can't lose that moment of potential. There's probably nothing more impactful to society than when someone says,

"I own this. I'm ready to change, but I need help."

> We can't force someone to walk through the door and be ready. But, when they're ready, we have to be there for them.

You can never predict that moment when someone decides it's time. That's entirely up to them. But, we have a conviction that if someone wants a second chance, we give them a second chance - no judgment. And, we offer a hand up, not a hand out.

What's it really worth if you don't invest yourself? We give them the tools they need to have a fulfilling, sustainable life. Does it get any better than that? I don't think so.

This is one of the most compelling and unique social enterprise models out there. I think FareStart is a bellwether for more programs to come. Our model starts and ends with respect - helping students see they are valued.

Being valued seems so fundamental, but it is the most powerful and necessary ingredient, along with hope, on the path to redemption.

DAVID LINTON

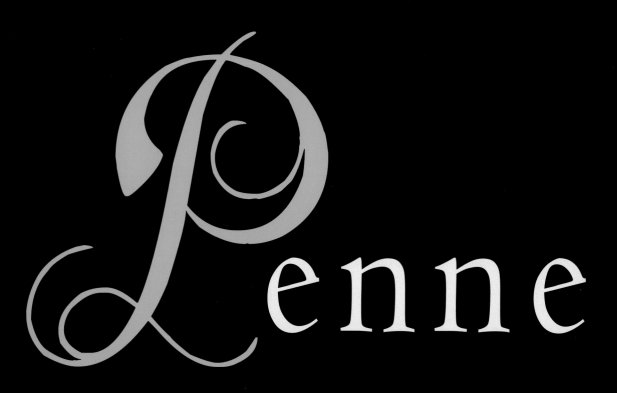

Penne

Pasta with Marinated Tomatoes

David Linton

INGREDIENTS

6 fresh plum tomatoes or tomatoes of your choice, chopped

2 cloves garlic, minced

½ yellow or sweet red pepper, seeded and diced

1 tablespoon basil, roughly chopped

½ cup olive oil

1 teaspoon salt

¼ teaspoon black pepper

1 pound pasta shells (penne or rigatoni)

8 ounces Mozzarella cheese, grated

Parmesan cheese, freshly grated

INSTRUCTIONS

Combine tomatoes, garlic, sweet pepper, basil, olive oil, salt, and pepper in a bowl. Mix well, and let stand at room temperature for 1½ hours.

Just before serving, cook pasta in boiling, salted water until just tender, about 3 minutes for fresh pasta and longer for packaged dry. Drain pasta, and place in a large serving bowl. Stir in Mozzarella cheese and the marinated tomatoes mixture.

Toss, and serve immediately with Parmesan cheese on the side.

One in seven Americans do
not have a reliable source
of food in their lives.

ORIGI

NS

DAVID LEE

"

I'VE ALWAYS HAD A SENSE OF MISSION.
THE PHILOSOPHY I INTRODUCED TO
THE ORGANIZATION IS SOMETHING
I FOUND IN MY SPIRIT.

When I founded FareStart, I didn't know where the end would be, but I was guided by an intention every step of the way.

The intention was to create something that would allow me to make my way in the world, to create more love, to build community, and to use food as a vehicle for change.

Food is a remarkable element. It's how we relate to the earth. It's how we breathe and take in the rain, sun, and the elements. It's how we view ourselves in relation to the earth.

A series of events led to establishing FareStart. I was taking stock of my life, when my uncle asked me if I had considered working with food. My first job out of high school was as a dishwasher. From there, I became a prep cook, then a cook. Food had been my background.

So, I was 28 years old, driving across America, when somewhere in Indiana, I had this moment. In that moment, I knew that I wanted to dedicate my life to be in-service with food.

When I arrived back in Seattle, I started Common Meals, now known as FareStart, focusing my talent with food on the everyday eating experience, not an exalted eating experience, but the everyday aspects of dining, incorporating the themes of subsidence and community.

I went through many iterations before Common Meals became FareStart. From the food brand, "Rice and Beans Forever," which sold to the co-ops around Seattle, to a food service for homebound elderly people to a contract to provide food to the **Downtown Emergency Service Center** (DESC). They are the largest publicly funded shelter in the area. Today, FareStart still provides food to that shelter.

FareStart grew out of my belief in the dignity accorded to the process of making food. I wanted to bring this consciousness to the food world. You don't hear the term **"institutional food"** anymore.

The dignity of preparing food makes you like a broker between the earth and life.

The term captured a sentiment that the homeless should only eat a certain quality of food and be grateful for what they receive. I came into that world with an intention of preparing the best food possible for them.

I was very resourceful, preparing 2,000 meals a day in my commercial kitchen, using all donated ingredients. Then, I went to the shelter to serve the food to the homeless. The dignity of preparing food makes you like a broker between the earth and life. You take raw materials from the earth and fashion them, making them even more beautiful.

WHEN YOU SERVE FOOD WITH LOVE AND RESPECT, YOU AFFORD THE ONE YOU ARE SERVING DIGNITY.

I came to a juncture to either transform Common Meals into a different type of commercial business or turn it into a nonprofit. I chose to start a nonprofit job training program to teach homeless men and women how to cook. I wanted to bring them into my kitchen, so they could see how I was doing it and show them they could do the same.

So many people feel disconnected from the kitchen. Bringing that experience back is what drives me.

FareStart was an affirming experience, bringing me confidence in my creativity, my heart, and my intentions. It evidenced the love I have in sharing.

I built Common Meals on my talent as a chef and my desire to serve quality food to homeless people - *people I felt honored to be among and to serve.*

When the organization became a nonprofit, a number of people joined me. These people made a big impact, helping build the curriculum, and securing funding from Housing of Urban Development. Megan Karch, the Board, and staff have made FareStart what it is today!

In 1997, I established Seattle-based Field Roast Grain Meat Company with Richard Lee, my brother. Field Roast vegetarian meats quickly gained national attention, and we've become recognized as a leader in the fast-growing segment of vegetarian food products. Field Roast products are now sold in grocery stores nationwide and are widely available at restaurants, universities, and stadiums.

I'm a long-time supporter of animal rights causes and organizations working to end farm animal suffering.

In 2011, this work culminated in a humanitarian award: Farm Sanctuary's Corporate Leader in Compassion Award.

Today, even though I've left the organization, my love for preparing and sharing food still guides me in what I do. For me, the future is always unwritten.

DAVID LEE

Common Meal...Soup!

Chef David Lee

INGREDIENTS

1 large piece kombu, approximately 3 by 3-inches

4 cups of chopped vegetables, such as:

- *3 stalks celery, sliced*
- *½ medium zucchini, quartered lengthwise and sliced*
- *3 mushrooms, sliced*
- *¼ quarter red bell pepper, cut into ½-inch strips*
- *3 small carrots, sliced*
- *1 head baby bok choy, chopped*

4 cups cold water

2 teaspoons salt, or to taste

1½ teaspoons sugar

INSTRUCTIONS

Place kombu in bottom of small sauce pan. Add all rinsed and chopped vegetables (should be approximately 4 cups) on top of kombu. Pour in cold water. Bring to just a simmer over medium heat. Do not boil. The longer it "sits" just below boiling (5 minutes or so) the better.

Remove kombu with tongs once the soup reaches a simmer. Add sugar and salt to taste. Cook vegetables to desired doneness. Season to your liking (see note below), and enjoy!

Note: This soup lends itself well to creativity and customization. Feel free to add whatever vegetables and seasonings you like, such as butternut squash, potatoes, dried mushrooms, fresh ginger, black pepper, miso, vinegar, tomato paste, truffle oil, soy sauce, rice, noodles, tofu, chicken, or fish.

Soup often summons thoughts of long simmering and slow cooking. I learned to make this quick, yet flavorful, soup from my experience living with a Buddhist monk. Based on kombu (dried kelp), it provides an amazing umami experience. Interestingly, MSG was an attempt to mimic the umami flavor of kelp. This simple, clean, healthy soup is especially welcome when you want something nourishing. You can use any combination of vegetables that you have at home, and you can season it however you want. You do not need to make a trip to the grocery store to get the ingredients for this soup, with the exception of the dashi kombu, which you can get at most Asian grocery stores.

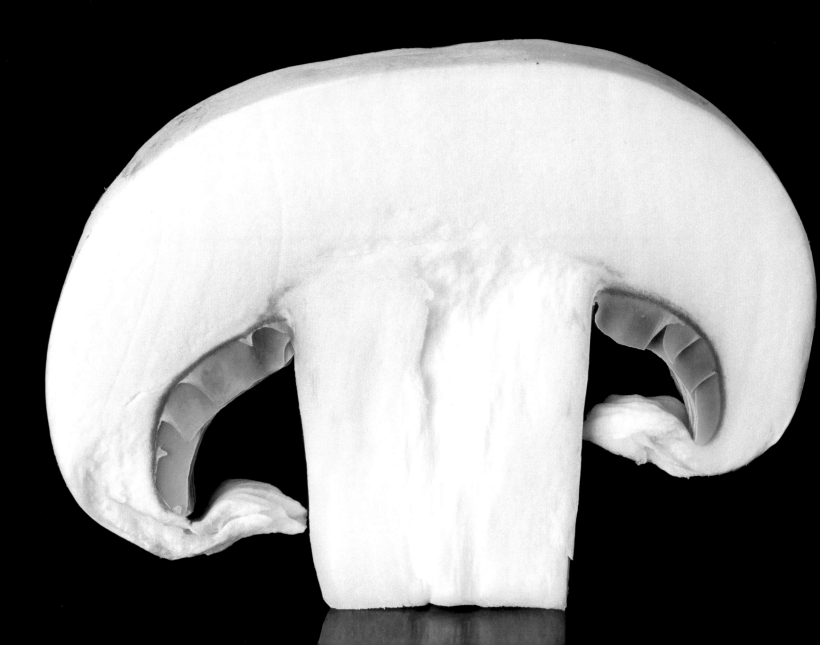

Mushroom

CELEBRATION ROAST PASTRY

WITH CRANBERRY CHUTNEY VEGETABLE MÉLANGE

Chef David Lee

INGREDIENTS

1 pound Celebration Roast

1 puff pastry sheet

⅓ cup celery, julienned

⅓ cup carrots, julienned

⅓ cup red bell pepper, seeded and julienned

1 tablespoon oil

½ teaspoon curry powder

2 tablespoons whole berry cranberry sauce

2 tablespoons chutney

Salt, to taste

INSTRUCTIONS

Thaw out puff pastry sheet if frozen.

Prepare mélange. In small frying pan on medium heat, heat oil, and sauté celery, carrots, and red bell peppers. Add a pinch of salt. Reduce heat to low, and cover; cook slowly for at least 15 minutes until vegetables are soft and wilted, stirring occasionally. Add curry powder, and cook for another 2 minutes. Add cranberry sauce and chutney, stir, and remove from heat. Let cool. Preheat oven to 350 degrees F.

Prepare puff pastry. Smooth rough edges and folds using a little water and your fingers. Be careful not to overwork dough. Cut puff pastry sheet into a 7 by 6-inch rectangle. Place ⅓ of the mélange in a pile in the middle of the pastry. Place a thick slice of Celebration Roast on top of the vegetable mixture. Fold the edges of the puff pastry towards the center and seal by pinching with your fingers and using water as needed.

Turn pasty onto baking sheet so that the side with the folds becomes the bottom. Bake for 30 minutes or until golden brown.

"Today, I am looking at my future,

and I have more confidence, hope,

and optimism than I've had in years.

The FareStart culinary training

program is a game changer, and now,

I'm here to play in the second half."

- FareStart graduate

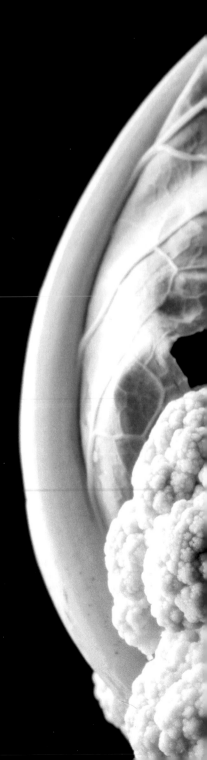

CAULIFLOWER

opening doors to end homelessness

FARESTART BEGAN BY SERVING MEALS IN THE DESC SHELTERS.

We got to know David Lee, the founder of Common Meals, now known as FareStart, through the Seattle Indian Foundation. When he decided to strike out on his own with Common Meals, we became his first contract.

He provided a very high quality meal, and he created the model of utilizing students to prepare meals that they brought to the shelter. That's how it works to this day. A FareStart van pulls up in our parking garage in the early evening, and the FareStart staff and volunteers serve the meals. Compare this to the other meal deliveries where the staff depart once the food is delivered.

> From the outset, David's food quality was way higher. This led to us asking David to handle all of the meals, seven days a week. FareStart continues, to this day, to provide the main meal in our shelter program.

We were mostly a shelter back when Common Meals started. Since then, we've become a much larger organization. I started with DESC on a one-year project and ended up loving it.

In our early days, we had a tiny budget for food service. As a qualifying organization serving poor people, we were entitled to access government surplus foods.

I remember the huge plain label cans. Not the kind of raw ingredients most of us could figure out how to make a meal out of. That's where the genius of David came in.

He took all of this food and supplemented it with the minimal amount of money we could afford to give him, and something beautiful came out. Everyone here was stunned.

DESC remains committed to serving men and women in our community who are most disabled and most vulnerable - the most often forgotten or ignored. These thousands of chronically homeless men and women are often severely and persistently mentally ill, chemically dependent, elderly, HIV-positive, medically frail, physically or developmentally disabled, or, most often, affected by some multiple combination of the above.

WE BELIEVE IT'S UNACCEPTABLE FOR ANYONE
TO EXPERIENCE HOMELESSNESS.

And, we know people living with disabilities become homeless more often, stay homeless longer, and are at the greatest risk for dying on the streets. **That's just wrong.**

Eliminating the chaos of homelessness for people restores dignity, it restores people's hope, and it restores people's will to improve their own lives. It is the humane thing to do.

DESC clients are men and women who are the most likely to be injured or victimized on the streets or to hurt themselves. They are the most "visible" homeless adults in our community and among the highest utilizers of publicly funded services, such as emergency rooms, jails, sobering centers, and psychiatric hospitals.

DESC has devoted research, creativity, and study to developing an innovative and effective approach to serve homeless adults with serious behavioral disabilities.

DOWNTOWN EMERGENCY SERVICE CENTER IMPACT:

- 279 emergency shelter beds at three locations
- 10 supportive housing sites, totaling over 750 state-of-the-art apartments
- Over 200 'scattered site' apartments rented from private landlords and enriched with comprehensive case management services
- Placement of nearly 600 homeless adults into housing each year - more than any other local provider

DESC housing and services benefit the broader community. People living on the street diminishes the quality of life for all of us. That's not fair, and it's not the kind of community we all want. DESC's services are made possible through the many partnerships we have in the community that help keep us running, such as local and federal government support, the local business community, and the hundreds of individuals who invest in our work regularly.

We help make life work for folks so that they can be part of the bigger community, be more accepted, and feel that they're not strangers in their own land.

I see there's plenty of reason to be hopeful. What we know is when we are able to give a person the right amount of help and attention, their individual situation of homelessness can be ended. *We do it all the time.*

DAN MALONE

"And, that's the cool thing about
FareStart. It's an all-encompassing
training, dealing with every
area of your life."

- *Kevin, 2008 FareStart graduate*

Carrot

PUMPKIN BROWN BUTTER SOUP

FareStart Restaurant

INGREDIENTS

—————— ● ——————

3 cups carrots, medium diced

1 shallot, roughly chopped

2 cloves garlic

1 stalk celery

1 to 2 cups pureed pumpkin

1 tablespoon fresh ginger, minced

2 cups vegetable stock

1 cup cream

4 ounces butter, medium diced and browned

2 teaspoons fresh thyme, minced

1 teaspoon fresh rosemary, minced

1 tablespoon fresh sage, chopped

Salt and pepper, to taste

Brown sugar, to taste

Cider vinegar, to taste

INSTRUCTIONS

—————— ● ——————

Simmer carrots with 1 cup water for 20 minutes in a covered sauce pan until soft. Drain, and set aside.

Add butter to sauce pan over medium heat. Whisk until melted and foamy. Whisk constantly until butter foams again. It should smell nutty and turn a caramel color.

In a 4 quart sauce pot, sweat onion, celery, garlic, and ginger until translucent and soft. Add simmered carrots, pumpkin puree, cream, and vegetable stock to sweated vegetables.

Puree with immersion blender until smooth and no chunks of carrot are left. Once smooth, blend in the melted brown butter and fresh herbs.

Season with salt, pepper, brown sugar, and cider vinegar.

**The Pacific Northwest loves its coffee, so I created this
Coffee Parfait Sundae with Butterscotch Sauce, Coffee Granita,
Coffee Whipped Cream, and Toasted Coffee Walnuts dessert
for Tulalip Resort's seafood restaurant, Blackfish Wild Salmon Grill.**

- Pastry Chef Nikol Nakamura

Parfait Sundae Assembly Directions

Use any tall glasses available and the amounts and/or the number of servings will vary accordingly. Technically, one can make a huge kitchen sink sundae with all of the ingredients or make individual portions for a dinner party.

Create layers, starting at the bottom: a spoonful of warm butterscotch sauce, 1-2 scoops of coffee ice cream, coarsely chopped toasted coffee walnuts, coffee whipped cream, scoop of coffee granita, coffee ice cream and repeat until ending with a big dollop of the coffee whipped cream on top to enclose all the goodness...with a final sprinkling of walnuts.

Cream

BUTTERSCOTCH SAUCE

Pastry Chef Nikol Nakamura

INGREDIENTS

●

1½ cups brown sugar

⅓ cup light corn syrup

½ -1 teaspoon salt

(I like salty caramel-based sauces to offset the sweetness, but add to individual preference)

2 tablespoons butter

¼ cup water

1 cup heavy cream

½ teaspoon vanilla extract

INSTRUCTIONS

●

Place brown sugar, light corn syrup, butter, salt, and water in a large sauce pot, and bring to a boil.

Add cream to boiling mixture, and cook until thick and syrupy, about 10 minutes.

Remove from heat, and stir in vanilla extract.

Place pot back on the burner, and cook for 3 additional minutes. Keep warm until ready to use.

Cool any remaining sauce, and refrigerate for up to two weeks.

TOASTED COFFEE WALNUTS

Pastry Chef Nikol Nakamura

INGREDIENTS

1 egg white

½ cup brown sugar

¾ teaspoon instant coffee granules

1 cup walnuts

INSTRUCTIONS

Preheat oven to 325 degrees F.

In a bowl, blend all ingredients, making sure to fully coat walnuts with egg white, brown sugar, and instant coffee mixture. Place on parchment-lined baking sheet pan, and cook for 10-12 minutes tossing walnuts halfway through to evenly toast.

The egg white mixture will begin to set on the walnuts when almost done. Another indicator of doneness will be the smell of toasted nuts. Cool completely. As the walnuts cool, they will become crunchier.

Stored in an air-tight sealed container, the roasted walnuts can last up to a week at room temperature.

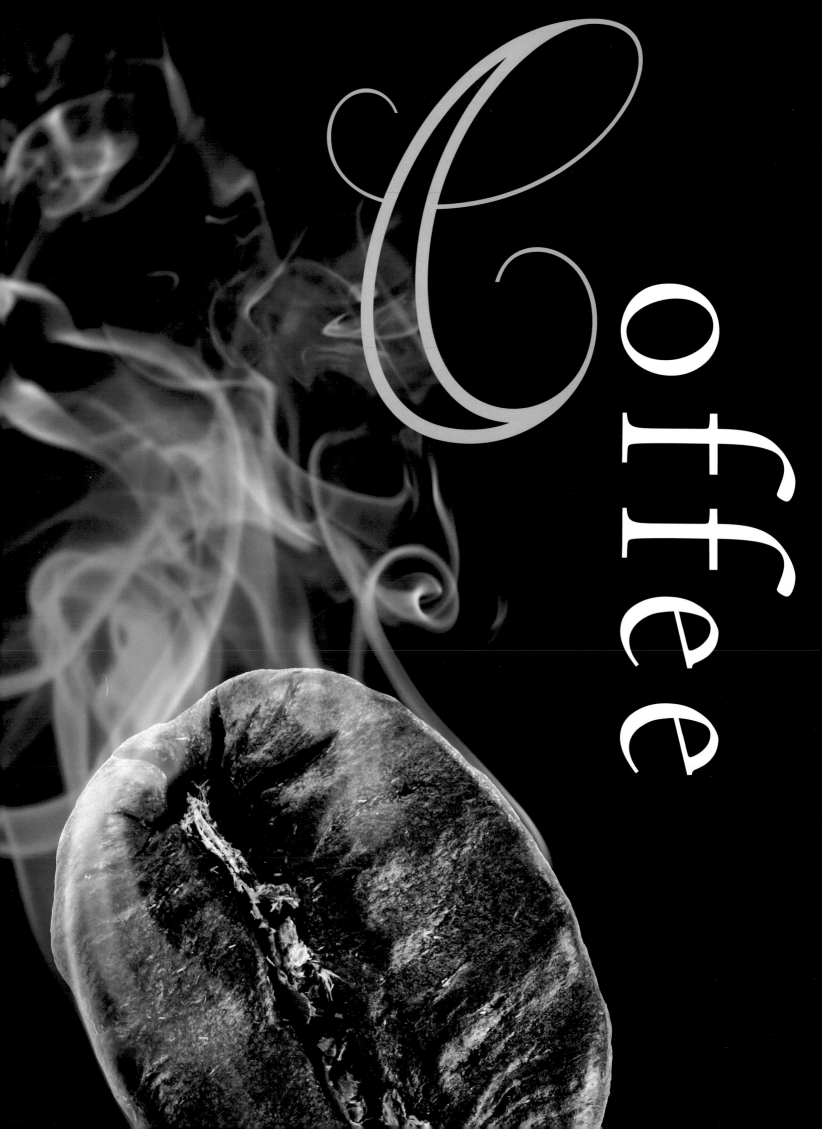

Coffee

COFFEE WHIPPED CREAM

Pastry Chef Nikol Nakamura

INGREDIENTS

1 cup chilled heavy whipping cream

3 tablespoons powdered sugar

1 teaspoon instant coffee granules

½ teaspoon vanilla extract

INSTRUCTIONS

In a chilled, large metal bowl, whip all
the ingredients until thick and fluffy.

Keep refrigerated until ready to use.

COFFEE GRANITA

Pastry Chef Nikol Nakamura

INGREDIENTS

●

2 cups fresh brewed coffee

¼ cup sugar

½ teaspoon vanilla extract

INSTRUCTIONS

●

Mix hot coffee with sugar and vanilla extract. Pour into a shallow glass or metal container, and begin freezing.

Scrape the surface of the granita every 20 minutes until icy and completely frozen. If not scraped periodically, the end product will not be as fine.

Store in a freezer bag or other container for long term storage; this can last for up to one month.

Sugar

THE NEED

MORE THAN 1 IN 8 AMERICANS LIVES IN POVERTY.

This situation poses huge obstacles to employment, such as lack of access to education, childcare, transportation, healthcare, and housing. Many also face additional barriers to employment, such as mental illness, homelessness, incarceration, or substance abuse. Subsequently, they are likely to experience unemployment rates three to five times higher than the general population (2006 Stuart).

FareStart enrolls 250 individuals annually; of these, 68 percent have a prior conviction, with 41 percent having served significant time in prison.

There are 6.7 million youth between the ages of 16 and 24 who are neither working nor attending school and over 630,000 people homeless on any given night in the United States (2012 Economic Value of Opportunity Youth, National Alliance to End Homelessness).

Breaking the vicious cycle of poverty and multiple barriers to employment requires a comprehensive approach that addresses each of these barriers while providing applied, technical job skills training, strong social support services, and, most important, training in life and employability skills that are critical to getting and keeping a job. FareStart's model provides all of these elements. More comprehensive, successful programs, like FareStart, are needed in many more communities to affect positive change on a national and, even, international level.

CARROTS ARE AN
INTEGRAL PART OF THE
FARESTART TRAINING
PROGRAM AND FOOD
SERVICE OFFERINGS.

They are cost-effective to purchase, valuable tools for building knife skills, and welcome in many culinary forms by our patrons. They also represent some the well- and lesser-known aspects of FareStart.

Like the tops of the carrot sprouting from the earth, FareStart's adult training program and restaurant are fairly well-known and widely respected, but much like the carrot itself, much of what we do is hidden from view.

Underneath the soil a lot of growth continues to happen.

FareStart prepares and delivers more than 825,000 meals to the Greater Seattle area community each year through our on-the-job training program.

LEAD

ZUCCHINI FLOWER

ERSHIP

CHERYL SESNON

EXECUTIVE DIRECTOR (1994 - 2000)

REINVENTING YOURSELF IS HARD WORK.

I grew up in a family with mental health issues, and I myself have had some issues with depression. I went down a path that was not a happy path. I knew I would have to figure out how to rewrite my life. So, I started the process of trying to determine what other people knew that allowed them to be happy.

In my late twenties, I got involved in the food business and owned a custom cake company. I would hire the people to do the cooking for the catering side of the business, but I didn't know much about that space. As a business owner, I figured I should know more about how it works in the kitchen.

So, I went to culinary school.

During my time at school, I heard there was a whole bunch of salmon that had been caught in Alaska. They had more than they knew what to do with, and it was being sent down to the food banks here in Seattle.

I put together a little cookbook with recipes on how to prepare salmon with very few tools and very little money. I gave copies of my book to the food banks, and this is how I found out about Common Meals, now known as FareStart.

I first joined Common Meals as a volunteer at one of their fundraisers. Then, later on, I was offered a position on the Board.

[
During the search for a new Executive Director, I offered to step in and help. This was the start of the road to me becoming Executive Director.
]

CS

MISSION:

FareStart provides a community that transforms lives by empowering homeless and disadvantaged men, women, and families to achieve self-sufficiency through life skills, job training, and employment in the food service industry.

During those days, there was tension between the mission of preparing quality diverse meals and teaching the homeless to cook. The training program was secondary, and we had mission confusion.

I'd been in the role of Executive Director a couple of weeks when I sat down with the staff and asked them how many thought of their job as training homeless men and women. **Not a single person raised their hand.**

At that point, I made it clear that training was our mission.

We also had some severe financial issues, and at one point, the Board had to decide whether to keep the doors open or close them.

I looked at all the things we needed to do and realized I needed to hire people who were much smarter than me.

I also had to alter my perception of leadership towards being in-service to my staff. **Everything shifted towards hiring.** I looked for the sort of people who would be able to take ideas and run with them. And, I found great talent.

WORKING WITH REALLY REMARKABLE STAFF WITH THEIR MANY SKILLS MADE FARESTART A SUCCESS. IT GREW BEYOND ANYTHING I COULD HAVE EVER DONE ALONE.

I also helped build the sense of community. I knew how important it was to feel like you belonged. We created a program where people would come and feel like a student of FareStart for life. You may graduate. You may move on. But, you'll be a part of FareStart for the rest of your life.

That made it more than a job training program...a lot more.

In the early days of Guest Chef Night, we had to plead and beg guest chefs to come. We literally went through the Yellow Pages, calling restaurants asking if they'd be willing to be a guest chef. Everybody turned it down. So, every week it would be "Great Cakes" Guest Chef Night, "Cheryl Bakes" Guest Chef Night, or "Catering" as Guest Chef. It was just me in many different forms.

I knew we had to get a program that worked in place first. We needed to build integrity and credibility. Through making things right with the program, everything else fell into place.

By the time I left FareStart, Guest Chef Night had a six-month waitlist of people wanting to be guest chef and an equally long wait for people wanting to volunteer in the restaurant.

CS

Along with the successes, I've seen so much sadness. You get really hopeful for people you bring into the program, but a few go back to their addiction and end up back on the streets.

My daughter looked at me and said,

"You are not God."

I remember there was a woman I got really attached to. She was doing so well and had been in the program for a long time. Suddenly, she relapsed. She actually went back on the streets and got pistol whipped. It broke the bones in her face. When she came back to talk with me, she was beaten up. It was heartbreaking.

I went home to my daughter, who was 8-years-old at the time, and sat on the couch and cried and cried. My daughter said, "Mom, what's the matter?" I told her a friend I was really close to, a student at FareStart, had relapsed on drugs, and I felt like there's something I should have done... that I should have been able to figure out what to do. My daughter looked at me and said, "You are not God."

That was a big moment for me. I started understanding that my job wasn't to fix people. My job was to lend a hand and walk beside them on the journey that they chose.

Looking back, I can see the impact I've had at FareStart, especially for building the life skills component of the program. I leveraged a lot of the content from other people, but a portion of it was from my own personal experience, having learned what it takes to reinvent yourself.

I LOVE DESIGNING PROGRAMS AND CREATING
ENVIRONMENTS WHERE PEOPLE CAN SPEAK HONESTLY
WITH EACH OTHER. *THAT IS WHAT I LIVE FOR.*

CHERYL SESNON

EDIBLE FLOUR, PANSY

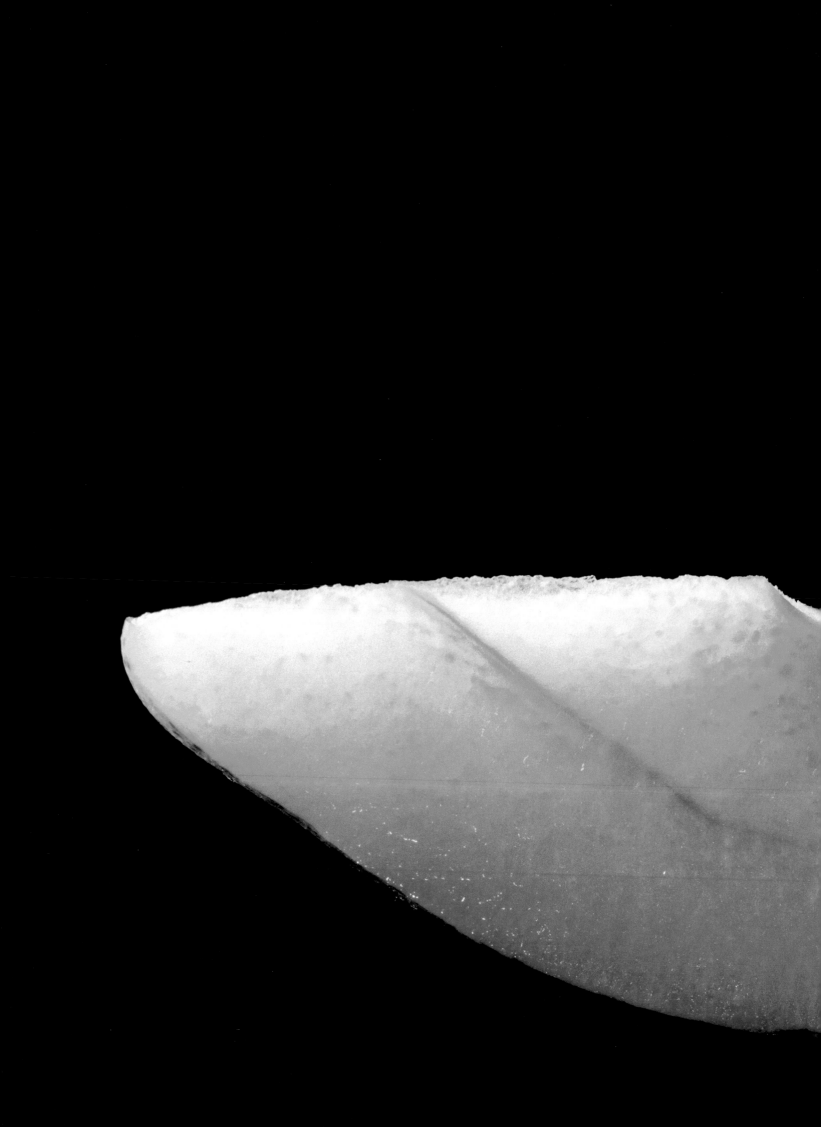

"There are no words that I can say to describe it. I feel like things are going to be okay, that I don't have to be afraid to speak up for myself.

It is okay to know my worth."

- Devona, 2010 FareStart Graduate

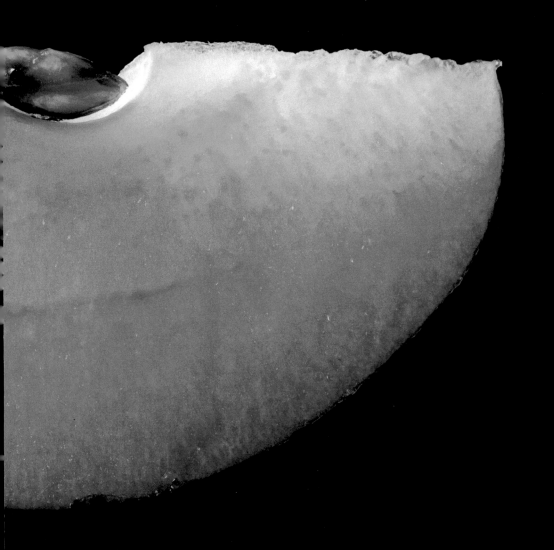

PEAR

Tomato

TOMATO MARMALADE

Cheryl Sesnon

INGREDIENTS

4 ounces butter

2 ounces olive oil

2½ pounds onion, sliced

¼ cup sugar

2 pounds tomatoes, skins and seeds removed, coarsely chopped or use canned, diced tomatoes

¼ cup red wine vinegar

12 teaspoons red pepper flakes

1 bay leaf

INSTRUCTIONS

Heat butter and oil in large pan, and add onions. Sprinkle with sugar and brown, and then, cook slowly for approximately 45 minutes.

Add chopped tomatoes, vinegar, pepper flakes, and bay leaf.

Cook over high heat until mixture is thick.

FLANK STEAK KÜLEUA

Cheryl Sesnon

INGREDIENTS

3 pounds flank steak

1 cup pineapple juice

⅓ cup soy sauce

⅓ cup salad oil

1 teaspoon ginger

1 teaspoon sugar

2-3 cloves garlic, minced

INSTRUCTIONS

Combine pineapple juice, soy sauce, oil, ginger, sugar, and garlic, and pour over steak. Marinate steak in the refrigerator at least 3 hours (overnight is the best). Grill until preferred doneness. Slice diagonally, and serve.

This is a family favorite!

Pineapple

Pecan

Pecan Chicken
with Sour Cream Mustard Sauce

Cheryl Sesnon

INGREDIENTS

2 boneless, skinless chicken breast halves

1½ tablespoons butter, softened and 2 tablespoons butter for frying

½ cup pecans, finely chopped

2 tablespoons Dijon Mustard

⅓ cup sour cream

INSTRUCTIONS

Place one chicken breast half, between two pieces of plastic wrap or waxed paper. Working from the center, gently pound chicken with flat side of meat mallet or rolling pin until about ¼-inch thick; remove wrap. Repeat with remaining chicken breast half. Pat dry with paper towels.

Place pecans in a small flat dish. Coat each chicken breast half with softened butter. Dip in pecans, and pat onto breast, coating both sides.

Melt remaining 2 tablespoons butter in medium nonstick skillet over medium-low heat. Add chicken, cook 3 to 4 minutes on each side or until chicken is fork-tender and juices run clear. Remove chicken from skillet, place on serving platter. Cover to keep warm.

Add Dijon mustard and sour cream to drippings in skillet; cook, stirring until mixture boils and thickens. Pour over chicken.

*I learned this recipe when working as an Assistant Manager
at the Shoalwater Restaurant in Seaview, WA.*

LILLIAN SHERMAN

DIRECTOR OF DEVELOPMENT (1999 - 2006)

MY CONNECTION WITH FARESTART WAS IMMEDIATE.

I got out of college and realized social work was not where I was going to land. I started working in the Pike Place Market in the 90's, handling all of their big events. It's funny, but I think my role at the Market did utilize my background in social work and in theater.

The chefs helped teach our students there was a community they could be a part of.

One of these events involved several other nonprofits in the area, and this included FareStart. I had been bringing people to the FareStart restaurant for lunch for some time. Later, I joined as a volunteer on the planning committee working with Barbara Hill.

At a lunch one day with Barbara, she told me she was writing grants, teaching, and running the restaurant. It was a lot of work. Barbara and Cheryl, the Executive Director, were holding the organization together, trying to make it viable.

Barbara asked if I'd join FareStart full-time, helping on the development side of things.

I had experience as an event planner but never as a development director. It was an amazing opportunity to create something new. We lacked the material needed to tell the story about what was happening in the restaurant and, certainly, no way to further engage potential donors in supporting it.

Early on, we knew we needed to build FareStart utilizing the chef community. The chefs helped teach our students there was a community they could be a part of.

Leading up to the capital campaign, I was involved in building the support material to tell our story to the consultants. We didn't have a lot of the data we needed in those days. **It was a massive leap of faith.**

In the old building, my office entered from the street, and the students would come and sit on the doorstep. I got to know them really well, and they would bring me things to eat that they'd made.

I would hear them talking about their experiences. It was very grounding to be that close to the mission. They each had a "moment" story when something happened to make them decide to do something different.

I remember listening to one woman, a single mom, and her story about how much she had to go through just to get to school that day. I remember it distinctly as I had just had my first child.

I never moved into the Virginia Street building. **My last day was at the Golden Sledge Hammer event when we invited all the donors to sledge hammer the wall, kicking off the renovations.**

FareStart changed me and allowed me to understand my mission in life. It helped me realize there's going to be little miracles along the way and, sometimes, a few roadblocks, too.

All you have to do is keep trying.

LILLIAN SHERMAN

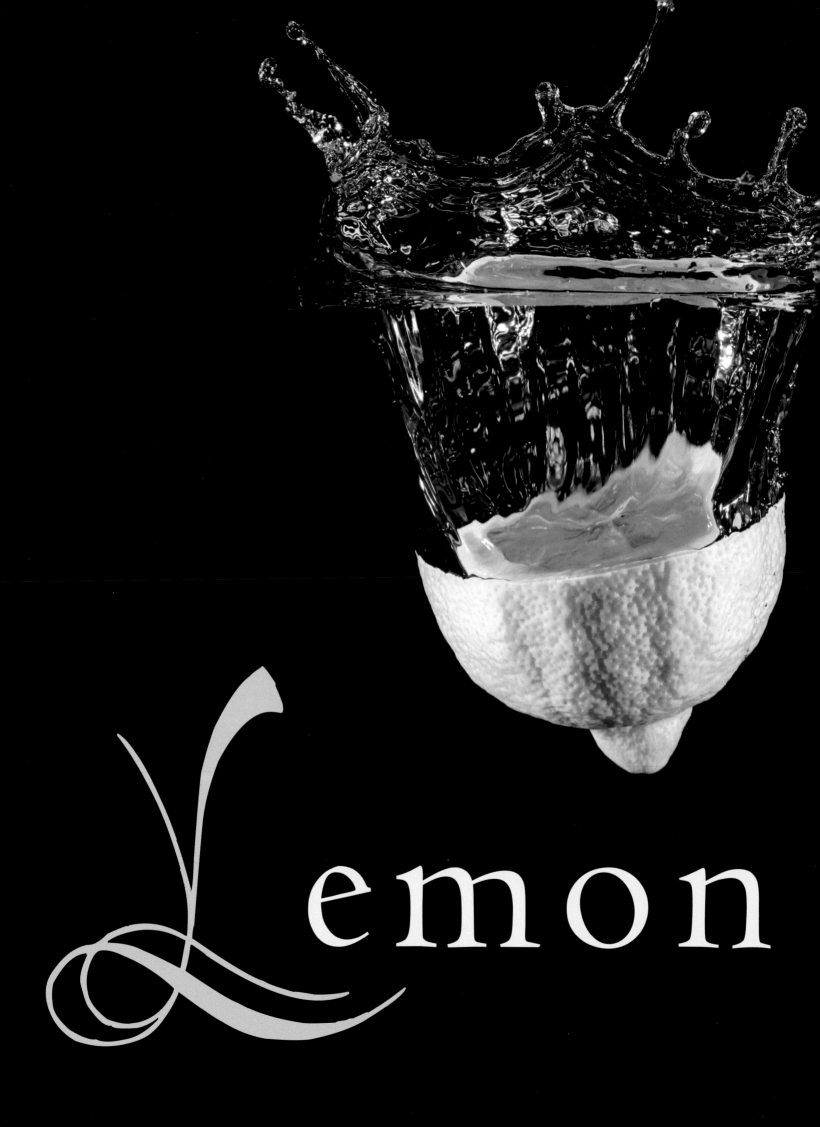

Lemon

LEMON CAPER AIOLI

FareStart Catering

INGREDIENTS

Zest and juice from 1 lemon

2 tablespoons capers, roughly chopped

1 cup mayonnaise

1 teaspoon blackening spice *(see below)*

1 teaspoon chopped garlic

Blackening spice

5 tablespoons paprika

3 tablespoons dried parsley

3 tablespoons black pepper

1½ tablespoon garlic powder

1½ tablespoons kosher salt

½ tablespoon each: dried basil, rosemary, and oregano

1 teaspoon cayenne

INSTRUCTIONS

Mix all ingredients in metal bowl.

Season with salt and pepper.

Southwestern Seasoning Mix

Chef John Howie
Adapted from Chef Howie's Cookbook - Passion & Palate: Recipes for a Generous Table

INGREDIENTS

2 tablespoons kosher salt

1 tablespoon plus ½ teaspoon ancho chili powder

½ teaspoon cayenne pepper, powdered

2 tablespoons plus ½ teaspoon mild chili powder

2 tablespoons plus ½ teaspoon sweet paprika

1 teaspoon ground white pepper

INSTRUCTIONS

Combine all ingredients together. Mix well.

Porcini Mushroom Soup with Truffle Crème

Chef John Howie

Adapted from Chef Howie's Cookbook - Passion & Palate: Recipes for a Generous Table

INGREDIENTS

½ cup butter

4 tablespoons flour

¾ cup assorted mushrooms, grated

¼ cup cremini mushrooms, sliced into ⅛-inch pieces

2 tablespoons Shiitake mushrooms, sliced into ⅛-inch pieces

1 ounce porcini mushrooms, dried

1 quart vegetable stock

2 cups whipping cream

1½ teaspoons kosher salt

¼ teaspoon ground black pepper

2¼ teaspoons fresh tarragon, chopped

Truffle crème *(recipe follows)*

INSTRUCTIONS

Soak the dried porcini mushrooms in the vegetable stock for 1 hour. Strain off the liquid, and reserve. Cut the porcini mushrooms into a fine mince.

Melt the butter in a large stock pot over medium-low heat. When melted, add the flour to create a roux, reduce heat to very low, and cook for 10-15 minutes, stirring constantly so the roux doesn't brown.

In a separate pot, heat reserved mushroom stock from the porcinis to approximately 160 degrees F. Then, slowly stir the stock into the roux; when all the stock has been added, increase the heat slightly, and bring to a simmer. The soup will begin thicken. Reduce heat, and let simmer for 20-30 minutes.

Add all the fresh and re-constituted mushrooms. Then, add the salt and pepper. Cook for another 10 minutes on a low simmer; add the tarragon and cream. Transfer, cool, and store refrigerated until needed.

TRUFFLE CRÈME

½ cup whipping cream
¼ teaspoon sea salt
1 tablespoon truffle infused olive oil

Place all ingredients into a mixing bowl,
and whip until creamy and medium stiff.
Hold refrigerated until needed.

To serve, place the appropriate amount
of soup in a cup or bowl, and top with
the truffle crème and chives.

Truffle

125

INSTRUCTIONS

———————— ● ————————

Begin by prepping all of your fish. If you are serving cod, remove the center strip of bones, set aside for stock, and then, cut the fish into strips about one-inch thick. If you're using halibut, debone, if possible, and then, cut the fish into similar-sized pieces.

Place the clams into a bowl of cold salted water to let them purge; beard the mussels by pulling or trimming the bearded part off of the shells, and put them into the same bowl of water. They will need about 30 minutes in salted water to spit out their sand.

Peel prawns, and discard the veins if there are any. Reserve the shells.

Make fish stock. In a medium-sized saucepan, heat a splash of olive oil over medium-high heat. Toss in the prawn shells. Sear them until they begin to become pink, about a minute, and then, add fish bones and ⅓ of the clams and mussels. Cover with 3 cups cold water, and bring to a boil. Turn off the heat. Let stand for 10 minutes, strain, and set aside.

In a large sauce pan or Dutch oven, heat another splash of olive oil over medium heat. Add the fennel seed, chili flakes, onion, and bell pepper, stirring continuously until they begin to sweat and the onions begin to brown. Add the garlic, and continue to stir until the garlic blooms and you can smell it cooking.

Keep the heat at medium. Add fish pieces to the pan, and sear them, cooking until they are about halfway done. Remove them from pan. Add the tomatoes, remaining clams and mussels, and your reserved fish stock. Bring to a boil, and reduce to a simmer. Cover, and cook until the clams and mussels begin to open.

Add the prawns and potatoes, and return the par-cooked fish to the pan. Simmer very gently until the prawns are cooked through, and clams and mussels have opened. Discard any clams and mussels that do not open. Season to taste with some crunchy salt.

Serve in bowls with lemon wedges, crusty baguette, saffron mayonnaise, and a lightly dressed salad.

Cioppino

Chef Matt Janke

INGREDIENTS

3 pounds whitefish filets, such as
true or ling cod or halibut

2 pounds manila clams

2 pounds mussels

2 prawns per person, shell-on

3 cups cold water for stock

Olive oil to cook

2 teaspoons fennel seed

1 teaspoon crushed red chili flakes

½ cup sweet onion, diced or sliced

½ cup red and orange bell pepper, diced

3 cloves garlic, minced

1 28-ounce can whole peeled tomatoes,
mashed by hand

½ cup fingerling potatoes, boiled, chilled,
and sliced

Salt, to taste

Since 1992, FareStart has helped nearly 8,000 people transform their lives.

COMM

POMEGRANATE

UNITY

ACIFIC TOWER

FARESTART PROGRAMS & RETAIL AT PACIFIC TOWER:

- Catalyst Kitchens
- School Meals Program
- Youth Culinary & Customer Service Program

  Assists "opportunity youth" - those who are at risk of dropping out of school, future unemployment, and homelessness - by combining culinary training with academic progress in the Interagency Academy's alternative high school programs.

- FareStart Café @ Pac Tower

  Provides on-the-job training for Youth Culinary program.

- Opening in 2017:

  A second location in Pacific Tower with expanded lunch options

  Provides on-the-job training for Adult Culinary program.

In 2015, FareStart became a tenant of the Pacific Tower, Seattle's iconic landmark Art Deco building on top of Beacon Hill, which has been transformed into a vibrant center for health education programs and a dynamic hub for some of our most vital and innovative **community nonprofits.**

"Being at Pacific Tower is all about the synergy," FareStart CEO Megan Karch says. FareStart provides all of the food service and catering for the tower and its tenants and operates its schools meals business there. In addition, FareStart students enjoy access to the on-site health care services and benefit from the exposure to a higher education environment.

10,000 square feet includes:

- 3,700 square feet of kitchen space

- 5,400 square feet of training/classroom/office space

- 900 square feet of retail space for a café and a quick-service "grab-and-go" facility

- FareStart has exclusive catering rights to the wonderful event space on the 8th floor of the building, which is appropriate for events of all kinds and can hold 130 people seated.

With anchor tenant Seattle College, longtime tenant Pac Med, and FareStart, the project attracted other nonprofit tenants. These include 501 Commons, which provides services and support to nonprofits, the Cross-Cultural Health Care Program, which helps ensure culturally appropriate health care services, Neighborcare Health, which provides free dental care for community members in need, and Building Changes, an organization that addresses the causes and prevention of homelessness.

CONSTRUCTED IN 1933, THE PACIFIC TOWER
BUILDING IS A DESIGNATED NATIONAL HISTORIC
PLACE AND SEATTLE HISTORICAL LANDMARK.

"

The Pacific Tower space has allowed us to more than double the number of students we're serving, but it also allows that growth to happen sustainably. It's a win-win!

Megan Karch

SOCIAL ENTERPRISE

A social enterprise is an organization that applies commercial strategies to maximize improvements in human and environmental well-being. This may include maximizing social impact rather than profits.

A social enterprise has two goals: to achieve social, cultural, community economic, and/or environmental outcomes and to earn revenue.

SEATTLE IS A CITY KNOWN FOR ITS INNOVATION. AND WE CHERISH BEING KNOWN FOR OUR GROUND BREAKING WORK IN THE SOCIAL ENTERPRISE ARENA.

This recognition amplifies our ability to meet community demands. But, we can't do it alone, and we must continue to work to maximize the relational capital in this region to affect change.

While focusing on empowering adults and youth to overcome their barriers to employment, we ultimately are working to eradicate homelessness, hunger, and poverty in our region and across North America.

We must continue to revinvent and look for opportunities to continue down this path of success, and we must never be satisfied with "good enough" until everyone in our community is fed, both stomach and soul.

This is all part of our story.
A story that we are proud to share.

Since 1992, we have prepared over 9 million meals for schools, healthcare centers, shelters, Head Start programs, and daycare centers.

DISADVANTAGED INDIVIDUALS

FareStart feeds the broken spirit and lives of the most disadvantaged people in our community by harnessing their drive to start over and providing them with wrap-around support to be successful in changing their lives. Our comprehensive training programs for adults and youth build a strong foundation and support system for every student who passes through our doors. We work individually with students, moving them toward successful re-entry into the community and enabling them to create a new life for themselves and their families.

AT-RISK COMMUNITY MEMBERS

We provide vital sustenance to thousands of people in our community every day. In preparing these meals 365 days a year, FareStart students work diligently to create nourishment for people who often go without. For many of our students, it is the first time that they experience pride in their work and connect with the people for whom they are preparing meals. In doing so, they start the process of building compassion for themselves and others. With over 800,000 meals prepared annually, the very activity that we were founded upon remains a key manifestation of that which we value most.

PEOPLE WHO LOVE QUALITY FOOD

FareStart feeds the food-loving greater Seattle community with a range of options, including the FareStart Restaurant, cafés, and catering. The quality of the food and customer service rivals the best in the city, creating a win-win opportunity to engage community members who appreciate amazing food and want to help make a difference in their community.

We serve 365 days a year!

FareStart menu items are fresh, culturally diverse, and seasonal. We appreciate that FareStart supports local growers, and their cooks are willing to listen to ideas and suggestions for new items.

South Seattle Community College Pre-School

ALL THE REVENUE WE RECEIVE
FROM THE COMMUNITY MEALS
AND SCHOOL MEALS
PROGRAMS GOES DIRECTLY
BACK INTO JOB TRAINING &
SOCIAL SERVICE PROGRAMS
FOR OUR STUDENTS.

COMMUNITY MEALS

Every day, FareStart produces hot, well-balanced meals for low-income people at shelters, health care facilities, transitional housing programs, and hospice centers.

Much of the high quality food we use in our Community Meals program is collected from "short shelf life" inventory through our Food Recovery Program.

SCHOOL MEALS

The children at your school or childcare center deserve the best. While many kid-focused meal programs offer processed food, FareStart provides healthy nutritious cuisine that kids love.

Each meal is painstakingly created by our students, from scratch, with the dietary needs and "special tastes" of kids in mind, including allergen free and vegetarian options.

"FareStart does a great job of exposing kids to new foods and using veggies in delicious ways.

The cauliflower mac 'n cheese is always a big hit!"

- Shannon, Teacher at University Temple Children's School

Programs like these help our students develop critical job and life skills they need to build a new future. They also offer a real opportunity to give back to the community.

"I wanted out, but my addiction prevented me from seeing the way out.

That is when FareStart came and offered a message of hope and the chance to start anew while protecting my sobriety.

Every chef, every staff member had something to teach along the way. All one needed was willingness for change."

- Jonah, FareStart 2014 Graduate

GRAPES

HOW TO GET INVOLVED IN THE FARESTART COMMUNITY

Volunteer by yourself or bring a group.

Donate cash, stock, or in-kind goods or services.

Dine at one of our restaurants or cafés.

Use our catering services and venues. You will experience exquisite food and support a great cause.

Feast at our weekly Guest Chef Night or other "foodie" events throughout the year.

Hire our well trained and motivated graduates.

Explore the possibility of corporate sponsorships with your company, such as hosting co-branded events or initiatives.

Collaborate with us as a food service partner.

If you live outside of the Seattle area, visit and support one of our Catalyst Kitchens members.

Connect with us on Facebook, Twitter, and Instagram.

Spread the word about FareStart to your friends, family, and co-workers.

Visit farestart.org for more information.

SEATTLE
FOUNDATION

the heart & science of philanthropy

I started at the Seattle Foundation in 1996, supporting the grant making program, so my original connection to FareStart was through work and the funding I was making. Cheryl Sesnon was the Executive Director at the time.

Who knew a child would eat black bean soup?

My association to them grew over time, becoming even more personal when I learned that the food served at my child care center was provided by FareStart. The FareStart truck would show up every day and deliver meals - healthy food with many different varieties. I think my daughter would still like it if food was delivered to her now. Who knew a child would eat black bean soup?

THESE EXPERIENCES CONNECTED ME
IN A DEEPER WAY TO THE ORGANIZATION.

The Seattle Foundation is among the largest of more than 700 community foundations in the United States. We help strengthen the health and vitality of the community by connecting generous people with well-informed philanthropic strategies. Unlike private foundations, community foundations invest and administer a pool of funds contributed by numerous donors. We provide support for donors wishing to take an organized approach to giving.

As stewards of the community's funds, we invest for the very long term. Few regions in the world can match Seattle's current growth and prosperity.

But, accompanying our good fortune are great challenges, including the widening disparities between rich and poor. Such inequities weaken the vibrancy of our community.

Using our philanthropic expertise, deep roots in the community, and network of partners, The Seattle Foundation develops targeted strategies to quicken the pace of progress toward a stronger community for all.

We are an agent of change.
Every day, we convene, communicate with, and catalyze our philanthropic partners to advance this ideal, uniting passion and discipline to create lasting impact.

For us, it's all about community impact.

It's been an amazing experience, and I've really enjoyed creating relationships and friendships with FareStart. From where FareStart began, back at the 2nd Avenue location to finding a space and transitioning into the location on Virginia Street to the inspirational Guest Chef Night and the celebration of individuals who are graduating, it's been an amazing journey.

**What a joy I experience waking up every day
and connecting nonprofits to resources
to help them achieve their goals.**

CEIL ERICKSON

PEOPLE THAT EXPERIENCE A GUEST CHEF NIGHT COME AWAY THINKING, " I WANT TO VOLUNTEER; I WANT TO SERVE."

Tomato

Tomato Basil Soup

FareStart Restaurant

INGREDIENTS

2 tablespoons olive oil

24-ounce can diced tomatoes

24-ounce can tomato sauce

5 ounces onions, medium diced

½ ounce garlic, roughly chopped

5 ounces heavy cream

5 ounces water

2 teaspoons dried basil

Salt and pepper, to taste

INSTRUCTIONS

Sweat onions and garlic in olive oil in a 4 quart pot on medium heat. When onions are translucent and garlic is fragrant, add tomato sauce and diced tomato.

Simmer for 10 to 20 minutes, stirring occasionally to keep the bottom from scorching.

Add water, cream, and basil. Puree with an immersion blender until smooth. Add salt and pepper.

JUDGE JUDITH HIGHTOWER

FORMER BOARD MEMBER

FareStart approached me to see if I'd like a position on their Board. As a judge, I can't fundraise, but that didn't matter to them. They wanted me for my ideas.

I first learned about FareStart when I was at work. There was a man who had been arrested on some old driving charge, and they booked him into jail.

He begged to be released, telling me he was graduating from this culinary program. If he could just make it to his graduation, he would get a set of knives, and he'd be able to work. The prosecutor was vigorously objecting because the man had been out on a warrant and had no address.

He was homeless.
I took a chance on him.

He came back afterwards to tell me he'd graduated and showed me his knives. He let me know how thankful he was.

So, when I got the call from Common Meals with the offer of a position, I said, "Of course, I'd love to be on the Board." This was not long after David Lee had transitioned out, and Cheryl had come in. She said we needed to build the Board, and we needed to move things forward and grow.

We were in this tiny little spot next to the Josephinum, and we revamped that space and how the meals were done. We continued to recruit, but in order to train and serve more people, we needed more space.

I'll never forget we had this Board retreat in a beautiful conference room looking over the water. We were told to envision what we wanted for FareStart. I drew a building.

I believe we can create what we envision.

The FareStart building on Virginia Street ended up looking like the building I drew.

I'm so honored to have been a part of the Board that raised the money and created the space FareStart is in now. Many things came together.

FareStart is a sense of family. There's a lot of people that care about you, that help you to be successful, help you learn to fly again.

I believe in the right for people to have opportunities. I came from a life where people didn't have bootstraps to pull themselves up. My father only had a sixth grade education, and my mother had graduated from college but stayed at home to raise us kids. They were very committed to education. Both of my parents had a firm belief in what was right and wrong in terms of how you treat people.

We lived in the housing projects. In that environment, we had every color, every religion, every race. There were students studying to be doctors and dentists, as well as students who were studying to be artists. There were people who were poor - single mothers, people on welfare, just about everybody. This was my neighborhood. This is where I grew up while going to Catholic school.

I lived in two worlds - the Catholic school and the housing projects. The Catholic school was primarily white, but there were a few black families, too. During the Civil Rights Movement, there was a lot of racist behavior, and I experienced some of that on the street. But, I always believed that, as people, they just didn't know any better.

I feel really lucky to be born black.

It's amazing how the people on the FareStart Board have bonded and become such good friends. I grew to love them so much. I was a part of hiring Megan Karch. Finding her was huge. When we met with her, we knew she was the one.

FARESTART ENRICHED MY LIFE THROUGH A DEEPER APPRECIATION FOR THE COMMUNITY.

I still love its mission to bring nourishing meals to shelters and to children. FareStart is a sense of family. There's a lot of people that care about you, that help you to be successful, help you learn to fly again.

*So picture yourself in the mist of this glory
and describe yourself as a part of this story...*

JUDGE JUDITH HIGHTOWER

Garlic

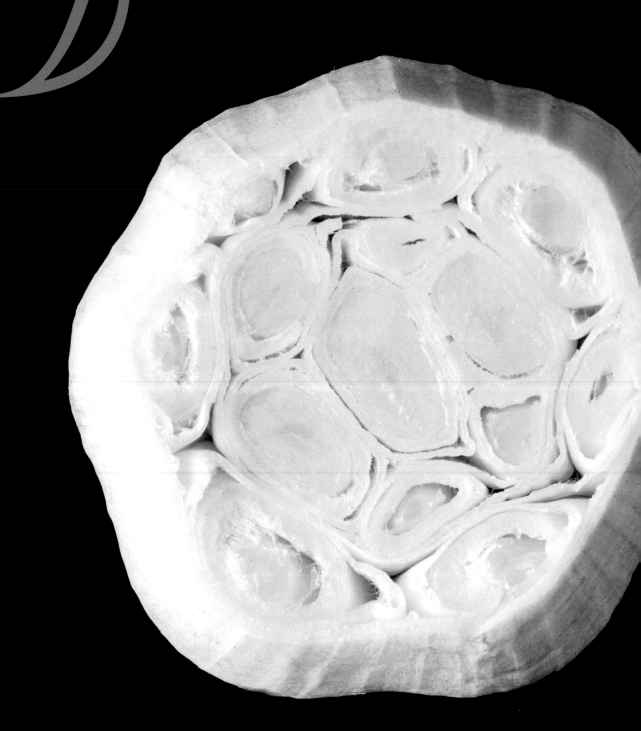

STRIPED SEABASS
WITH GARLIC AND GUINDILLA DONOSTIA STYLE

Chef Joseph E. Jimenez de Jimenez

INGREDIENTS

1 whole striped seabass (3-3½ pounds)

1½ cups olive oil

6 cloves garlic: 4 finely chopped, 2 sliced

3 lemons, juice only

1 chili pepper sliced, seedless

½ cup flat parsley, finely chopped, for garnish

Salt, to taste

INSTRUCTIONS

Preheat oven to 475 degrees F.

Clean the fish from the backbone, leaving the tail on. Wash the fish. Dry the fish very carefully with a towel. Sprinkle with lemon juice and salt, and add ½ cup of olive oil. Marinate for 40-45 minutes in a cool place.

In a small baking pan, place the fish skin-side down, and bake for 10 minutes. Turn the fish over, and bake for another 6 minutes. While baking, baste often with olive oil. Place the fish on a platter.

Meanwhile, in a sauté pan, sauté the remaining oil, garlic, and chili pepper. The result will be a very hot, flavored oil.

Salt the fish to taste, and pour the flavored garlic oil over the fish. Garnish with fresh chopped flat parsley. Serve very hot.

DAVID COFFEY

RECOVERY CAFE

A core of our program is our recovery circles.

WHEN I THINK OF AMAZING THINGS, I THINK OF FARESTART.

When I moved to Seattle in 2005 to work at Recovery Café, FareStart was on the radar as a partner. We were both located in the Josephinum, and Megan Karch's office was across the atrium from mine. She was always so generous with her time.

I got involved with Recovery Café by pure grace. Someone forwarded my resume to the founder and that led to me being interviewed and hired. I've been with them now for 10 years.

I can't believe I get paid to do what I do; it's the best job in the world!

> We help each individual reclaim life as a person worthy of giving and receiving love.

Recovery Café was founded as a direct response to the critical, unmet need for those who suffer on the margins – to provide long-term recovery support.

We offer a fundamental service that helps break the cycle of destruction and despair for individuals who have suffered trauma, homelessness, addiction, and other mental health challenges.

Whether in crisis, newer to recovery, in long-term recovery, after a relapse, during a difficult life change, or during mental health transition, the Café is a refuge of care and healing. We provide support, resources, and a community of care along the entire continuum of a person's need for recovery assistance. We teach people ways to manage mental health, maintain sobriety, and build community. We help each individual reclaim life as a person worthy of giving and receiving love.

A core of our program is our recovery circles.

These are small, loving support groups that meet every week. People in places of isolated loneliness come to these circles and begin to be known and loved again.

I remember in one circle, there was a young woman, and she shared with the group her joy to have to decide between two different jobs. She had enrolled several months before in the FareStart program and that decision was a new beginning. From there she got housing, her life moved forward, and she came back to seeing herself as a person of dignity and value.

In a book I love, called *Tattoos on the Heart* by Greg Boyle, the author talks about returning people to themselves, to who they once were.

There's a lot of overlap between that concept, FareStart, and the Recovery Café.

84% report Recovery Café has increased the amount of hope in their lives, and 75% report that since being at the Café, they have become a better advocate for themselves.

70% report that the Café has helped prevent relapse. Of those who report having a relapse since coming to Recovery Café, 69% report that Recovery Café helped them maintain longer periods of drug-and alcohol-free time, and 45% believe that Recovery Café has helped them get back on track more quickly.

53% report experiencing suicidal behavior before coming to the Café, and 31% believe Recovery Café helped prevent suicidal behavior. Of those, 55% reported visiting the ER before coming to Recovery Café, and 31% report that their visits to the ER have decreased since coming to Recovery Café.

When people ask us who we partner with, we are happy to say FareStart. Megan Karch was a great resource with regard to our New Market Tax Credit and our capital campaign.

I was riding on the bus one day, and there were two young people sitting next to me. I listened to them talk about how they were going to the FareStart Tuesday orientation.

By the conversation, I could tell they had turned a corner in their lives.

They were going to make a new path.

And, suddenly, it felt like I was riding next to hope.

DAVID COFFEY

Recovery Café was founded on the knowledge that every human being is precious and beloved regardless of past trauma, mental and emotional anguish, addictive behaviors, or mistakes made. They provide a beautiful, safe, warm, drug and alcohol free space and loving community to anchor Members (our most closely-supported consumers) in the sustained recovery needed to gain and maintain access to housing, social and health services, healthy relationships, education, and employment.

The program is designed to help people maintain recovery, reduce relapse, and fulfill their potential.

They provide support, resources and a community of care along the entire continuum of a person's need for recovery assistance. Whether in crisis, newer to recovery, in long-term recovery, after a relapse, during a difficult life change, or mental health transition, the Café is there as a refuge of care with evidence-based addiction support and love.

They teach people ways to manage mental health, maintain sobriety, and build community. They help each individual reclaim life as a person worthy of giving and receiving love.

Through their work, Recovery Café prevents individuals from another potentially life-ending crisis, to help them stabilize, and allowing mental health and addiction support professionals to focus on health maintenance and addiction prevention.

DOW-JAY, NGOW-YOK-SOONG (CHOPPED BEEF AND STRING BEANS)

David Coffey

INGREDIENTS

2 cups rice

1-pound bag frozen cut green beans or more to taste *(use fresh green beans if preferred)*

1 cup water, boiling

1 teaspoon beef boullion

½ to 1 pound hamburger

2 tablespoons olive oil

1 garlic clove, minced

1 small onion, diced

1-2 eggs, slightly beaten

Soy sauce, to taste

INSTRUCTIONS

Cook rice according to package instructions.

Meanwhile, cook green beans with a two tablespoons of water for 5 minutes in microwave. (Don't add salt - that's added later with the soy sauce.) Set aside.

Add bullion to boiling water. Set aside.

Heat oil in pan, add hamburger, garlic, and onion, and brown. Add beans and bullion water. Cover, and cook 5 minutes over medium heat. Stir in eggs, and cook over low heat, stirring constantly but gently, until eggs thicken; add soy sauce, and stir for a few seconds.

Serve over hot rice.

This is one of my favorite recipes that comes from my wife, Hilary's, family

EDIBLE FLOUR. SWEET PEA

Norton Clapp, founder of
Medina Foundation, wrote:

The world we live in is not static.
It is dynamic, it's exciting, and it presents
us with great opportunities. Thus, while
what we learn in school is good, we must
never forget the fact that it is only the
beginning of a great and continuing
learning process...

FareStart teaches their students self-sufficiency, concrete culinary skills, and life skills. They meet the needs of the whole person by investing in a holistic way. That's why so many of the graduates are still working years after their training.

Their model is innovative, and there are so many benefits to so many people - from the students going through the program to the people who eat food at the FareStart Restaurant to those who eat the meals that are cooked for the shelters and care centers to the restaurant owners that employ the graduating chefs.

The FareStart model puts all the money generated from the meals and the restaurant back into the organization. In the funding community, we look for good work to scale, and the FareStart Catalyst Kitchens program does just that.

FareStart is the gold standard of what a nonprofit should look like.

Medina funds basic human services, helping people towards self-sufficiency. Everything that FareStart is doing aligns with the Medina mission.

MEDINA
FOUNDATION

When the Medina Foundation began in 1947, our grants went to help the recipient buy a new pair of shoes or pay tuition for a medical student. Some grant applications were handwritten.

Our strategies have greatly evolved since then. More recently, we can see that the way we looked at hunger in the 1980's is different from the way we look at it today. We now address homelessness with supportive services rather than housing alone.

Today's nonprofits have strategic plans, and they measure results. One thing remains constant, though. The Medina Foundation has consistently been willing to undertake new ventures and initiatives, especially those of unusual scope and complexity.

THROUGH THREE GENERATIONS OF
TRUSTEES, OUR STORY IS
ONE OF LOOKING EVER FORWARD.

FareStart is highlighted as a long-term grantee in our 60th anniversary annual report. In this report, we refer to FareStart as a "Kitchen classroom. A recipe for a better community." Medina has been involved since FareStart's beginning, and to date, we've given over $600,000 to support their mission.

We go on site visits and meet with Executive Directors, like the inspiring Megan Karch.

At Medina, we share the vision of ending homelessness, but we focus our efforts on trying to make homelessness a rare, brief, and one-time event. If homelessness does happen, it should happen infrequently. Only once. And, we need to get people housed as quickly as possible.

We consider our support to organizations, like FareStart a vital part of addressing homelessness.

There are systemic problems that work against what we're trying to do - income inequality, the cost of housing, and the cost of living - but that doesn't mean the work we're supporting isn't worthwhile.

We go on site visits and meet with Executive Directors, like the inspiring Megan Karch. On these visits, we hear about the good work being done, the innovation, and the concrete stories of people who have been helped.

Through these stories, we see that our founder, Norton Clapp, was right... We are only at the beginning of a great and continuing learning process...

JENNIFER TEUNON

SALMON ROASTED IN BUTTER

Jennifer Teunon

INGREDIENTS

4 tablespoons (½ stick) butter

4 tablespoons chervil, parsley, or dill, minced

1½-2 pounds salmon fillet

Salt and freshly ground black pepper, to taste

Lemon wedges

INSTRUCTIONS

Preheat the oven to 475 degrees F.

Place the butter and half the herbs in a roasting pan just large enough to fit the salmon, and place it in the oven. Heat about 5 minutes, or until the butter melts and the herbs begin to sizzle. Be sure to preheat the butter along with a little bit of the herbs in a roasting pan in a hot oven. This preheating causes the fish to sizzle the instant it's set into the pan, so that it browns before it overcooks. If you start the fillet in a cold pan, it will simply turn a dull pink and will not brown until it is as dry as chalk.

Add the salmon to the pan, skin-side up. Roast 4 minutes. Remove from the oven, and remove the skin. If the skin does not lift right off, cook 2 minutes longer. Sprinkle with salt and pepper, and turn the fillet over. Sprinkle with salt and pepper again.

Roast 3 to 5 minutes more, depending on the thickness of the fillet and the degree of doneness you prefer. Cut into serving portions, spoon a little of the butter over each, and garnish with the remaining herbs. Serve with lemon wedges.

Variations

The basic recipe can easily be varied. An equal quantity of extra virgin olive oil can be substituted for the butter, and 2 teaspoons basil or thyme leaves or 2 tablespoons marjoram leaves can be substituted for the dill, chervil, or parsley.

Peanut oil can be substituted for the butter with a teaspoon of dark sesame oil for flavor if you like, and cilantro or mint can be substituted for the dill, chervil, or parsley; with this version, use lime instead of lemon.

HOW YOUR DONATIONS HELP

Many people in our community struggle with hunger and
unemployment, and homelessness is rising in the current
"haves and have-nots" climate of our economy.

Breaking the cycle of poverty requires a comprehensive approach
to transforming lives, and FareStart does this by providing people
in need with the tools - the renewed confidence and the regained
hope - required for a successful, self-sustaining future.

Examples of what a donation makes possible:

$25,000 - A year-long Catalyst Kitchens team can turn a nonprofit's fledgling job training program into a success

$10,000 - All the services and support required to a years worth of training and job retention services

$5,000 - All the services and support required to provide 16 weeks of adult culinary training

$2,500 - 8 weeks of Barista Training, or enough consulting time to replicate our model in another community

$1,000 - 8 months of job retention support, so our students have the best possible chance of success

$500 - Funds a student's housing, job placement services, and a full month of culinary training

$250 - Supports a student's counseling services, life-skills classes, and two weeks of culinary training courses

$100 - A full week of culinary training courses & clothing for a student to wear during interviews

$50 - Buys hot lunches for a youth barista during the 8-week program

$25 - A healthy meal for a student's family while he/she is in training

ONION

"Today, I am looking at my future,

and I have more confidence, hope,

and optimism than I've had in years.

The FareStart culinary training

program is a game changer, and now,

I'm here to play in the second half."

- FareStart graduate

One in eight Americans lives
below the poverty line.

HOMELE

SSNESS

NICHOLAS PRIOR

Award-winning Photographer

I had not made a habit of photographing the homeless prior to this FareStart project, and the truth is this is not a project I would have undertaken on my own. But, knowing that these images would benefit **FareStart** and could in some way benefit the homeless of Seattle helped me to overcome my concerns with respecting the privacy of others and my fear of approaching strangers.

The photographs were taken over a week in October 2005, and during this time, I attempted to meet as many homeless people as possible. They were not hard to find. My photographic process began, not with a camera, but by offering of food.

A FACE CONTAINS ITS OWN HISTORY, AND EYES CONTAIN THEIR OWN EMOTION.

I showed respect to the subjects by asking them how they wished to be depicted. Some chose to look helpless; some chose to highlight their indomitable fortitude.

Sympathy without action is useless.

Overcoming homelessness is challenging because too many people feel disconnected to the problem. Most people have never known life on the streets. It is something that happens to people you feel are different.

In the end, I hope that you see these people as I came to see them - *as people.*

**Homeless conjures a very particular image of being
"unsheltered." But, a home is more than shelter.**

A home is warmth, comfort, privacy, and security. It's the family and the
people you love; it's companionship. Home is birthday parties, raking
leaves, and the sound of music playing. It's the smell of a meal cooking.

Home belongs to all the senses. It's timeless. It is what we think of when
we think of the past and what we think of when we think of the future.

A home is more than a thing that surrounds us; it's inside of us.
And most important, home signifies dignity.

This photograph illustrates the collaborative nature of many of these photographs. I asked to take Ron's picture, but I did not ask him to pose, and I did not ask him to hold up that sign that he wrote. In writing that sign and holding it up, I believe that Ron helped me to make a very compelling photograph.

Initially, I was struck by the Mini-Storage sign itself. The idea that was interesting to me was that some of us have so many physical possessions that we literally pay rent to store them.

RON'S SIGN, IT TURNS OUT,
IS A HAND DRAWN COLLEGE DIPLOMA
TO REPLACE HIS ORIGINAL, NOW LOST.

Ron's sign, I think, serves to remind us about our preconceptions about the homeless. It's interesting also because when I first printed the photograph, I printed it small, and you couldn't read the sign that Ron was holding. This troubled me a bit, but then, I decided that I liked it that way as well. I think the small sign is a nice counterpoint to the big sign, and I think it serves as a good metaphor for the homeless problem in general.

Here we have a big sign, that everyone can read, and it's really about nothing at all; it's about something rather superficial. And, then we have this small sign that says so much.

The fact that we can't easily read the small sign is a reminder that we have to go beneath the surface of things, dig a little deeper, and reach out and try to get to know someone, not just take things at the level of first impressions, that it's rather easy to overlook the more important things in life.

NICHOLAS PRIOR

Onion

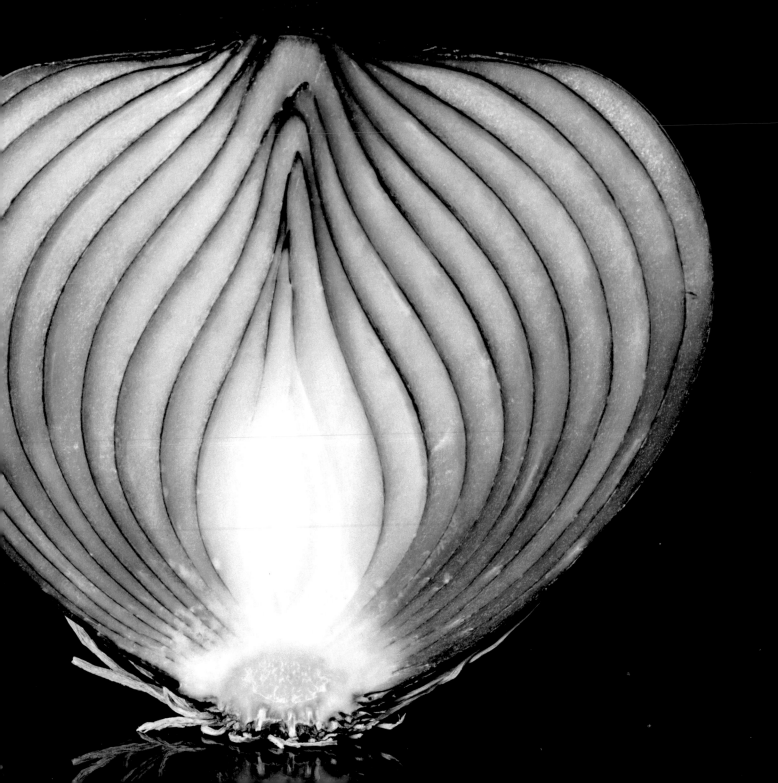

CHEF BUCK'S TARRAGON CHICKEN SALA

FareStart Restaurant

INGREDIENTS

———————— ● ————————

1½ pounds cooked chicken, medium
diced

⅔ cup sour cream

1 cup mayonnaise

4 teaspoons Dijon mustard

4 sprigs fresh tarragon, finely chopped

½ red onion, finely diced

2 celery stalks, finely diced

Salt and pepper, to taste

White wine vinegar, to taste

INSTRUCTIONS

———————— ● ————————

Mix all ingredients together, and add
salt, pepper, and white wine vinegar.

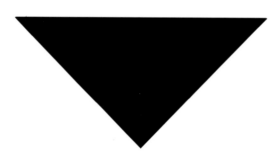

"Coming to FareStart made me feel like I
was worth something. They accepted me and
gave me something to do. And, there was so
much love...

I've never seen so much love
in one building."

- Clint, FareStart 2005 Graduate

STAND UP!
FOR THE
HOMELESS

BUT FIRST,
FINISH YOUR PIE.

BILL & MELINDA
GATES *foundation*

THE MOTTO OF THE GATES FOUNDATION IS
"EVERY LIFE HAS EQUAL VALUE."
THAT'S OUR CORE PRINCIPLE.

I am an accidental philanthropist, a social worker by training. I had been supporting the Bill & Melinda Gates Foundation as a consultant, **helping them develop their family homelessness strategy. I provided research on homelessness in Washington State.** This work led to me being asked to interview with the organization. There aren't too many social workers at the Foundation.

My first encounter with FareStart was food.

One of the people who interviewed me was Bill Gates, Sr. He sat down with my resume in front of him and said, **"Looks like you're interested in inequity. That's what we do here, and we have resources."** That's a pretty compelling pitch!

Prior to the Gates Foundation, I was working at King County in the Department of Human Services overseeing mental health and a variety of other service programs. The FareStart Restaurant on 2nd Avenue was near my office, and I think it was Bill Hobson from the Downtown Emergency Service Center that said we should grab lunch over there. Bill ran one of the largest homeless programs in the city and his was one of the contracts I was responsible for managing.

After this, I would take the people I was meeting to FareStart for lunch, but I didn't become more deeply involved with FareStart until I moved to my current position with the Bill and Melinda Gates Foundation.

One of the first grants the Foundation gave FareStart was a capital grant to help them purchase their current building on Virginia Street.

That's when I learned how much FareStart actually did for the community - so much more than a restaurant.

Over the years, we've continued to support FareStart. Most recently, we provided additional capital funding to help them mobilize their kitchens in the Pacific Tower.

There's almost no one I speak to that doesn't have homelessness somewhere in their lives.

As a funding provider, I realized FareStart is, at least, a triple bottom line operation and a critical resource for people who are homeless. FareStart helps the homeless find meaning, stability, and employment in a very important way. **They help people figure out who they want to be and who they are.**

FareStart helps the homeless in an incredibly innovative and respectful way. In addition to the culinary training program, they also provide services for the community in terms of the meals they serve and the programs they cook for. This is an important piece of the social services fabric of our community.

FareStart is a successful business, giving homelessness a positive and forward looking face to the diners that come into their restaurant.

They provide an interface between the general public on the issue of homelessness - one that educates, informs, and enlightens. And, their Catalyst Kitchens program demonstrates thought leadership and replication, moving the model out to cities across the country.

H O M E L E S S N E S S

There's almost no one I speak to that doesn't have homelessness somewhere in their lives, where it hasn't touched them directly. But, some people distance themselves from the problem intellectually and emotionally, and that's when implicit bias surfaces and becomes an obstacle.

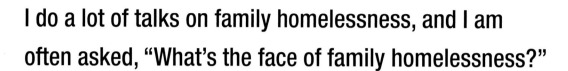

I do a lot of talks on family homelessness, and I am often asked, "What's the face of family homelessness?"

I say...

"Do you have a mirror? Take a look. That's the face of homelessness. It could be any one of us." When you pretend this isn't true, you distance yourself from the issue.

Not long ago, I went to a day center for homeless women, and I sat down with a group of about 20 of them to have a conversation about their experiences.

I was overwhelmed by the stories of survival - the incredible strength, power, and resilience each of those women needed to mobilize.

Sitting with these 20 women, it was acutely clear to me that I was still learning about homelessness from their wisdom, experience, and knowledge. By comparison, I've never even spent one night on the streets. I'm not sure how long I could survive if it were me.

Our goal at the Gates Foundation is to be catalytic with our investments. We look for an impact from our investments far disproportional to the dollar value of what we're investing. We invest at a system level with the goal of transformation.

FareStart is catalytic, transforming the lives of their students, preparing nutritional food for the hungry mouths they feed, and scaling their model through Catalyst Kitchens. When you dine at the FareStart Restaurant, you are only seeing the very tip of the iceberg.

You see something that needs fixing,
you fix it. It doesn't matter how
important you are, how tall
you are, how old you are.

I LEARNED A LIFE LESSON FROM A CAN OF SODA...

When the Gates Foundation was in the building at 1551 Eastlake, the cafeteria there was run by FareStart. Bill Gates Sr. would have lunch in the cafeteria every day. Off to the side of the cafeteria, there was a little refrigerator case that had sodas in it. It was on wheels, so there was space underneath it.

I remember Bill Gates Sr. getting up after finishing his lunch, busing his plate, thanking the FareStart staff for a nice meal, which he always did, and leaving. I'm still sitting there eating when, 2 or 3 minutes later, he comes back in with a yardstick in his hand. I was thinking, "Who still has a yardstick in their office?"

Bill, who was 81 at the time, six foot six inches tall, gets down on his hands and knees and, with his yardstick, pokes under the refrigerator case. Out rolls a can of soda. The can had fallen under the refrigerator and rolled to the back.

I saw it, so it was my responsibility to do something about it.

He picked it up, took it to the sink, washed it off with soap and water, and then, put it back in the refrigerator case. As he was leaving the cafeteria, I stopped him and said, "Bill, you know there's 300 people in this building that would have gotten that can of soda for you if you'd just asked us to do it."

He looked at me and said, "I saw it, so it was my responsibility to do something about it."

Who else could give you a life lesson with a can of soda? You see something that needs fixing, you fix it. It doesn't matter how important you are, how tall you are, how old you are. If you need to get down on your hands and knees and roll a can of soda out from under a refrigerator case, you do it. If you see it, you take care of it.

In the ambition of wanting to solve big, audacious problems, there's a bit of hubris, and it's hubris that allows you to be bold. We must all be bold.

Every life has equal value. That's what I believe.

Simple Vegetarian Corn Chowder

David Wertheimer

INGREDIENTS

●

2-3 tablespoons olive oil

2 sweet onions, chopped

3-4 large carrots, sliced thinly

3 stalks celery, sliced thinly

2 red peppers, chopped

Kernels removed from 6 ears of steamed sweet corn or a one-pound bag of frozen sweet corn
(more if you need to stretch to serve guests!)

1-2 cups vegetable stock

Salt and pepper, to taste

Dash of cayenne pepper

INSTRUCTIONS

●

Heat olive oil, and sauté the onion until wilted. Add the carrots, celery, and red pepper, and cook until slightly softened but not overcooked.

Add the corn, salt, pepper, and cayenne, and stir until warmed. Add vegetable stock until ingredients are just covered, and cook gently for 10-15 minutes.

When the ingredients are softened (but not mushy!), place about ½ to ⅔ of the mixture in a blender or food processor, and blend. Be sure to leave enough chunky veggies to give the chowder texture and bits of color.

Continue to warm on the stove until you're ready to eat!

This recipe dates from my graduate school days when I was living on a shoestring and needed to make something that was inexpensive but filling and tasty enough to lift my spirits even when contemplating dense reading assignments and term papers.

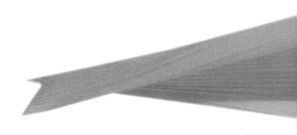

orn

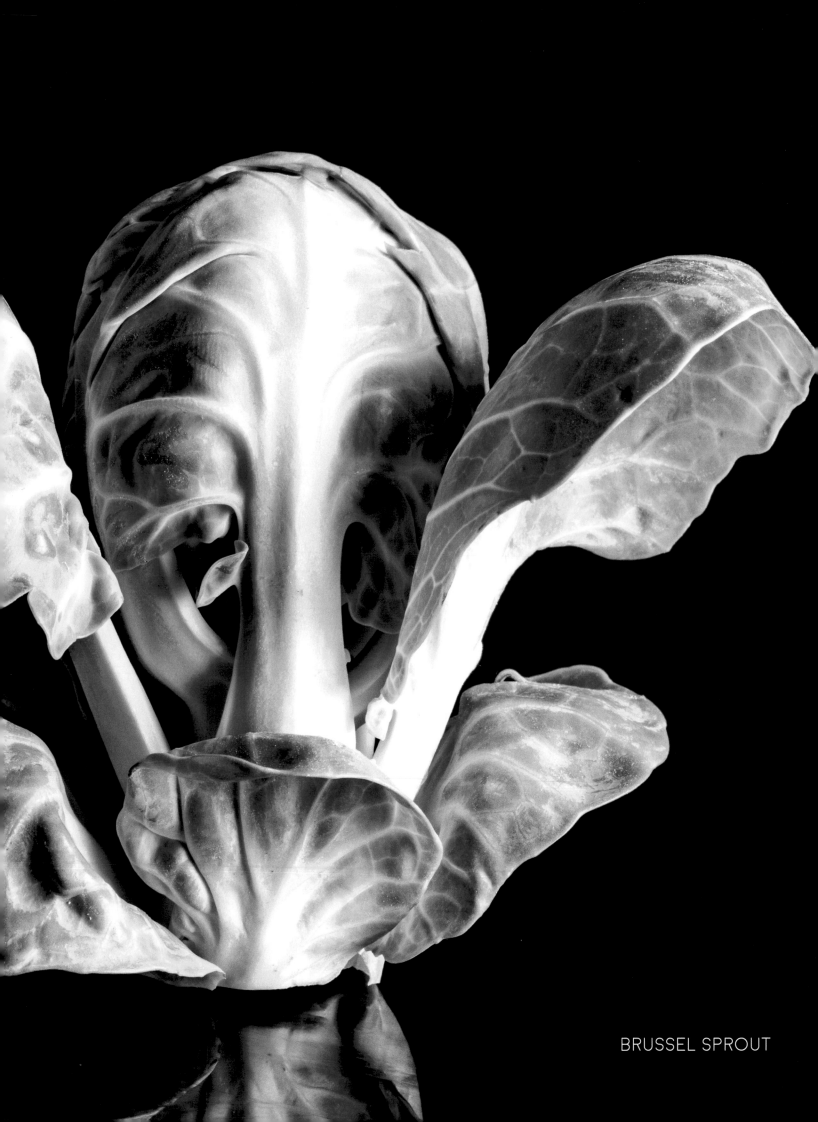

BRUSSEL SPROUT

"Before the Barista program, I was lost. I had only finished 9th grade, dropped out of school, and had no idea what the real world was like.

Once I entered the Barista Program, I felt at home among the smell of gourmet coffees. It was a safe place for me, so I could be who I am - 'Queer.'"

- Mandy, Youth Barista Program Graduate

JUDGE MARY YU

BOARD MEMBER

> ## My mission and purpose in life is serving a remedial or corrective function - correcting injustices, lifting the yoke that's placed on others, making it a level playing field for everybody.

As a lawyer and now, as a judge, I see myself serving this purpose. I am correcting the injustices that exist just because we are human and reforming the institutions that intentionally oppress and those that unintentionally do so.

An attorney friend invited me to consider being on the FareStart Board, and with hindsight, I see it was because I was a judge in contact with the population they were trying to serve. So many of the individuals that come in front of me often find themselves without a home for a variety of reasons.

I know how complicated it all is - releasing people from jail in the middle of the night with nowhere to go begins a whole cycle of being put at a disadvantage. Living without shelter, economic resources, and emotional support creates chronic homelessness.

I've never met anyone that came in front of me that didn't want a job, that didn't want self-sufficiency, that didn't want the chance to be successful.

When you serve on a nonprofit Board, you're on a working Board. This means commitment. As a Board, we stretched one another. Looking at the organization, our mission, and our community and its problems, we found common agreement, and we found differences of opinion. What makes our Board so great is the different opinions, life perspectives, and approaches.

I find myself personally growing and thinking outside of my box or comfort zone. I hope I offered insight into the population we serve because I saw these individuals every single day and knew how difficult it was to move from being homeless or disadvantaged to being self-sufficient.

Entrepreneurship and commitment to social progress

- those are the values that make FareStart successful.

At every single Board meeting, the FareStart mission is a part of the conversation. We look at everything we propose to do and ask if it really aligns with our core mission. At a Board retreat, we participated in a life skills training class similar to one our students go through. It reminded us that the people who come to the FareStart program sometimes just need a gentle loving hand to walk with them through the process of recovery. We can help individuals believe their life has value and is worth living.

Gentle, loving, small steps.

I came from a very simple family background. My parents were working class, and both came to this country as undocumented individuals - my mother from Mexico, my father from China. They didn't have access to resources or education but wanted to ensure that their children would have such access. They were hard-working and proud that their work would provide opportunities for their children.

I believe my Catholic background fostered my sense of social responsibility. I learned the value and dignity of the human person and that each one of us bears responsibility for doing something to promote that dignity. I grew up in a time where the church was a leader on issues of civil rights and racial equality, and this is where the primary values of social justice were instilled in me.

EDIBLE FLOUR. WHITE FREESIA

FareStart provides the opportunity for people to transform their lives. That's more than just giving a person a place to sleep. We enable and empower them to discover their talent and abilities and to find self-respect through self-sufficiency. Employment and economic independence restores hope and confidence - we provide reasons for believing.

That's what makes the program unique.

Graduation really embodies FareStart. Every student serves to remind us that like springtime, there's going to be a flower that blooms, there's going to be the regeneration; our students can emerge anew with optimism and hope.

As human beings, we are fragile and, sometimes, putting us back together can take a lifetime. FareStart is about rebuilding our human capital. FareStart helps individuals believe in themselves and enables them to rediscover their inherent dignity.

And, that's a very different way of looking at homelessness.

JUDGE MARY YU

RE-ENTRY PARTNERSHIP

In 2014, FareStart implemented a partnership with the Washington State Department of Corrections to streamline the entry into our adult training program from incarceration for eligible and interested men and women, bringing them directly upon their release to FareStart with no time or services gap in between.

The challenges in adjusting post-release and securing employment for those with criminal records are many, and the barriers to success are high. But, a seamless transition to FareStart ensures that the services and opportunities needed for this special group are in place.

In particular, FareStart's life-skills training and the availability of counseling are vital for those coming from incarceration to develop new attitudes and beliefs about themselves and reorient them to life and behavioral norms outside of the prison system. The direct transition, immediate basic needs services, and wrap-around support services that we provide serve to ensure that the risks of postincarceration homelessness, joblessness, and re-offending are minimized.

FareStart has always served students with criminal records *(historically, about 40 percent of our student population)*. The aim of this partnership is to remove obstacles that might impede their successful, long-term outcomes and ultimately, to reduce recidivism for ex-felons through job training and stable employment.

Of the initial group of graduates who came from the Department of Corrections partnership, 100 percent have been placed in jobs, and our DOC enrollees' retention rate in the program is higher than our overall adult program retention rate.

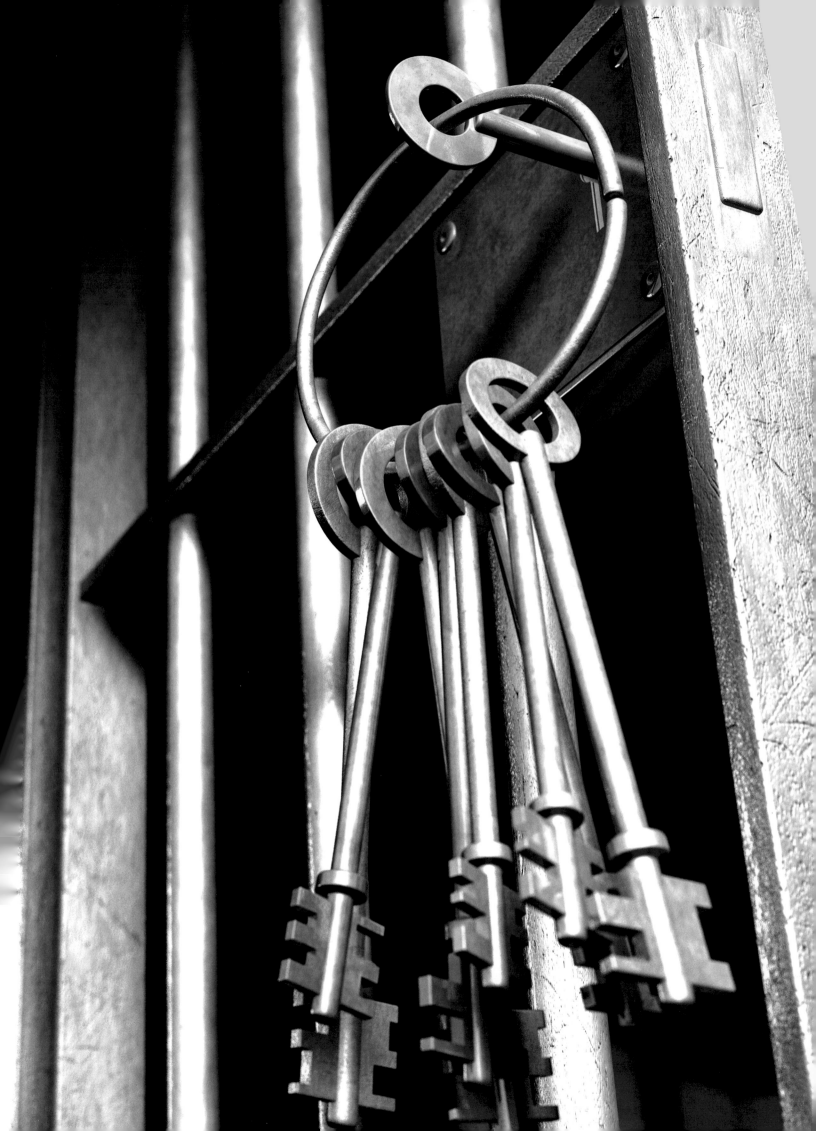

Scallops

Curry Paste

¼ pound fresh galangal, peeled

¼ pound ginger, peeled

¼ pound fresh turmeric, peeled

½ pound shallots, peeled

1 head garlic, peeled

1 bunch cilantro

Juice from 2 limes

5 dried Thai chilies, soaked in hot water
to soften

Peanut oil

Place all ingredients, except peanut oil,
in food processor, and grind. Add just
enough peanut oil to make paste.
Continue to grind until paste is smooth.

This recipe makes more than you'll need
for the sea scallops recipe. It's versatile
and can be used in many recipes. Freeze
it in small batches, and pull it out as you
need it!

Thai Curry Sea Scallops

Chef Chris Keff

INGREDIENTS

●

20 large sea scallops

1 tablespoon peanut oil

⅔ cup chicken stock

½ cup coconut milk

3 tablespoons curry paste

Salt, to taste

INSTRUCTIONS

●

Place peanut oil in a large non-stick skillet. Heat to smoking. Remove from flame, and quickly add scallops to pan, one by one.

Return to flame; sear scallops approximately 2 minutes on each side.

Remove scallops from pan, and discard excess oil.

Add curry paste to now empty pan, and sauté briefly. Add chicken stock, and reduce by half. Add coconut milk, and continue to simmer until sauce is thick enough to coat a spoon.

Pour sauce over scallops, and serve.

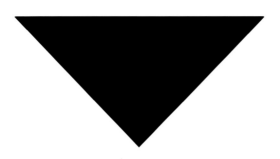

"FareStart literally gives people
second chances. They say, "We
believe in you and where you can go."

They give you a genuine shot. It's an
act of kindness in its greatest form.

I can't begin to say how
thankful I am for FareStart."

- Diana, 2016 FareStart graduate

Hunger, shelter, and clothing are basics. no one should be struggling for the basics, especially in America.

CHEF THIERRY RAUTUREAU

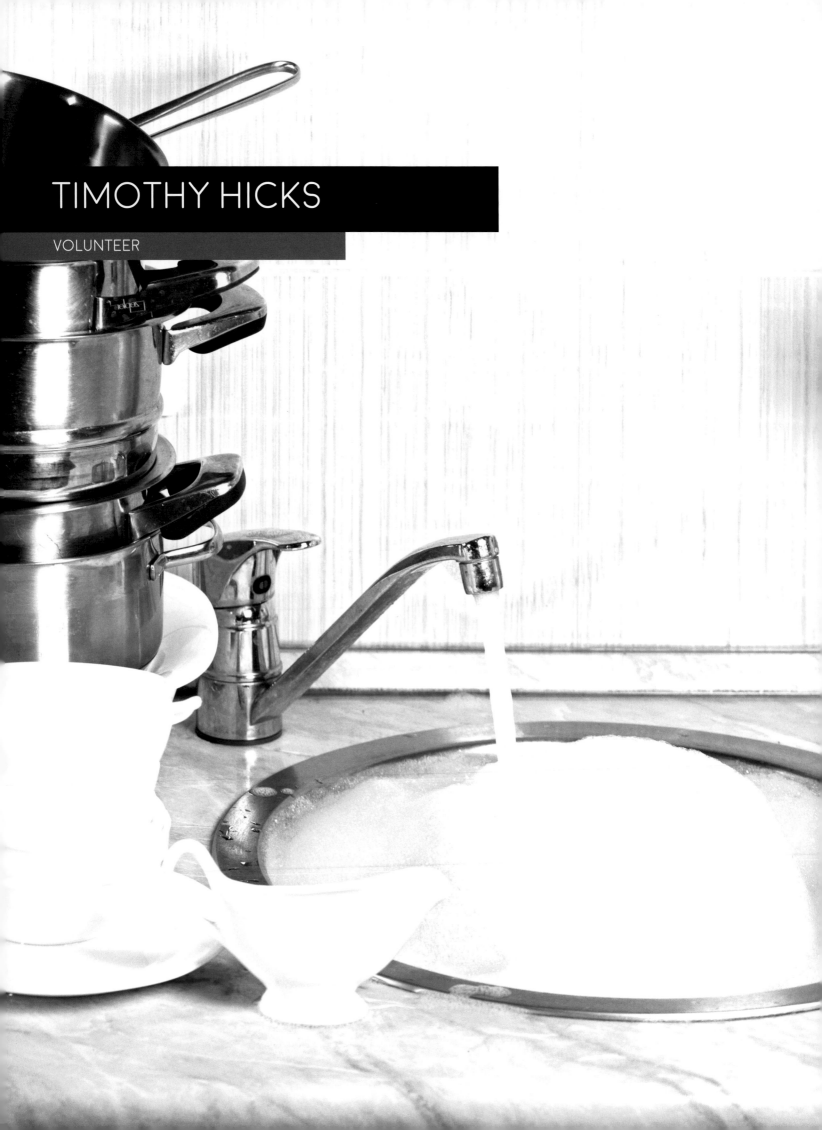

TIMOTHY HICKS

VOLUNTEER

A LONG TIME AGO, THERE WAS A PLACE I HAD NEVER HEARD OF CALLED FARESTART.

A friend took me out to dinner at the restaurant on 2nd Avenue. In that facility, most people had to wait outside for their table - rain, snow, or shine. It was such a compelling event, and I didn't even realize that some of the people I talked to were just volunteers. I started going on a weekly basis.

My first job at FareStart was as a busboy, replacing paper table cloths. I find when you volunteer doing something you like that you meet people you like. I met some great people! For example, I met Bob through my service to FareStart.

Bob was a Boeing airplane painter during the day, and all he ever really wanted to do was wash dishes. He was THE dishwasher there for years.

About 4 years ago, I started coming down to FareStart to do practice interviews with students about to graduate. It changed my view of the world. I found that the more I interact with the students, the more meaningful the experience is for me. Later, when I got home, I started looking through resumes, and I understood my view of homelessness had completely changed.

When I looked at the resume of the first person I interviewed, a well-spoken man, I saw he'd been in prison for 25 years. Another had been at Microsoft for 15 years. And one, just this last year, had Bachelors from Clemson and a Masters from Stanford. He spoke five different languages.

My assumptions of homelessness were out the window.

Addiction doesn't care what it says on your 1040, what your IQ or zip code is, or how many degrees you have after your name.

And, neither does homelessness.

To me, FareStart is one of the more dynamic nonprofits I've run into. They run businesses. They're always thinking "what's the next step; what's the business model; how do we get more students involved?"

**On this Board, nobody just writes a check;
they're actively involved.**

It's one thing for an organization to say we do 750,000 meals, but when you see behind the scenes, it becomes a much more meaningful experience. So, I started giving people tours of the FareStart building.

There was a couple that came in for a Guest Chef Night, and I found out it was their first time. I was chatting with them, and they thought it would be interesting to have a tour.

So, I did the tour, and the couple was very interested and asked lots of questions. When we got back to their table, they said they'd like to make a donation. I found out about a week later that this couple donated $200,000.

You just never know!

FARESTART HAS CHANGED MY VIEW OF THE WORLD.

TIMOTHY HICKS

arlic

FALL GREENS
WITH TOMATO CHERVIL VINAIGRETTE

Chef Lisa Dupar

INGREDIENTS

Mixed greens

2 cloves garlic

1 tablespoons Dijon mustard

¼ cup tomato paste

¾ cup white wine vinegar

2 teaspoons kosher salt, plus more

¼ red onion, thinly sliced

½ cup pumpkin seeds

Dash of sea salt

1 tablespoon cracked black pepper

1 cup canola-olive oil blend

2 tablespoons chervil, chopped

INSTRUCTIONS

In a food processor, combine garlic, Dijon mustard, tomato paste, white wine vinegar, kosher salt, and pepper. Puree until smooth. Drizzle oil, and blend until smooth. Fold in chopped chervil.

Toss onion slices with a little olive oil and a touch of kosher salt. Grill on a rack until tender and golden.

In a hot skillet, heat olive oil, and then, sauté pumpkin seeds until they pop like popcorn. Sauté until golden. Season with sea salt. Drain on paper towels.

To assemble, toss mixed greens with dressing, grilled onions, and toasted pumpkin seeds.

FENNEL RUBBED STEAMED SALMON

Chef Tom Douglas

INGREDIENTS

Spice Rub

1 tablespoon fennel seeds

2 teaspoons grated lemon zest

1½ teaspoons kosher or sea salt

¾ teaspoon freshly ground black pepper

Salmon

1½ pounds salmon fillet, preferably wild,

cut into 4 portions

2 cups chicken broth

2 cups water

Zest from 1 lemon, removed in long strips

with a vegetable peeler

2 bay leaves

Fennel Salad

1 small fennel bulb with fronds

Extra virgin olive oil

1 lemon

Kosher or sea salt, to taste

Freshly ground black pepper, to taste

Fennel

INSTRUCTIONS

To make the spice rub, in a small pan over medium heat, toast the fennel seeds until fragrant. Allow to cool, and then, grind seeds in a spice grinder. In a small bowl, combine the ground fennel, zest, salt, and pepper. Pat the fennel spice rub evenly over the salmon, using all the rub.

Place chicken broth, water, lemon peel, and bay leaves in the bottom of your steamer. Bring to a boil. Lay the salmon fillets in the steamer basket. Pick some of the fronds from your fennel bulb, and place them over the salmon. Cover, and steam until the salmon is just done, about 5 to 6 minutes.

Meanwhile, make the fennel salad. Cut off the remaining fronds from the fennel bulb, and set a few of them aside. Cut the fennel bulb in half, remove the core, and very thinly slice. Put the fennel in a bowl with a few of the fronds. Dress the salad to taste with olive oil, squeezes of fresh lemon juice, salt, and pepper.

When the salmon is cooked, transfer to plates, and top each piece of salmon with some of the fennel salad.

Note: You can grind the spices in a clean electric coffee bean grinder. For steaming the fish, Chinese bamboo steamers work well and are not very expensive, but any steamer setup is fine. Steaming is a fast cooking method, so check your fish often, and don't let it overcook.

On average, 90% of FareStart Adult Culinary Program graduates secure employment within three months of graduation.

TRANSF
LIVES

ORMING

Transforming Lives through Three Training Programs

Adult Culinary Program

FareStart's comprehensive training program incorporates a full range of services that provide disadvantaged men and women with job and life skills, meet their basic needs while they are in the program, and enable them to make positive life choices during and after they complete the program. The program includes the following components:

• Hands-on culinary job training in FareStart's contract kitchen, restaurant, and catering social enterprises

• Comprehensive case management

• Life and financial skills training

• Job readiness, placement, and retention services

• Stable housing, two meals a day on-site, and access to transportation

• Wrap-around support, including access to continued education, mental health/recovery services, and counseling

Youth Barista and Customer Service Training Program

Our Youth Barista program targets hard-to-serve street youth. This program offers job training and placement, life skills, employment counseling, classroom, and on-the-job training in the competitive espresso industry. Our partner, YouthCare, provides comprehensive support services for homeless youth as they progress through the program. On-the-job training is provided at the FareStart Café @ 2100 in the Rainier Valley.

Youth Culinary and Customer Service Training Program

In partnership with Seattle Public Schools' Interagency Academy, students in our Youth Culinary and Customer Service Training Program will learn practical culinary and barista job skills while earning high school credit. At press time, this program was in the pilot phase as we refine our best practices. To learn more, visit farestart.org.

Both youth programs use a comprehensive approach to address the current needs of this demographic by increasing opportunities for employment and wage progression, employment while in high school with schedule flexibility, and more diverse job opportunities. The aim of these programs is to connect youth with jobs, internships, and educational advancement opportunities in order to instill a strong skillset that will prevent a lifetime of poverty. On-the-job training is provided at the FareStart Café @ Pacific Tower on Beacon Hill.

More than a decade ago, when YouthCare and FareStart came together to start the Barista Training and Customer Service Program, we knew it was inherently a good idea, but the learning and successes have been even more than we could have expected.

Each agency brings their best skills to the table in this partnership, and together, we ensure homeless young people have the technical training, customer service skills, support, and confidence to move forward in their lives.

Now, our program model has found its way across the nation, being modified and replicated in cities, including New York, NY, Chicago, IL, and Gulf Port, MS.

Each student cohort names their group, so as YouthCare raises a cup of coffee to our friends and steadfast partners at FareStart to celebrate their 25th Anniversary, so too lift the mugs of hundreds of graduates from teams, including the Love-A-Lattes, Fuel Force, and Bean Buddies.

A very heartfelt congratulations!

MELINDA GIOVENGO
EXECUTIVE DIRECTOR, YOUTHCARE

IT'S A LONG STORY...

Lived in Vegas.
Got in trouble.
Ended up becoming homeless.
Not a fun place to be.

I'd been out of contact with my daughter at the time for about 8 years. I went to the library, got online, and found out she lived in the Seattle area. So, I saved enough money to get on a bus. I had about $60 in my pocket. I arrived not knowing anybody but not ready to get in touch with her again.

I was living under Cherry Street by I-5, going to Connections, a place where you could bathe and get your clothes washed, when **I saw a poster for FareStart.** So, I applied and was accepted. Shortly after, I moved into housing.

I went to interviews every week, and I didn't give up.

When I was in Phase 2 of the program, my FareStart Chef Instructor was doing prep work in a restaurant down on the pier to make a little extra money. I kept bugging him to take me down to the restaurant to see if I really wanted to be a cook. After 3 weeks, he said, "My chef says, 'okay.'"

I went and spent a whole day just doing seafood. It was hard work, but it was fun work. In my past life, I'd been a carpenter, so hard work never scared me. This was better than being outside lifting beams, especially with my crushed disc. You see, I have some wear and tear.

After I graduated, there weren't a lot of jobs out there; the economy wasn't doing too good. It took about 6 months to get a job. I went to interviews every week, and I didn't give up.

Finally, I got a job in a sports bar, moving up the ranks quickly due to my work ethic. I ended up becoming a manager after about a year. Later, I joined the owner in a startup venture, opening a Brazilian seafood bar in Ballard.

We used to do Guest Chef Nights at FareStart, but the bar was failing miserably. I was only just making enough money to pay my rent. I was eating as much as I could at the bar, saving spare food to eat later. I could only eat so much seafood. You know it's bad when you're looking forward to McDonald's but can't afford to go to one.

At Guest Chef Night, I met a chef that was here when I was going through the program. He told me that they had an opening. I remember when I left the program, I told them I'd come back and work at FareStart one day. **So, I applied for the job and got it.**

Since then, I've moved into a position as a chef instructor in Phase 2. That was about three and a half years ago.

When the students graduate, I stand up on the stairs, and it sometimes brings tears to my eyes. I remember what it feels like.

I have my own apartment now and joined Facebook even though I'm not a Facebook guy. I sent an invite to my daughter. Her initial response was "Why now?" So, I stepped back. About a week later, she sends a message and says, "How about we do lunch?"

Today, I'm close to my daughter again, my granddaughter who just turned sixteen, and my two grandboys, eleven and twelve, that I go fishing with. And, that's pretty much what I live for.

I love this job. Not only am I giving back, but I'm helping people that are walking in the shoes I wore.

I don't have the couple of years' worth of culinary school that some of the other chefs have. But, what I bring to the table is a whole other thing. When the students come into Phase 2, they get shown around the kitchen, and they learn the rules on how we do things. Then, I welcome them to Phase 2.

I tell them how FareStart really works, that I graduated this program in 2008. That gets their attention. I tell them if they work hard and put in the effort, they'll succeed.

I have some students come back and talk to me because of my background. Some of them are ready to quit.
I ask them if they want to go back out on the street.
I didn't. I haven't.
I tell them to work hard, put their head down, grind away. I've had them come back later to thank me for it.

I can't believe they pay me to do this.

CHEF GARY HALLER

Chowder

Corn and Bacon Chowder

Chef Gary Holler

INGREDIENTS

7 ounces bacon, medium diced

Oil for frying bacon

1⅛ cups corn

1 cup celery, medium diced

1 cup yellow onion, medium diced

1 russet potato, medium diced

1 cup carrots, medium diced

¼ cup flour

¼ cup butter

1 teaspoon dill, in a spice bag

1 teaspoon thyme, in a spice bag

1 bay leaf, in a spice bag

1 teaspoon garlic, minced

2 cups heavy cream

1¾ cups milk

½ jalapeno, small diced

Salt and pepper, to taste

INSTRUCTIONS

Coat bottom of sauce pan with oil, and render bacon until crispy around the edges.

Add garlic and jalepeno, and cook for 3 minutes. Melt butter, add flour, and mix. Cook rue for 5 minutes, stirring frequently. Add milk and heavy cream, and mix well.

Add spice bag; simmer over low heat for 30 minutes, stirring frequently.

Remove spice bag. Season with salt and pepper.

CHEF GARY'S PUMPKIN MUFFINS

FareStart Restaurant

INGREDIENTS

Dry Ingredients:

14 ounces all-purpose flour

1 teaspoon salt

1 teaspoon nutmeg, grated

2 teaspoons ground cinnamon

2½ teaspoons baking soda

½ tablespoon baking powder

Wet Ingredients:

22 ounces sugar

17 ounces pumpkin puree

8 ounces canola oil

⅔ cup water

4 eggs

INSTRUCTIONS

Preheat oven to 325 degrees F.

Sift dry ingredients together. Using the paddle attachment in a stand mixer bowl, mix wet ingredients until uniform and smooth.

Add dry ingredients, and mix until just incorporated.

Pour batter into lined or well-greased muffin tins.

Bake for 25 minutes or until a toothpick inserted in the center comes out clean.

Pumpkin

FOCACCIA BREAD

FareStart Restaurant

INGREDIENTS

440 grams all-purpose flour

338 grams water

10 grams salt

2½ teaspoons instant yeast

Olive oil for drizzling

INSTRUCTIONS

Mix the water and yeast for two minutes on medium speed in a stand mixer with the paddle attachment. Slowly incorporate the flour into the water/yeast mixture, and mix for two more minutes. Add salt, and mix another four minutes.

Rest dough for 10 minutes.

Remove paddle attachment, and replace with dough hook. Knead for six minutes on medium speed. Proof in a greased bowl until it doubles in size.

Grease a 9 by 13-inch baking sheet pan with pan spray or olive oil. Spread dough on pan, dimple with fingertips, and drizzle with olive oil. Let dough rise until it doubles in size. It should be light and pillow-like.

Preheat oven to 425 degrees F.

Bake dough for 15 minutes until golden brown. Cool for 10 to 20 minutes.

Cut into squares, and serve.

ONION

"I tell people I came to this town

with $10 in my pocket and now,

live in a nice apartment. I've never

owned my own place before."

- John, 1997 FareStart Graduate

Celery

VEAL BROTH

Chef Mauro Golmarvi

INGREDIENTS

●

2 pounds of various cuts of lean beef or veal with bones *(e.g., neck, shoulder, short ribs, or brisket, etc.)*

1 spongy bone *(knee)*

1 2½-inch piece of bone marrow *(optional)*

2 celery stalks, with leaves, broken into 3 pieces

2 medium carrots, peeled and cut in half

1 medium onion, quartered

6 sprigs fresh Italian parsley

3 bay leaves, broken into small pieces

6 black peppercorns

2 tablespoons salt

2 tablespoons tomato paste *(optional)*

4 quarts plus 2 cups cold water

INSTRUCTIONS

●

Rinse the bones quickly under cold running water. Place meat and bones in a very large pot. Add celery, carrots, onion, parsley, bay leaves, peppercorns, salt, and tomato paste.

Add cold water, and simmer, uncovered, over medium-low heat for 3 hours. Skim surface foam occasionally with a slotted spoon. More salt can be added at this point if necessary.

Strain broth, and discard solids. Broth can be separated into containers and frozen for later use.

JOHNNY

It was 48 square feet, three walls of concrete, one row of bars. **The Washington State Department of Corrections calls it solitary; Johnny called it home.**

"I was content. No one bothered me. I had my own space. I was going to get a television. I was fine with spending the rest of my life there," explains Johnny.

THE LONG ROAD TO FARESTART

To say Johnny has had a tumultuous life is an understatement. Born into a high-profile Filipino family, Johnny's early life seemed idyllic. Then, when he turned four, his life changed. His mother left the family, creating a scandal in the tight-knit, Catholic family.

"My father couldn't deal with it and turned to drinking, gambling, and eventually, heroin. I still remember him leaving me and my brother in a car all night in Chinatown while he went gambling. When he came back and drove us home, he was driving fast and weaving all over the road. I didn't understand what he was doing. At that time, I thought it was fun. It wasn't until a few years later that I figured out he was drunk," said Johnny.

Although Johnny was a smart child and easily excelled in school, his home life "changed his compass," and he soon found himself lured to life on the street.

"I was smart but precocious. I'd get sent to the principal's office for questioning the teachers. Eventually, I dumbed down and acted like everyone else,"

School boy misbehavior turned grown-up when his girlfriend became pregnant. The couple married and had a second child, but the marriage was short-lived. By this time, Johnny's street life was in full swing, as he hustled to earn money and street cred every way he could.

"All I wanted was my father to be proud of me, to earn his love and respect. My brother took the high road - college, athletics, family. My dad had a plan for me, but I didn't want to do it. I thought I could make him proud by owning the streets."

Johnny's "success" on the streets soon caught the attention of Seattle police, and Johnny began his new career as a prison inmate.

FareStart Graduate

"All together, I've spent more than 20 years in prison," said Johnny, who was turning 48. "I became a made man in prison. Eventually, I became the 'chief' or 'El Jefe.' I had lieutenants. The times when I got out of prison felt like a furlough; prison was my home."

THE TURNING POINT

"I was in solitary when my father died. However, I was able to go to his funeral in shackles and with two armed guards. At the funeral, this one boy kept walking past me, giving me the eye. I thought someone had put a hit out on me." The "hit man," it turns out, wasn't a hit man...it was Johnny's son.

"My own son. I didn't even recognize him. I went back to jail and (later) learned that my son had changed his name. He didn't want anything to do with me.

My dad had just died, my son didn't want to know me... I just wanted to disappear. Then, it hit me. I remembered the look in my son's eye. Even though my kids hated me, I knew they needed me.

They needed to know me, to know how they got their traits, their chin, their smile. I knew I couldn't go on the way I was."

Determined to change his life when he got out of prison, Johnny tried a variety of services and programs in the Seattle area. He did "the Home Depot thing" and sponsored others at the shelters he stayed in. But, it wasn't working. "I was older, and there just weren't any opportunities for me. The doors were closing. **I thought I'd just go back to prison and be king of the mountain again.** Then, my brother offered to let me live with him and his family if I enrolled in FareStart. I had cooked before, so I wasn't that interested in a culinary program. But, I wanted to reconcile with my family, so I did it."

"At first, I was cautious. I thought it was going to be an 'us vs. the man' type thing. Then, I really watched and listened, especially in Phase 1 of the program, and realized that they [the chef trainers] are everyday people. They serve as an example. **Some of them have had the same issues, and if they can make it, I can make it."**

Although Johnny enjoyed the culinary training, it was the life skills classes that changed his life.

"The life skills class gave me inspiration and encouragement without being patronizing or condescending. It taught me that you just have to be accountable and responsible and do what needs to be done, and you can change your life."

"FareStart trains anybody who is willing to do the work on how to be employed in any professional kitchen or restaurant in the food service industry. But, you have to be determined, once and for all, to make that decision to change your life."

It wasn't only the training and classes that helped Johnny transform his life. "Knowing that you are part of a family, they have your back, and they are always going to be there for you - that gives you balance. It helps you take the shackles off."

LIFE AFTER FARESTART

Not only has Johnny reconnected with his brother ("now my second favorite person after my mom"), his children, and many of his extended family, he also reconnected with his second wife. "Even though, I wasn't able to reconcile with my father, everyone here knows I love them. When I was asked to speak at (FareStart's) Gala, Mom was so proud of me. She even posted to Facebook!"

Within a week of graduating from FareStart, Johnny had a job offer. Within nine days, he had two more. Now, almost a year later, Johnny still gets calls for interviews.

"FareStart is very effective at breaking down a lot of barriers. The stigma of homelessness, and incarceration is almost reversed. People know we come from disadvantaged backgrounds, have barriers like criminal history or substance abuse, but they know that if you make it through FareStart that you are trained to be a professional."

Although Johnny continues to work in the food service industry, his goal is to serve others looking for a new life.

"I've always had a love for people, but I needed to excise my own demons. Now, I have an obligation to pay it forward. Whatever is in my power, I will do.

To tell people that they are okay, that there are no limits. It's not going to happen overnight. You can have do-overs, but you just can't quit. The chefs at FareStart taught me this."

"I know I am a part of something. Most of us just chased our tails and did nothing but destroy ourselves. With FareStart, there's hope.

If you want to do something besides be inside a concrete box, as long as you have breath in your lungs, you have a chance."

JOHNNY

LEMON COUSCOUS

Chef Thierry Rautureau

INGREDIENTS

1 cup couscous

1 cup boiling water

Juice from 1 lemon

2 preserved lemons, diced

¼ cup olive oil

Salt and pepper, to taste

INSTRUCTIONS

Pour hot water over the couscous, add the lemon juice, and cover for about 10 minutes.

Add the olive oil and the preserved lemon, and gently fluff with a fork.

Season with salt and pepper.

I also recommend a side of harissa sauce.

MUSHROOM

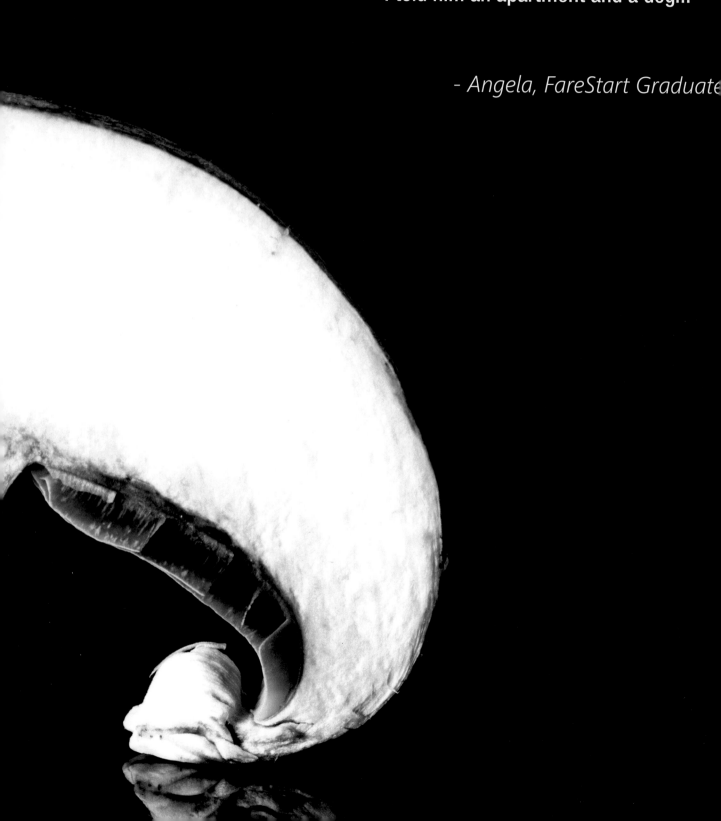

"When my boss interviewed me, he asked me what I wanted in the next five years. I told him an apartment and a dog..."

- Angela, FareStart Graduate

At one point in my life, I had to decide not to give up. All my life I've cared about people. It's in my heart. My co-workers call me "Mom" because I take care of everyone. *And, I've learned to take care of myself, too.*

I ENTERED THE FARESTART TRAINING PROGRAM AND GRADUATED IN 2005.

After graduating, I got a job but kept a relationship with FareStart. I would come back to volunteer. The chef manager that trained me asked me if I'd like to work with FareStart once they moved into the building. I said that I would love to.

It doesn't matter if the homeless are black or white or whatever - if you're poor, you're poor.

I put my energy and my heart into FareStart. I show other students that with hard work they can make it, too, that everyone can change. But, I know that no one can change another person's life...they have to want it for themselves.

Every day, there's something new to learn. FareStart is like family, and they welcome you. You come and learn from each other.

When I walk home, I always carry some food in my hand to give to the homeless. I also give them the orientation details, and tell them to come and change their life. I really want them to be able to work, to help their families. It doesn't matter if the homeless are black or white or whatever - if you're poor, you're poor.

I share my story with the students, letting them know that once I lived on the street. I help them see they should never give up. You have to believe in yourself. You have to love yourself.

JENNIFER ROSE

Sage

PAN SEARED POLENTA
WITH ROASTED CHESTNUT AND ROMANO

Chef Ericka Burke

ROASTED CHESTNUTS

1 teaspoon garlic, minced

1 teaspoon shallot, minced

3 tablespoons butter

½ ounces chestnuts, chopped and roasted

½ cup walnuts, roasted

½ cup chicken broth

½ cup vegetable stock

½ cup grated Romano cheese

1 teaspoon sage, chopped

1 teaspoon Italian parsley, chopped

Salt and pepper, to taste

In a pan, sauté garlic and shallots in butter until softened. Add chestnuts and walnuts, and toast briefly. Deglaze with chicken broth, and then, add vegetable stock. Cook down liquid by half, and then, add Romano, sage, and parsley.

POLENTA

4 cups polenta

10 cups water

4 ounces butter

5 ounces Romano cheese, grated

2 tablespoons sage, minced

2 tablespoons salt

Corn meal for dredging

Oil for frying

Sage leaves, fried, for garnish

Bring salted water to a boil. Slowly add polenta, whisking constantly. Lower heat to medium. Cook approximately 20-30 minutes. Add Romano and butter. Season with salt and pepper. Pour into a baking pan. Dip spatula into hot water, and spread polenta evenly. Set aside to cool. When cool, invert pan, tapping on counter to loosen. Cut into triangles, or use a cookie cutter for desired shapes.

Dredge in corn meal. Heat oil in sauté pan, but do not allow it to smoke. When hot, add polenta shapes, and sear on each side. Remove from pan when polenta is golden brown on each side, and place in oven at 350 degrees F for about 5 minutes.

Place two pieces of polenta in the center of each plate, and pour warm chestnut sauce over them. Garnish with large shavings of Romano and a single fried sage leaf.

CHOCOLATE ESPRESSO TORTE WITH CINNAMON HAZELNUT CRUST

FareStart Restaurant

INGREDIENTS

Crust:

1¾ cups hazelnuts, chopped very fine

⅔ cup sugar

¼ cup butter, melted

Filling:

2 cups heavy cream

16 ounces semi-sweet chocolate chips

1 tablespoon ground espresso

INSTRUCTIONS

Preheat oven to 350 degrees F.

Stir all crust ingredients together. Firmly press on bottom and up sides of 10-inch tart pan with removable bottom. Place tart pan onto baking sheet. Bake 15-18 minutes or until lightly browned. Cool completely.

Heat 2 cups whipping cream in 2-quart saucepan over medium heat for 5-8 minutes or until mixture just comes to a boil. Remove from heat. Add espresso and chocolate chips; stir until completely melted.

Pour into cooled pie crust. Chill at least 2 hours before serving.

Chocolate

Garlic

Peanut Sauce

FareStart Restaurant

INGREDIENTS

———————— ● ————————

2 tablespoons garlic

2 tablespoons ginger

1 cup water

½ cup soy sauce

2 tablespoons sugar

2 tablespoons rice vinegar

1 teaspoon Sriracha

1 cup coconut milk

½ bunch cilantro, finely chopped

1½ cup peanut butter

INSTRUCTIONS

———————— ● ————————

Leaving the peanut butter aside, mix all other ingredients together thoroughly.

Slowly whisk the other ingredients into the peanut butter, adding a little at a time, mixing until incorporated before adding more.

Or, you can add all ingredients in a blender, and process until smooth.

It was the Youth Barista Training program that brought me to the door of FareStart.

I was operating two not-for-profit cafés, called Habitat Café, on Capitol Hill. The first café was on Broadway, and every day, there were kids shooting up in the bathrooms. This was the mid-nineties. It was Seattle on Broadway. It was bad.

I would go to business association meetings, and the solution being proposed the most was to hire private security. We were trying to build and give back to the community. This didn't seem like the right approach.

I sat with my team, and from our brainstorm conversations, we came up with the idea for a barista training program. It was this idea that led me to the door of Megan Karch.

Megan loved the idea, and we collaborated on developing a training program. I brought over some existing relationships with YouthCare and New Horizon Ministries. We spent a couple of months working on the idea when the owner of Habitat Café decided to sell.

Megan hired me and one of my baristas with the goal of continuing to develop the program. I'm very proud of what we created.

THE PROGRAM INCLUDES:

8 weeks of training, direct work experience with expert baristas, resume and computer skills, coaching for interviews, help looking for a good job, and 10 months of support to help our students keep their jobs.

MG

We tell our students...

"You don't have to be perfect, but you have
to give this your best every day. You need to
show up on time and be willing to learn,
work hard, and stay with the program."

If they don't give up, neither do we.

MORE THAN 75% OF OUR YOUTH BARISTA GRADUATES HAVE GOOD JOBS WITHIN 90 DAYS OF FINISHING THE PROGRAM.

I came from a fairly protected home environment and grew up in a very
safe neighborhood. I was in school to get a degree in economics, thought I
had the world figured out, and imagined that after college, I would go on to
make a ton of money. But, the college experience showed me there was
so much more to the world. Three-quarters of the way through school, I
realized economics and being a stock broker were not for me.

During this time, I fell in love with cooking and decided I wanted to own a
restaurant. I went to culinary school, and this path led from being a prep
cook to management positions, eventually leading to Habitat Café.

I have empathy for the students coming into FareStart and think they are just as deserving of opportunity as anybody else. If I were to fall on hard times, I would want a community to embrace me and help me find new opportunities.

The seeds were always there for me to become a more community-engaged person, but this really solidified when I saw the first class take our training and graduate. I don't get to work directly with students anymore, but I find renewal at every Friday graduation that I attend.

I've been at FareStart for 15 years, and these days my role is aligned to ensuring the long-term success of the organization. Helping students get jobs, re-engage with their families, or go back to school - that's success.

My joy comes from facilitating and growing this community, making it sustainable, and transforming lives.

MATT GURNEY

Braised Beef

Chef Robert Spaulding

INGREDIENTS

1 tablespoon sea salt

4 tablespoons extra virgin olive oil

2½ pounds beef chuck roll, cut into large cubes

Salt

3½ cups yellow onions, large diced

3 tablespoons garlic, chopped

¾ cup grape juice

¼ cup brewed coffee

1 cup orange juice

2½ tablespoons brown sugar

3¾ teaspoons cocoa powder

⅓ teaspoon ground cinnamon

⅓ teaspoon ground cloves

2½ teaspoons ground cumin

¼ teaspoon ground allspice

2¼ teaspoons ground black pepper

2¼ teaspoons ground chipotle pepper

INSTRUCTIONS

Preheat oven to 275 degrees F. In a large pot, heat olive oil over high heat. Salt the beef, and sear in two batches. Do not stir the meat while it is cooking; let it caramelize on each side before turning.

After caramelizing both batches, remove the beef, and reduce heat to medium high; add onion, and cook for 1 minute. Add garlic, and cook 30 seconds, stirring constantly. Add the liquid ingredients, and then, add the dry ingredients and browned beef.

Bring to a boil, cover tightly, and place in oven to cook for 4 hours.

Remove beef from pan, and reduce the liquid to a sauce like consistency. Add the beef. If not using immediately, refrigerate, and warm prior to serving.

Coffee

Sugar

SHERRY VINAIGRETTE

Chef Wayne Johnson

INGREDIENTS

———————— ● ————————

2 cups sherry vinegar

3 tablespoons sugar

3 tablespoons Dijon mustard

2 shallots, roughly chopped

1 tablespoon salt

1 teaspoon black pepper

5 cups oil blend

1 teaspoon fresh thyme

INSTRUCTIONS

———————— ● ————————

In a plastic container, mix all ingredients, except oil, with emersion blender until well mixed.

Slowly drizzle in oil while blending.

Radicchio-Belgian Endive Mix

Chef John Howie

Adapted from Chef Howie's Cookbook - Passion & Palate: Recipes for a Generous Table

INGREDIENTS

●

1 tablespoon olive oil

½ head radicchio, cut in half

1 head Belgian endive, cut in half

INSTRUCTIONS

●

Baste the endive and radicchio with olive oil. Place on a pre-heated grill pan, and grill both sides until grill marks appear. Don't let it get soft.

Remove from the grill, and cool on a sheet tray in a refrigerator. Cut the radicchio and endive into pieces that are ¼-inch by 1-2-inches long, toss together, and refrigerate until needed.

JAY

SOMETIMES, HELP COMES FROM THE LAST PLACE YOU CAN IMAGINE.

As a teenager, the last place Jay imagined working was in a restaurant. He vividly remembers his mother coming home and complaining about her job as a waitress. So, it's ironic that a restaurant is where Jay found his calling.

It didn't come easy, though. At age 15, Jay was kicked out of his house and began living on his own.

After dropping out of school, he slept on a lot of couches, doing and dealing drugs, surrounded by people who were anything but good role models. He spent time in and out of jail and, eventually, wound up in the state prison.

He grew up with the belief that he would never amount to anything. In prison, every inmate is assigned a job, and for Jay, it was helping in the kitchen. "I liked the kitchen because I didn't mind getting up early and having afternoons to play basketball and softball."

Over time, Jay earned the head cook's trust and was one of only four inmates trusted to work in the kitchen's slicing room with the knives. While they worked, they were locked in the room, and the knives were chained to the counters.

Knowing that Jay's release date was coming up, the head cook told him about FareStart - that it was an organization that could help with housing. Jay knew he needed a permanent, "approved" address before he could be released, and FareStart sounded like his ticket out. He didn't know about the job training. "I figured I'd be back doing the same old thing before long" - the drugs and dealing that had defined his life for over a decade.

"Honestly, I used FareStart just to get out of prison."

After being released, Jay went directly to a shelter in Seattle. Now, with a roof over his head and a permanent address, he would learn what FareStart was all about.

FareStart Graduate

What he didn't know was that his life was about to change dramatically.

Not only did he have a place to stay, but FareStart provided him with toiletries, bus passes, a Goodwill voucher, and stipend cards to local stores - everything he needed to start again.

"After my first week working with the chefs, it was different [than I expected]. They listened and were very cool. They broke down how to do something, so it was easy to understand."

All the positive feedback gave him hope. His biggest challenge had always been asking for help or instructions.

At FareStart, they made it easy for him. "If you want to change your life, FareStart will help you. They put you in a shelter, so you don't have to worry about where you're going to sleep. They give you whatever you need.

If you want to change your life, FareStart will help you.

When I see people I used
to know living on the
street, I tell them to check
out FareStart.

I never thought I could do
it. It seemed too hard.
The program's free,
and it works.

For me, it was the positive attitude of the chefs that made me realize this could work. I realized the people at FareStart were there to help, and I was anxious to finish the program.

I learned about measurements and conversions, knife and cutting skills - all the basics that are helpful when you go to a new kitchen."

FareStart also coached Jay in computer and life skills, and, most important, he got positive feedback from the chefs that developed his confidence.

Jay had one small setback but overcame it and was back after a month. He was determined to graduate. He gives credit to Chelsea Van Rask, his employment specialist at the time. She helped him get his first job at Morton's Steakhouse in the pantry doing salads. That proved to be a double learning experience because he also had the opportunity to help the pastry chef.

"Jay was one of the first to go through our graduate support program, which is now the norm," said Van Rask. "It allows us the time to follow up with our graduates for up to six months and, sometimes, even longer."

When Morton's cut back his hours to three days, Jay moved on to Spitfire where he sharpened his grilling skills and then, moved to Elliott Bay Café.

Once again, FareStart was looking out for him when Chelsea called and told him there was an open call for a line cook at Purple Café and Wine Bar. At Purple, he hit his stride.

Within a year and a half, he became a manager as lead line cook. "When I see people I used to know living on the street, I tell them to check out FareStart. I never thought I could do it. It seemed too hard. The program's free, and it works."

These days, when he's not working at Purple, you'll find Jay poring over cookbooks. His favorite is *Modern Grilling.*

With the skills and confidence that he acquired at FareStart, it's not just a fantasy that he could open a restaurant someday - perhaps Northwest American that specializes in grilled foods.

With a new house, a new baby daughter, and a manager's job as lead line cook at Purple in Bellevue, Jay says, "It's the best it's ever been, and it's only getting better."

JAY

COFFEE

"I really think the Barista Program

might have saved my life."

- Kat, FareStart Youth Barista 2011 Graduate

Romaine

Fennel, Apple, and Celery Salad

Chef Matt Janke

INGREDIENTS

½ fennel bulb

Fennel fronds, trimmed and chopped

3 celery stalks, chopped

1 Gala or Braeburn apple, peeled and chopped thin

1 head romaine lettuce, cut to preference

¼ bunch Italian parsley, rough chopped

Splash of honey

1 tablespoon walnut oil

3 tablespoons good, fruity olive oil

2-3 tablespoons sherry vinegar

Crunchy sea salt, to taste

INSTRUCTIONS

Slice the fennel bulb as thin as possible. This works best if you have a mandolin, but a sharp knife will work. Toss the fennel bulb, apple, and celery in a small bowl with walnut oil and a pinch of crunchy salt.

Toss romaine in a bowl with the chopped parsley and some of the chopped fennel fronds. Toss in the fennel-apple-celery mix. Add the sherry vinegar and a splash of honey. Adjust the vinaigrette proportions to your taste; you may need to add more vinegar or olive oil. Season with good crunchy sea salt.

This is one of my favorite salads!

Hollandaise Sauce

Chef John Howie

Adapted from Chef Howie's Cookbook - Passion & Palate: Recipes for a Generous Table

INGREDIENTS

3 egg yolks

2 teaspoons lemon juice

1 teaspoon water

2½ ounces salted butter, cut in ½-ounce chunks

Dash of Tabasco™ sauce

INSTRUCTIONS

Add egg yolks, lemon juice, and chicken and broth to a stainless steel or copper bowl over double boiler. Whisk constantly until just warm, and then, add butter.

Continue to cook, whisking constantly, until the mixture thickens to a thick ribbon consistency. Remove from the heat. Hold warm until needed.

g g

JOVIEN

When you talk to Jovien, you can't help but notice the big vocabulary, high energy, and smile. You wouldn't imagine that at one point, he didn't speak.

"When I started school, even though I didn't have speech problems, when I talked, no one could understand me. As a result of not being understood, I eventually just stopped talking."

Jovien spent his early school years in silence, cutting himself off from other students. As a result, he was lured by the world of books. "At first, I liked magic, goblins, all the stuff that kids like. Then, I got into hard facts. When I was in third grade, I started reading dictionaries - I still do. Even today, I have seven dictionaries on my phone."

Finding his voice wasn't the only challenge Jovien faced as a child. Adopted as a baby along with his twin sister, his adoptive parents divorced when Jovien was in grade school.

For the next several years, his adoptive mother suffered a series of job losses, eventually forcing the family into homelessness.

"We moved around a lot. One year, we moved to a different hotel every night. We lived in our car; we slept outside. It was a struggle."

By the time Jovien reached high school, he was working to help support the family, but his grades were slipping, and he was getting into fights at school. Then, as a sophomore, he was expelled and sent to the Interagency Academy at Orion Center, a small, alternative high school program designed to support students who have different needs than what standard public schools can support.

Once at Orion, he discovered another lifeline - FareStart's Youth Barista Training and Education Program (BTEP). "Once I got to Orion and BTEP things started happening for me. I went from failing school to all A's.

I found people who were like me, had the same struggles. **I no longer had to put on a façade and pretend that I had it all together.** People saw me as I am and genuinely wanted to teach me. I no longer had to put a mask on for other people."

FareStart Graduate

The barista program was amazing!

My career coordinator and I talked about everything - not just the program but about emotions as well as decisions that I had made and those that I needed to make."

One of the decisions Jovien had to make was what he wanted to do after he graduates from high school this June. "I always wanted to be a surgeon, but I didn't think I wanted to spend another 13 years in school. But, after going through the program and seeing other kids go through the program, I knew I could do it. It will be a challenge but also rewarding," explains Jovien.

Public speaking?
Yes," explains Jovien, "One day, I started talking, and people could finally understand me. It just happened; I don't know why. And, I haven't stopped talking since!"

JOVIEN

I went from failing school to all A's.

I found people who were like me, had the same struggles. I no longer had to put on a façade and pretend that I had it all together. People saw me as I am and genuinely wanted to teach me. I no longer had to put a mask on for other people.

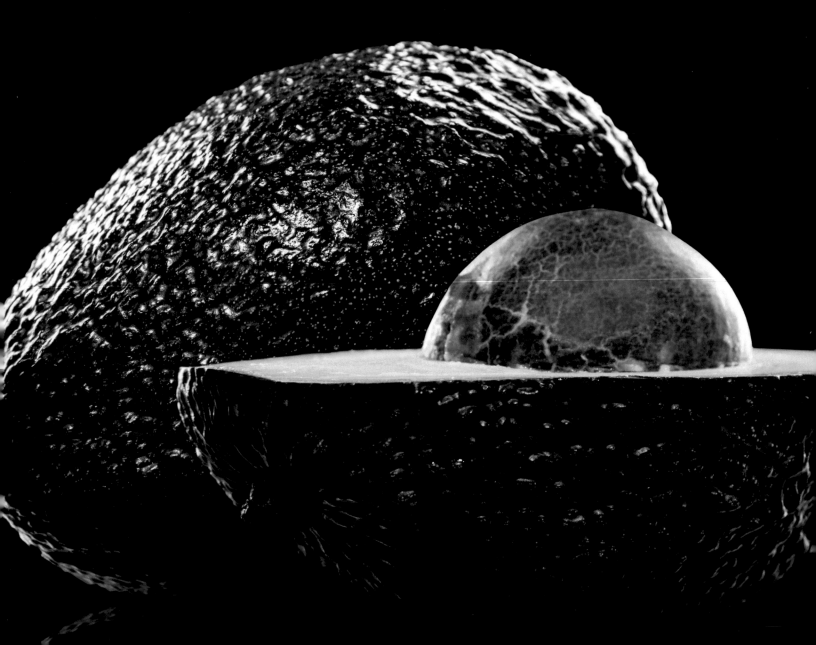

KASPAR'S HEALTHY NO OIL AVOCADO GREEN GODDESS DRESSING

Chef Kaspar Donier

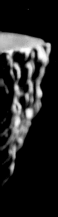

INGREDIENTS

2 large avocados

¼ English cucumber

¼ green apple, core removed

1 small shallot

1 garlic clove

4 sprigs tarragon or basil

1 teaspoon Dijon mustard

2 teaspoons honey

½ cup lemon juice

1½ teaspoons salt

¼ teaspoon ground black pepper

1 cup water

INSTRUCTIONS

Cut avocados in half, remove pits, and scoop the flesh into a tall blender cup. Add all the other ingredients, except the water, and blend with an immersion blender for about 1 minute until smooth. Add the water to dilute the dressing, and blend for 15 seconds. Taste, and season with more salt and pepper, if necessary. Dressing can be stored in the refrigerator for up to a week in a bottle or jar.

At Kaspars, we love to bottle dressings as hostess gifts.

CHEF'S SPECIAL BING CHERRY SALSA

Chef Don Curtiss

INGREDIENTS

1 pound Bing cherries

1 medium shallot, peeled and minced

½ medium onion, diced in ⅛-inch pieces

3 ounces balsamic vinegar

½ teaspoon harissa paste

1 cup basil leaves, finely chopped

1 cup Italian parsley leaves, finely chopped

½ teaspoon salt and pepper mix

¾ teaspoon sugar

INSTRUCTIONS

Wash, stem, pit, and quarter the cherries.

Combine with shallot, onion, vinegar, harissa paste, basil, parsley, salt mix, and sugar.

Refrigerate until ready to use.

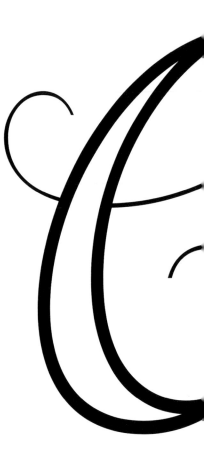

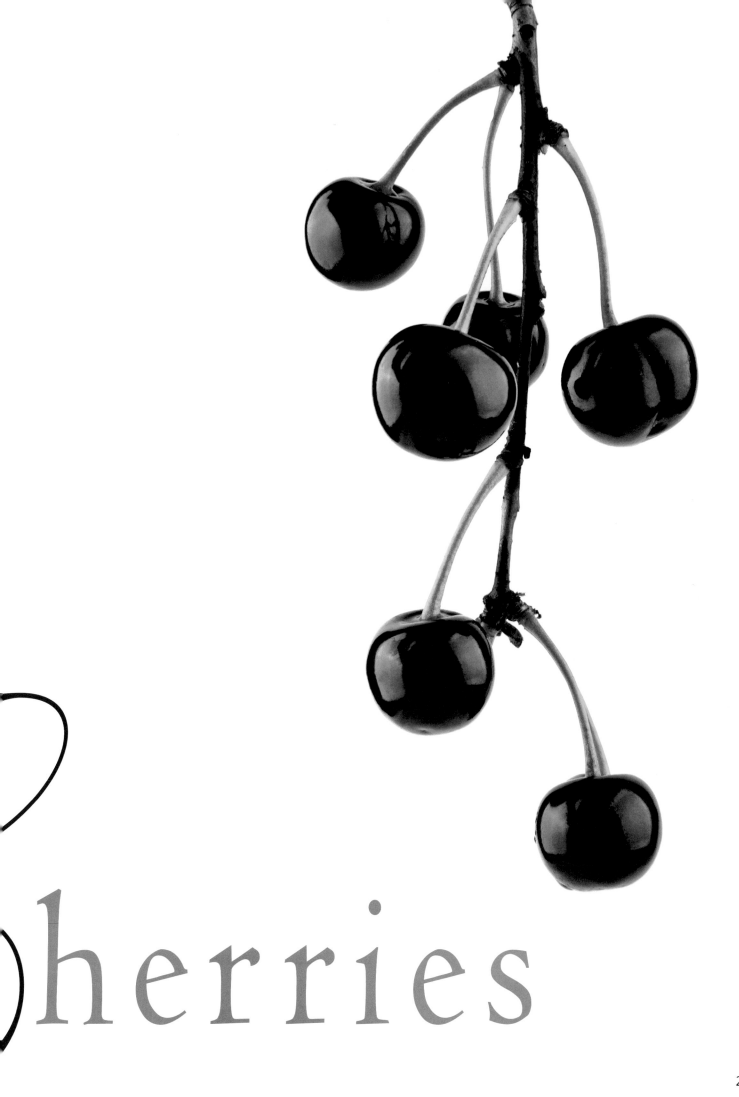

herries

KEVIN

Kevin came to FareStart in need of a place to live and help regaining focus in his life. "I tried everything my way, and I was ready to sober up and try something new," he said. Kevin found that having a place to be every day - FareStart - was just the kind of focus he needed to stay on track for the first time in years.

"At FareStart, I found a place that I thrived in. I was able to complete the program on time, which made me feel like I had really accomplished something. And, now I have a job prepping, cooking, and packaging food, which I love!"

Before FareStart, Kevin had been struggling with day-to-day life for a very long time, living in a tent at one point. "I had not worked in five or six years. I had purchased a tent and was ready to move to the street again when a friend told me about FareStart.

I went for an interview, and within five days, I had started the program," said Kevin. "FareStart gets you ready to work, and it gets you ready to be a valued member of society again. It sounds simple, but it's so important!"

Life skills classes were a high point of Kevin's training at FareStart. "It was phenomenal because I learned a lot about goal-setting," he said.

"Living on the streets for so long is a day-to-day struggle. There are no goals on the street; you are just living for the moment."

Learning the proper way to do things was also important to Kevin because it gave him a sense of professional confidence. "After my training, I could walk into any employer and hold my head high. Because of FareStart, I have a job, and money in my pocket, and my bills are paid. I've worked hard to do that, and it's huge! I feel like I'm going somewhere. It's scary, but it's also exciting."

Since leaving FareStart, Kevin says he has set many goals and has met every one of them so far, including holding his current job for almost a year.

FareStart Graduate

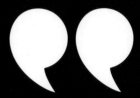

At FareStart, I found a place that I thrived in. I was able to complete the program on time, which made me feel like I had really accomplished something.

And, now I have a job prepping, cooking, and packaging food, *which I love!*

"It's not just a cooking school.

They're teaching me things and preparing me for life. It's being able to make somebody else happy. I've never had that."

- Joel, 2015 FareStart graduate

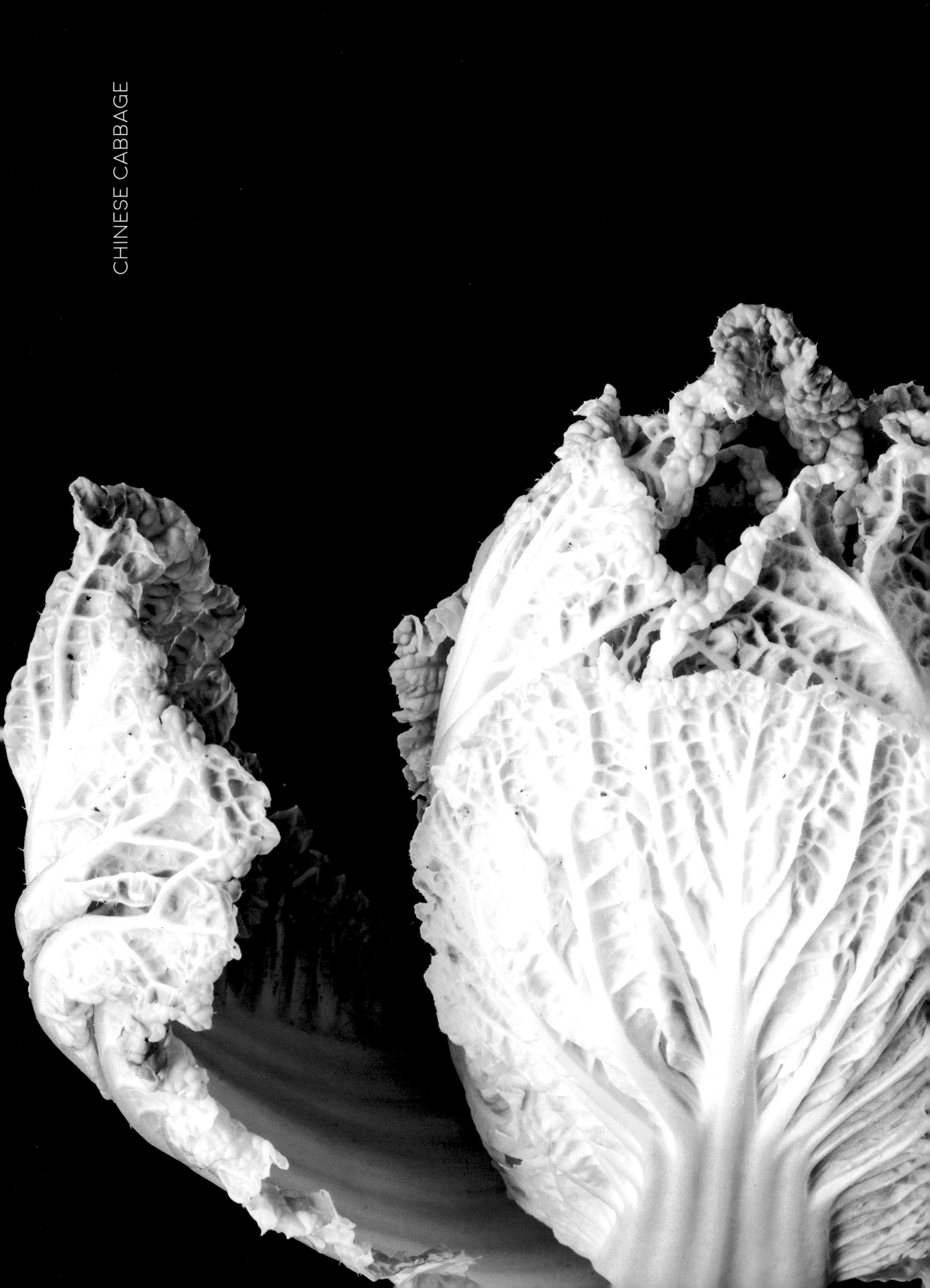

CHINESE CABBAGE

DEVONA

After the birth of her fifth child, Devona knew she wanted to leave a better legacy for her children.

Following years of enduring domestic violence and nearly five years on welfare, Devona knew she needed a new path but didn't know where to start.

She had known about FareStart for many months, but it wasn't until she overheard a conversation at her WorkFirst office that she knew that the program was the opportunity she had been waiting and looking for.

Devona says she wasn't nervous at all for her first day in the adult training program; she was ready to absorb and learn everything she could. From the beginning, she says that she felt a sense of family with the other students and FareStart staff, a sense of belonging that she had never known.

FareStart was the first place that she didn't feel judged for her past, which had been fraught with bouts of homelessness, alcohol abuse, and starts and stops with several job training programs.

Because of that sense of community, Devona says that she did everything she could not just to complete the program but to excel at every aspect of her training.

With the steady support of her mother, who helped with childcare, Devona graduated from the program having already secured employment as a cook at a local shelter.

Devona says that she was proud to graduate from FareStart, which she says demonstrated to her children that she could achieve something great despite considerable barriers.

FareStart Graduate

At the shelter where she works full-time, Devona prepares meals and teaches women to cook - many of whom share a similar background to her own. "I'm not going to work every day," she says. "I'm going to my second home."

Since her graduation, Devona has also launched her own catering business, which she operates in her spare time.

She hopes to one day open a restaurant featuring her signature spin on sophisticated soul food with a Latin flair.

Devona likens her transformation to that of an ugly duckling to a beautiful swan. "We come to you broken, from all walks of life ... you take us in and you nurture us, give us new skills and confidence, and then, send us out into the world as these beautiful creatures. And, I thank you from the bottom of my heart."

DEVONA

From the beginning, I felt a sense of family with the other students and FareStart staff, a sense of belonging that I had never known.

Veal Sweetbread and Maine Lobster
with Fava Beans
and a Curry Honey Ginger Glaze

Chef Thierry Rautureau

INGREDIENTS

½ pound veal sweetbread, skinned

1 to 1½ pounds Maine lobster, blanched for 3 minutes in water, shelled and sliced into medallions

2 ounces cumin oil

1 tablespoon shallots, chopped

1 teaspoon garlic, chopped

1 tablespoon chives, sliced

1 tablespoon curry

1 teaspoon ginger, grated

1 tablespoon honey *(fireweed recommended)*

½ pound Fava beans, peeled and skinned

2 ounces butter

Salt and pepper, to taste

INSTRUCTIONS

In a hot sauté pan, melt the butter, and add the fava beans.

Cook for 3-4 minutes.

In another hot saute pan, add the cumin oil, and sauté the sweetbread until colored. Add the lobster and then, shallots, garlic, and chives. Sauté quickly. Add curry, and finish with honey.

Cook for 20 seconds, and season to taste.

Serve hot on top of the fava beans. Drizzle the pan juices over the dish.

obster

Since 1994, Guest Chef Night
has raised more than $5 million,
and chefs have contributed
over 25,000 hours of their time.

GUEST

CHEF

NIGHT

> **Guest Chef Night has been a weekly highlight for the FareStart community since its initial launch in 1994.**

Our Thursday Guest Chef Night is a unique opportunity for our students to work with premier chefs from the Seattle area, for our supporters to enjoy an excellent meal, and an opportunity to share the transformative work of FareStart with the greater Seattle community.

Hundreds of chefs from our area's finest restaurants have volunteered their time and resources to offer our students a tremendous training opportunity. For FareStart supporters, it's a great opportunity to enjoy an excellent meal, introduce new supporters to the organization, or volunteer as a server.

Our "guest chefs" are deeply committed to us.

They want to produce an amazing three-course meal for our patrons, but more important, they look forward to partnering with the talents and passion of our staff and students, factoring the cost of this support into their annual budgets and showing up with a team ready to give their all to students.

The restaurants who participate in "Guest Chef Night" become trusted partners - members of an almost "secret society" privy to the inner workings of a top-notch organization (with a state-of-the-art kitchen) and directly engaging with the people they serve. Through this experience, their souls are fed, and a stronger web is built among the culinary arts community.

FareStart adds diversity to the Seattle restaurant community - it isn't business as usual. We want to help grow a community that takes care of each other but does so in creative and cutting-edge ways.

Since 1994, Guest Chef Night has raised more than $5 million in direct support of our student job training and placement services - proof that our food, our value, and our place in the community is, indeed, sacred.

CHEF THIERRY RAUTUREAU

EXECUTIVE CHEF, LOULAY KITCHEN & BAR AND LUC

"

There is nothing that resonates more
with me than FareStart's emphasis
on giving everyone a chance.

I don't care how tough you are;
everyone deserves a chance. Bad
breaks can happen to anyone.

I STARTED WITH AN APPRENTICESHIP
AT 14 YEARS OLD IN ANJOU, FRANCE.

After I graduated two years later, I decided to learn as much as possible about the different types of cooking in France. I explored cooking techniques at Mont Saint Michel in Normandy, Chamonix in the Alps, Hendaye in the Basque country, and finally, in Orleans just South of Paris. In 1978, after finishing my required time in the Army, which was necessary as a citizen of France, I moved to Chicago and worked in a restaurant called La Fontaine.

Again looking to learn as much as possible about different cooking techniques in America, after 3½ years, I moved to Los Angeles, California, and worked at an Italian restaurant called Mangia. **This is where I met my lovely wife, Kathy.** My next kitchen called, and I took a position at The 7th Street Bistro, where I was the sous-chef to Laurent Quenioux for 4 years.

In 1987, we moved to Seattle. I found a small restaurant that was only 10 months old in Madison Valley that had been reviewed in the *LA Times*. I couldn't resist but to buy it and start a family in the Pacific Northwest with the idea of sharing my passion for food with the people in Seattle.

This was a giant leap of faith, but seeing the popularity and soul of Pike Place Market, I figured that the people here must love food.

In 2010, we opened Luc, our French/American neighborhood bistro, and in 2013, we opened Loulay Kitchen & Bar, an urban, modern brasserie in downtown Seattle at 6th and Union at the bottom of the Sheraton.

Why do I want to help and support the community?

I am a fortunate man with a beautiful wife and two healthy boys. I am healthy and have two restaurants. I already feel like the luckiest man alive. Why wouldn't I give something back to the community and help the less fortunate?

TR

I have been working on hunger-related causes for about 30 years, and it really upsets me that this problem is not going away any faster than it is.

HUNGER, SHELTER, AND CLOTHING ARE BASICS. NO ONE SHOULD BE STRUGGLING FOR THE BASICS, ESPECIALLY IN AMERICA.

In 1992, David Lee, founder of Common Meals (later became FareStart), called me and said, "We have a chef come once a month on Thursdays to do a dinner. Would you want to come? We are working to help get people off the streets."

He said, **"I was thinking of charging $12 for a four or five course meal!"**

He explained that they were close to losing the lease on the building they were in, and he was looking for ways to raise money. We decided to hold an auction to raise some real money. I couldn't believe the situation.

I went on stage and sold a couple things to help build the foundation. It was an amazing night. The event was small, fun, and had huge impact. The first year we raised approximately $7,000.

I did this for another couple of years and feel really proud of how the whole organization had grown. I am glad that we were able to help this great organization not lose their lease and restart on a great path. My memory of the old place on 2nd Avenue is fond, but their growth still has me in awe, how they transitioned into what FareStart is now.

I love the feeling you get from being in the kitchen with people who are doing something meaningful to change their lives, knowing that they are grateful for the opportunity. I also love to teach the students in the kitchen and give them a different perspective on cooking techniques. That's why I look forward to Guest Chef Nights.

WHEN THE PEOPLE IN THE KITCHEN DON'T REALLY KNOW WHO YOU ARE, AND THEY ARE SMILING, HAPPY, AND NOT TAKING A LESSON OR MOMENT FOR GRANTED... IT FEELS GOOD TO BE A PART OF THAT.

I am looking forward to the future of FareStart. They have done great things, but there is more to be done. The hunger problem and the issue of helping people will never stop.

I have also been on the Board of Food Lifeline for some years, which is gratifying, and falls in the same realm as FareStart - helping people in bad times. **Thanks to FareStart, people are getting a chance to change their lives. We need more FareStarts in this world.**

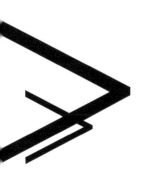

Food is the only language that allows you to communicate without speech. You can sit on a rock eating food out of a shell, smiling at the person next to you who is doing the same, and you are communicating without saying a word. Food is the great connector of the world.

We all experience great feelings around the table, and for me, this is one of the greatest pleasures of life.

GRILLED LEG OF LAMB MOROCCAN STYLE

Chef Thierry Rautureau

INGREDIENTS

1 3-pound leg of lamb, boned and butterflied

Tapenade:

2 cups green and black olives, pitted and chopped

4 tablespoons shallots, chopped

1 tablespoon garlic, chopped

3 teaspoons harissa *(for spicier result, add more harissa)*

3 red bell peppers, roasted, skinned, and diced small

1 teaspoon thyme, chopped

1 tablespoon chives, chopped

¾ cups Moroccan olive oil

Salt and pepper, to taste

INSTRUCTIONS

Toss all the tapenade ingredients in a salad bowl, and season with salt and pepper. Spread half the tapenade on the top of the lamb meat, patting gently. Then, turn the meat, and spread the remaining tapenade on that side. Let marinate for at least 1½ hours.

Place coals in the center of your grill and light. When the coals are hot, move them to the side, close the lid, and allow the grill to get hot.

Remove most of the tapenade from the lamb. Reserve.

Place the lamb in the middle of the grill with skin-side down, and once grill marked, turn over and close lid to finish cooking. Once the lamb reaches about 120 degrees F, spread the tapenade on top of the lamb, close the lid, and cook for 15 minutes or until it reaches 130 degrees F. Place on a platter, and let the lamb rest for about 20 minutes before slicing. Rewarm the sliced meat briefly, if necessary. I recommned serving this with lemon couscous *(Recipe in Book)*.

Olives

INSTRUCTIONS

———— ● ————

Bend each asparagus stalk near the base, breaking the spear at the natural spot where the tough base gives way to the tender upper portion. Trim away about 3 inches from the tops of 12 spears to use for garnish.

Bring a large pot of salted water to a boil, and prepare a large bowl of ice water. Add the asparagus spears to the boiling water, and cook until bright green and nearly tender, 1 to 2 minutes. Scoop out the spears with a slotted spoon, and immediately place in the ice water to quickly cool. Return the water to a boil, add the reserved asparagus tips, and cook until bright green and nearly tender, about 1 minute. Scoop the tips out with a slotted spoon, and cool in the ice water as well. When the asparagus is cold, drain well, and arrange on paper towels to dry. Set aside the asparagus tips for later use, and cut the remaining asparagus spears into 1-inch pieces.

Heat the butter in a medium saucepan over medium heat until melted and foamy white. Add the onion, thyme, and garlic, and cook, stirring occasionally, until the onion begins to soften, 2 to 3 minutes. Stir in the asparagus pieces, and then, add the vegetable stock. Bring the stock just to a boil over high heat, and then, reduce the heat to medium-low, stir in the crème fraîche, and simmer until the asparagus is very tender, 15 to 20 minutes.

Strain the asparagus, returning the liquid to the saucepan. Bring to a boil over medium-high heat, and boil until reduced by one-third. In the meantime, purée the asparagus in a blender or food processor until very smooth. If the purée is quite thick, add a couple of tablespoons of water to lighten the purée. Pass the purée through a fine sieve, pressing with the back of a rubber spatula to remove any fibrous bits. Stir the puréed asparagus into the cooking liquids. Taste the soup for seasoning, adding salt and pepper; keep warm over low heat. Cut the reserved asparagus tips in half lengthwise unless the tips are already quite thin.

To make the goat cheese cream, whip the cheese and cream until soft and smooth. Season with salt and pepper, whisking to fully blend.

To serve, ladle the asparagus soup into warmed shallow soup bowls. Place a large dollop of goat cheese cream in the center of the soup. Lean the reserved asparagus tips against the goat cheese. Scatter the chives over the cheese. Drizzle the top of each soup with argan or hazelnut oil, and serve immediately.

WASHINGTON GREEN ASPARAGUS SOUP
WITH GOAT CHEESE AND ARGAN OIL

Chef Thierry Rautureau

INGREDIENTS

1 pound asparagus spears

4 tablespoons unsalted butter

½ onion, chopped

1 teaspoon thyme leaves

½ teaspoon garlic, minced

3 cups vegetable stock

1 cup crème fraîche or heavy cream

Salt and freshly ground white pepper, to taste

Goat Cheese Cream

4 ounces soft goat cheese

1½ ounces heavy cream

Garnish

Argan oil or hazelnut oil

1 teaspoon chives, chopped

ASPARAGUS

BAKED WASHINGTON HALIBUT
WITH MORELS, RAMPS,
AND SMOKED BACON BUTTER SAUCE

Chef Thierry Rautureau

INGREDIENTS

5 ounces Applewood-smoked or regular bacon strips, cut into ¼-inch pieces

8 to 10 ounces ramps or small leeks

8 tablespoons unsalted butter

4 ounces morel mushrooms, cleaned and halved *(or quartered, if large)*

2 teaspoons minced shallot

½ teaspoon minced garlic

(or 1 teaspoon, if using leeks)

¾ teaspoon thyme, minced and divided

1¾ cups fish stock, divided

1 pound skinless halibut fillet, cut into 4 portions

Salt and freshly ground white pepper, to taste

2 teaspoons chives, minced

Olive oil for drizzling

Morel

INSTRUCTIONS

Cook the bacon in a skillet over medium-high heat until crisp and brown, 5 to 7 minutes, stirring occasionally. Spoon the bacon into a small sieve set over a bowl to drain; reserve the bacon fat if you like.

Trim the root ends from the ramps, and cut each ramp in half where the white gives way to the green tops. Cut the white portions into ¼-inch pieces, and leave the ramp greens whole. If using leeks, trim to the white and pale green portion, then halve crosswise and cut into ¼-inch wide strips.

Preheat the oven to 350 degrees F.

Heat 2 tablespoons of the butter (or use some of the bacon fat) in a skillet over medium-high heat until melted and slightly nutty smelling. Add the morels, and sauté for 30 seconds. Add the white portion of the ramps (or all of the leek strips) with the shallot, garlic, and ½ teaspoon of thyme. Sauté, stirring often, until the ramps begin to soften, 2 to 3 minutes. Add three-quarters of the bacon with the ramp greens and 1¼ cups of the fish stock. Bring just to a boil, and then simmer to reduce by three-quarters, 8 to 10 minutes. Add another 4 tablespoons of butter, swirling the pan so it melts creamily into the sauce; keep warm over very low heat.

Put the remaining ½ cup fish stock in a large ovenproof skillet and warm over medium heat. Whisk in the remaining 2 tablespoons of butter, and add the remaining bacon and remaining ¼ teaspoon of thyme. Season the halibut pieces with salt and pepper, and add to the skillet. Spoon some of the cooking liquids over the top of the fish, and bake until just nearly opaque through the center, 5 to 10 minutes, depending on the thickness of the fish, basting with the cooking liquid once or twice.

Pour the halibut cooking liquids into the skillet with the sauce, and bring just to a low boil. Stir in the chives, and season the sauce with salt and pepper.

To serve, spoon some of the ramps, bacon, mushrooms, and sauce onto warmed plates. Top with the halibut pieces, and spoon the remaining sauce over the top of the fish.

Drizzle olive oil around, and serve immediately.

CHEF TOM DOUGLAS

EXECUTIVE CHEF, SEATTLE KITCHEN

SOMETIMES IN LIFE YOU JUST DON'T GET THE SAME SHOT THAT ANOTHER PERSON DOES.

My involvement with FareStart dates back to the David Lee early days. Pamela, our current CEO, was one of the Board members for Common Meals (now FareStart). I thought the concept was a good idea then, and I think it's a good idea now.

I've always wanted FareStart to be successful, and it's nice to see the organization continue to prosper. Megan Karch is so committed and thoughtful.

I tell my team that it's about being a pillar of the community. I've had involvement with my good friend, Thierry Rautureau, over the years, and we've supported both FareStart and Food Lifeline. I remember a benefit we held for FareStart several years ago; it sold out within several hours, and reminded me the power we have as chefs to change people's lives.

A hand out is not the same as a hand up. People don't appreciate how important it is being a stop gap in someone's life.

FareStart does that – it has its arm out ready to pull someone out of the abyss. And, they provide an easy way for young chefs to get a taste of what it's like to be a part of the community.

Sometimes in life you just don't get the same shot that another person does. It's not always about taking a wrong turn in life; sometimes, it's just the hand you're dealt. I've always tried to teach my daughters that it's about options. And, if you put in the effort, like getting good grades, it gives you options.

MY PASSION HAS ALWAYS BEEN HUNGER RELIEF. I JUST FEEL I'M HERE TO FEED PEOPLE. THIS DESIRE HAS ALWAYS BEEN INSIDE ME.

ROASTED CIPOLLINI ONIONS

Chef Tom Douglas

INGREDIENTS

●

1 pound Cipollini onions, peeled and quartered

2 tablespoons olive oil, plus more as needed

1 tablespoon butter

Kosher or sea salt, to taste

Freshly ground pepper, to taste

2 teaspoons fresh herbs, such as thyme leaves, parsley, and rosemary, chopped

INSTRUCTIONS

●

Preheat the oven to 425 degrees F.

In a bowl, combine the onions with enough oil to coat lightly, and season with salt and pepper.

Spread the onions on a rimmed baking sheet, dot with butter, and roast in the oven, stirring every 10 minutes, until browned and tender, about 30 minutes.

Sprinkle with herbs, and serve.

nion

russels spro

CHEF ETHAN STOWELL

EXECUTIVE CHEF, ETHAN STOWELL RESTAURANTS

> When my dream career of being a body builder
> started looking like it wasn't going to ever fully
> materialize, I knew that I loved cooking and working
> in restaurants and started thinking about ways
> I could do things my own way.

I started off young and cocky and learned a lot of things the hard way, but I was fortunate to have great help from the beginning and throughout the years. I don't think I'd change anything really if I could go back now. One thing I never shy away from is asking people what they think and how they would do things. You learn a lot by asking questions.

I HAVE ALWAYS LOVED COOKING FOR PEOPLE. I COOKED THE DINNER AT MY OWN WEDDING.

I continue to bring friends and family together around the dinner table as often as possible because it's where I feel like I'm providing and doing my best for them. I know that bringing family and friends together to share a meal is important in lots of cultures around the globe. The feeling of comfort that it brings is something that all of us have in common, which just feels good.

When I was a 28-year-old chef right out of the gate, owning my first restaurant, I got talked into doing a Guest Chef Night at the old FareStart on 2nd Avenue.

I have to tell you, I was a little scared when I saw that old run-down kitchen. I didn't have a lot of experience with the homeless population, so I don't think I really knew what I was getting into. It was an eye-opening experience that made me appreciate a lot of things, and I was proud when they put my chef photo on that wall.

ES

When FareStart moved to the new building in Denny Triangle I think that, like a lot of chefs, I was blown away at how clean and spacious the kitchen was. I know most chefs would be envious of that prep space alone.

One thing I noticed right away, though, is that it allowed the students to step up, to start acting like they were in a "real" kitchen, and they began taking it a little more seriously. And, when you walk into that dining room, see all the guests on the two floors, see how many people can take part in the experience, it's really amazing.

Watching the homeless population in my hometown grow in the recent past is troubling. For years now, we've watched Belltown, and now Ballard, experience problems that affect our guests and employee's safety, and its scary.

I know that it's going to take a lot of people getting involved with solutions to make a real impact at this point – not just a few people with some sandwiches and a parking lot.

We need more programs like FareStart that have stood the test of time in helping people find a way out of their current situations.

I'm always awe-struck when I hear the stories of people working so hard just to learn a new trade and accomplish something. The pride that's earned and shared with the community is extraordinary and makes me very humble to be standing next to them.

In the past few years, my wife and I have spent more time looking at ways to give back to the community and finding opportunities that will have the most impact. She is really the leader when it comes to championing those in need. In addition to our own big fundraiser that we put on each year for fetal health-related causes, we encourage our managers to find ways to get their restaurants involved in the community and help out.

Last year, Angela joined the Board of the United Way of King County, and we've spent a lot of time visiting homeless camps and talking to folks living there. I think before when I did an event, like Guest Chef Night, I didn't necessarily get the full impact, but now, when I cook at Union Gospel Mission for homeless teens and their moms or make sandwiches for tent city or hold a fundraiser at one of the restaurants, I know it's not for "those people" but for an actual guy named "John" who I might have just met, who has a real story and real family, who is trying really hard to make everything work out day to day, and it's a lot harder than I ever realized.

**Those are definitely the real heroes out there.
It feels good to play a small part in that.**

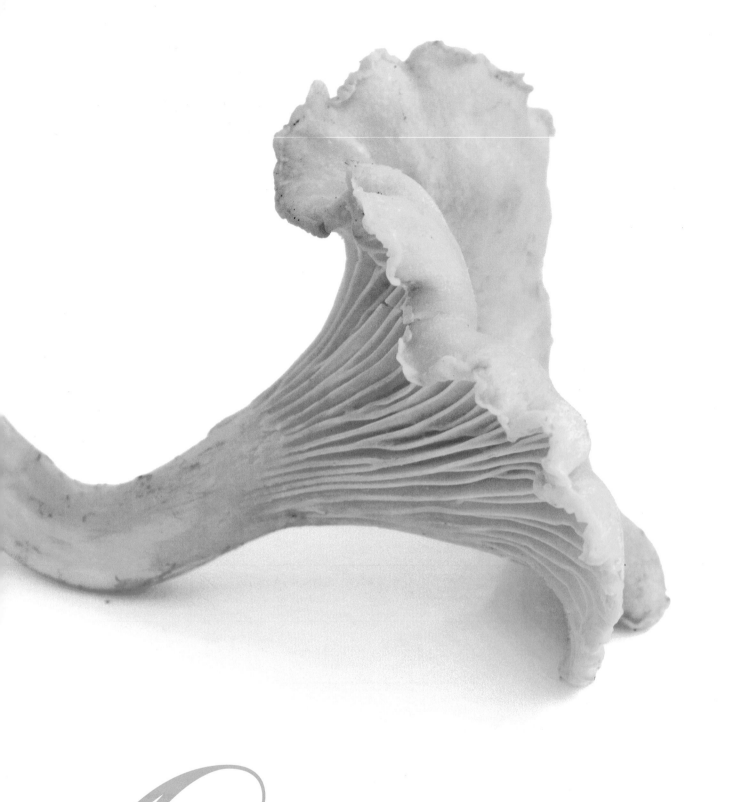

Chanterel

Beef Tenderloin
with Corn and Chanterelle Mushrooms

Chef Ethan Stowell

INGREDIENTS

4 6-ounce center-cut beef tenderloins

2 cups corn kernels, cut off the cob

2 cups small chanterelle mushrooms, cleaned and quartered

1 tablespoon shallot, minced

1 tablespoon Italian parsley, chopped

2 tablespoons butter

2 cups beef broth, reduced by half

1 cup veal demi-glace

1 tablespoon thyme leaves

Salt and pepper, to taste

2 tablespoons olive oil

INSTRUCTIONS

In a medium sized sauté pan, add the butter, corn, and chanterelle mushrooms. Sauté on medium heat until the corn and mushrooms are cooked and any released liquids have evaporated, about 4-5 minutes. Add the shallots and parsley, season with salt and pepper, and set aside to keep warm while you cook the beef tenderloin.

Preheat oven to 400 degrees F.

In a large sauté pan, heat olive oil over medium-high heat. Once the pan is hot and the oil is just about to start smoking, season the steaks with salt and pepper, and place in the pan. Cook on each side until very brown and crispy, about 2-3 minutes per side. Once both sides are browned, place the entire pan in the oven to cook the steaks evenly, about 4-5 minutes for medium rare to medium. Remove pan from the oven, and place the steaks on a platter to rest for about 6-8 minutes while you finish the sauce.

Heat the broth and the veal demi-glace in a small pot. Season with salt and pepper.

On four warm plates, divide the corn and chanterelle mixture, and place a steak on top of each pile. Add the thyme leaves to the sauce, and spoon over the steaks. Serve immediately.

CHEF JOHN HOWIE

CHEF, JOHN HOWIE RESTAURANT GROUP

I believe FareStart makes a genuine difference in the lives of people who might otherwise never have an opportunity to improve their situation.

WHEN I WAS INTRODUCED TO FARESTART NEARLY 25 YEARS AGO, IT WAS CALLED "COMMON MEALS."

I was asked by the director at the time to do a chef dinner, and, in the process, I learned about the program. **I was very impressed with what they were doing and wanted to support their outreach. I have been involved ever since.**

It's great anytime you can give someone a hand up rather than a hand out. I believe FareStart exemplifies this approach and makes a genuine difference in the lives of people who might otherwise never have an opportunity to improve their situation.

I've had many challenges in my family life and have always known that, except for the grace of God and few good mentors, I could be in the same position the FareStart students are in now.

Every Guest Chef Night is special, but mostly, it is seeing the tears in the eyes of the family members as they watch their children, brothers, sisters, or even, mothers or fathers transform their lives!

I get the same thing out of Guest Chef Night as the families do - seeing that the work we do changes lives for the better.

I've had many challenges in my family life and have always known that, except for the grace of God and few good mentors, I could be in the same position the FareStart students are in now. So, I want to help and believe it is what I have been called to do.

JH

I have been involved in the Seattle restaurant scene since 1975. I worked at many popular Seattle restaurants, including stints at Emmett's, The Butcher Restaurant, Boondocks, Sundeckers, and Greenthumbs. I also worked for Sundays, 13 Coins, Simon's Restaurant & Piano Bar, Scott's Bar & Grill in Edmonds, and Triples Bistro on Lake Union.

I loved working for Restaurants Unlimited and never thought I would leave. I have great respect for Rich Komen, the founder, but after he sold the company, I decided that starting my own company, with roots in the RUI philosophy was a natural next step.

In June 1992, I was the opening Executive Chef for Palisade Restaurant; this is also when I was first introduced to Common Meals (FareStart's original name).

I was at Palisade for ten years until I opened my first restaurant, Seastar Restaurant & Raw Bar, followed by SPORT Restaurant & Bar, Adriatic Grill, John Howie Steak, The Beardslee Public House and Brewery, and Wildwood Spirits Co.

IT'S BEEN QUITE AN ADVENTURE!

I always thought owning a
restaurant would be my future.

Thank God I waited, or was made
to wait, until I was older and a little wiser.

Whether it's my mom's spaghetti sauce, beef stroganoff, green pepper steak, or my grandma's simple tomato sandwich, the way to my heart has always been through my stomach.

My favorite memories involve food; from the corn feeds we had with neighbors in my home state of Illinois to the digging and steaming of clams and catching Dungeness crab during childhood vacations at Hood Canal to my wife's favorite activity – having friends over for dinner or a backyard BBQ – food is an important part of the moments that I remember and cherish.

I have been blessed with so much - my relationship with God, a healthy family, our strong business, and the heart to be there for others.

IT'S PROJECTS, LIKE FARESTART, THAT GIVE A HAND UP THAT I WANT TO BE A PART OF FOREVER. THEY HAVE MY HEART, MY SOUL, AND MY MIND!

CHEF JOHN HOWIE

ROASTED CORN RECIPE

Chef John Howie

Adapted from Chef Howie's Cookbook - Passion & Palate: Recipes for a Generous Table

INGREDIENTS

6 ears corn on the cob, husk peeled back, silk removed

¼ cup olive oil

2 teaspoons kosher salt

INSTRUCTIONS

Baste each ear of corn with olive oil, and then, season with salt.

Roast the ears on the wood chip broiler, BBQ grill, or in an oven until golden brown and slightly charred; some of the kernels should be caramelized through the skin and some exposed kernels will be slightly charred.

Remove from the grill. If you are not eating immediately, cut the kernels off the cob. Refrigerate until needed.

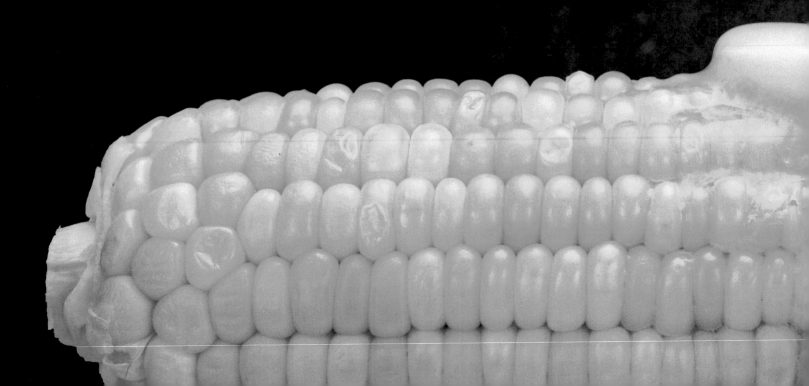

SOUTHWESTERN ROASTED CORN MASHED POTATOES

Chef John Howie

Adapted from Chef Howie's Cookbook - Passion & Palate: Recipes for a Generous Table

INGREDIENTS

10 ounces Yukon gold potatoes, mashed

2 tablespoons salted butter

6 ounces sweet corn, roasted and cut from

the cob *(Recipe on previous page)*

1 teaspoon Southwestern Seasoning mix

(Recipe in Book)

INSTRUCTIONS

Place butter into a sauté pan over medium high heat; let melt, and add the roasted corn kernels. Sauté until tender. Add the mashed potatoes and Southwestern seasoning, and heat through. Serve.

Lime

Lime Cream

Chef John Howie

Adapted from Chef Howie's Cookbook - Passion & Palate: Recipes for a Generous Table

INGREDIENTS

●

¼ cup sour cream

1 tablespoon lime juice.

1 teaspoon lime zest

INSTRUCTIONS

●

Mix ingredients together, and keep refrigerated until needed.

Ancho-Chili Rubbed Salmon
with Sweet Chili Hollandaise

Chef John Howie

Adapted from Chef Howie's Cookbook - Passion & Palate: Recipes for a Generous Table

INGREDIENTS

●

7-ounce salmon filet

¼ teaspoon canola oil

1½ teaspoon ancho chili rub, such as Chef Howie's 3 Chefs in A Tub Brand™

1½ ounces sweet chili hollandaise *(Recipe below)*

Southwestern roasted corn mashed potatoes *(Recipe in Book)*

1 tablespoon lime cream *(Recipe in Book)*

1 sprig cilantro

Sweet Chili Hollandaise

¾ cup hollandaise *(Recipe in Book)*

¼ cup BBQ base *(Recipe in Book)*

½ teaspoon ancho chili powder

Combine and blend ingredients. Store in a warm area until needed.

INSTRUCTIONS

●

Rub each salmon filet with the ancho chili rub. Let sit for 2-3 hours uncovered in the refrigerator. This will allow the dry rub to penetrate the salmon. If desired, place the salmon in a smoker and cold smoke for 15 minutes. This will add a smoky richness to the filet, but it can be prepared without doing this.

Preheat oven to 500 degrees F. Place the salmon filets on a cookie sheet and bake for approximately 10-12 minutes. If a crisp crust is desired, finish the last few minutes under the broiler. Salmon should have a crisp exterior with a tender interior. Remove from the oven, and let cool slightly, 1-2 minutes.

Place the Southwestern roasted corn mashed potatoes on the plate. Place the salmon filet on the potatoes.

Pour the sauce over the top of the fillet, and then, drizzle the lime cream over the sauce. Garnish with a cilantro sprig, and serve.

Salmon

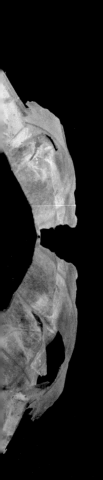

"FareStart was the perfect place for me during my early recovery.

It provided a solid foundation and community to support my new life."

- Dante, 2011 FareStart Graduate

CHEF MAURO GOLMARVI

EXECUTIVE CHEF. ASSAGGIO RISTORANTE

"If you're a chef and you feed people, you have to love people. It is so natural to me to help and feed other people."

I LOVE THE FARESTART PROGRAM AND BELIEVE IN WHAT THEY DO.

I believe FareStart is a great organization that takes people off the streets and puts them in a great working and learning environment, gives them a great education, and helps them find jobs. It is really important for the restaurant industry because it is growing so fast, and the employees are much needed.

Every single time I do an event with FareStart, I feel special about it.

It's always a wonderful experience. Teaching someone how to cook the right way is one of the most rewarding things for me. I love having the opportunity to help impact other people's lives.

I grew up around the tradition and culture of sharing food. My mother always did things that way. Whoever showed up at our house, no matter who it was, whether she knew them or not, she asked them to eat with us. It's a way of bringing people together.

I opened Assaggio Ristorante in 1993. In Italian, Assaggio means "taste," and the menu has been designed to give guests a taste of my culinary passion, Italian style. Our menu is not about fancy spices or complicated dishes; it's about simplicity, honesty, and the freshest ingredients you can find.

Growing up in Ancona, Italy, people ask me "How did you learn to cook?" I tell them, "My stove and my oven are my masters - they teach me everything; they are like my gods. They are not fancy, but they are mine, and they allow me to express the passion of cooking."

CHEF MAURO GOLMARVI

PORCHETTA CON PORTOBELLO

STUFFED PORK CHOPS WITH PORTOBELLO MUSHROOMS AND RISOTTO

Chef Mauro Golmarvi

INGREDIENTS

4 pork loin or veal chops, bone-in,
2½ to 3-inches thick

4 thin slices prosciutto

4 thin slices fontina cheese

8 fresh sage leaves

Olive oil

Salt, to taste

Black pepper, freshly ground, to taste

Sauce:

2 tablespoons olive oil

2 garlic cloves, coarsely chopped

Salt, to taste

Black pepper, freshly ground, to taste

2 medium Portobello mushrooms,
stemmed and cut into ¼-inch slices

1 teaspoon honey

⅜ cup water

1 cup veal broth *(Recipe in Book)*

2 tablespoons unsalted butter

1 tablespoon flour

Risotto:

2 tablespoons unsalted butter

½ cup diced onion, cut into ¼-inch slices

1 cup Arborio rice

1 teaspoon honey

1½ cups water, at a rolling boil

½ cup hot veal broth *(Recipe in Book)*

Salt, to taste

Black pepper, freshly ground, to taste

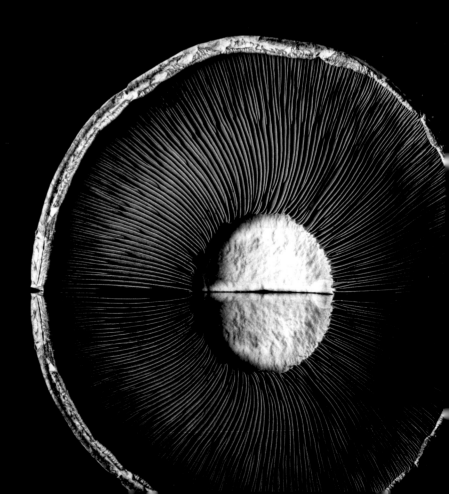

INTRODUCTION

INSTRUCTIONS

Prepare a gas or charcoal grill for medium heat.

Lay each pork or veal chop flat on a cutting board. Make an opening in the side of the chop to the bone. Hollow out the inside to about ¼-inch from the edges, being careful not to pierce the sides. For each chop, stack 1 slice of prosciutto, 1 slice of fontina, and 2 sage leaves, and fold over once. Brush with olive oil, and season with salt and pepper. Place on a plate, set aside, and prepare the sauce.

To prepare the sauce, heat olive oil in a heavy-bottomed sauté pan over medium heat. Add garlic, salt, and pepper; cook until garlic is golden brown. Add mushrooms, and sauté for 1 minute. Stir in water and honey, and reduce by half. Add veal broth, and reduce by two-thirds.

In a small sauté pan, melt butter over low heat. Add flour, and cook, whisking for 2 minutes. Stir into the sauce, and cook until the sauce is fairly thick and shiny. Set aside, keep warm, and prepare the risotto.

To prepare the risotto, melt 1½ tablespoons butter in a heavy-bottomed sauté pan over low heat. Add onion, and sauté until translucent. Add rice, water, and honey, and cook, stirring constantly until all liquid is absorbed. Add hot veal broth, salt, pepper, and remaining butter. Simmer until the rice is just cooked and has a creamy texture.

Grill the stuffed chops until just cooked through, about 4 to 6 minutes per side. Cooking time will vary according to the size of the chops. When the chops are nearly finished grilling, place some risotto in the center of each plate. Place a chop on the mound of risotto with the bone side facing in. Divide the sauce equally among the plates. If the sauce has become too dry, add water or veal broth.

CHEF BRENDAN MCGILL

EXECUTIVE CHEF. HITCHCOCK

I have dreamed of opening my own restaurant since I enrolled in culinary school in 2001.

I did my first FareStart dinner in 2009 while working for Via Tribunali; it was funny because we couldn't do Trib food there (no wood-fired oven), but the owner, Mike McConnell, a longtime FareStart supporter, just let me cook Italian food under the Caffe Vita/Via Tribunali banner. **I opened Hitchcock in 2010 and have been a guest chef every year since.**

As somebody who has worked in restaurants in a time and place before it was cool, romanticized by books and television...really before cooking was glamorized, I fell into it as a trade as a young person who needed a job and was willing to work hard. And, the kitchen rewards that hard work, regardless of your race, gender, creed, orientation, or criminal background.

I don't have a high school diploma, but the kitchen has taken me around the world and made a good life for me here.

THE ONLY THING THAT GETS YOU TO THE NEXT LEVEL IS YOUR ABILITY TO DO THAT HARD WORK, WHICH MADE IT AN INCREDIBLY VIBRANT AND EGALITARIAN UNDERGROUND SOCIETY.

It was also a haven for every misfit. In other words, it was lots of fun.

It's fun to demonstrate where the trade/craft can take you; I don't have a high school diploma, but the kitchen has taken me around the world and made a good life for me here. It can be the same for any of the students if they have the raw material and the fortitude to go after it.

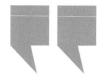

Food informs almost every decision I make, from my professional goals to where I live to what I do in my spare time. It is the center of all activities with my friends and family, how I define a region or culture, and an endless source of learning and inspiration.

My most powerful experiences around dining are usually the simplest; I took over Thanksgiving for my extended family 5 or 6 years ago, and it always shapes up to be my favorite holiday. I equate cooking rituals with places - making an arroz al horno in a hearth, burning Catalan pine cones for fuel, staying with hosts/friends outside of Barcelona.

A restaurant friend of mine was murdered after a Sounders game in a large crowd right on Jackson by the train station. His killer had untreated schizophrenia, and his disease got the best of him.

At a FareStart graduation, I spoke in my friend's memory, knowing that if his killer had found his way to FareStart from the street, he would have been counseled and given medication; he would have had tools to deal with his disease and have the ability to work toward a career that would keep him safe from the streets.

It is the story of so many FareStart students. Watching them graduate in front of formerly estranged family, giving the student a reason to be proud and make their loved ones proud, is really incredibly moving.

In regards to Guest Chef Nights - obviously, I get a lot back. We tend to sell out, and I see lots of faces from all stages of my cooking career and different aspects of my life and, of course, lots of fresh faces who support FareStart and don't have the slightest idea who I am or what I'm about. I can invite my friends, family, and colleagues and introduce them to the program. It really puts a lot of good energy "out there," and it can't help but bounce around and come back.

> I'VE ALWAYS HAD A PASSION FOR SOCIAL JUSTICE. I GREW UP IN FAIRBANKS, ALASKA, WHICH IS A WORKING-CLASS TOWN FOR THE MOST PART. GETTING RECOGNIZED AND REWARDED THE WAY I HAVE BEEN FOR COOKING PEOPLE DINNER SEEMS LIKE A GREAT BOON TO ME. I GUESS YOU COULD SAY I'M GRATEFUL.

MY FARESTART MEMORIES...

I've had some services that went perfectly - perfect execution, great group of students, wonderful guest chefs helping me out.

I've also miscalculated my proteins and came up short, having to send a runner to Whole Foods for pork loin to fill the last orders.

I've courted disaster by planning a meal requiring a nearly unrealistic amount of prep.

I found the best lessons came from the rougher ones. Even when it goes great, there's usually a story to tell.

And, I am always moved by the graduate's story.

I have dreamed of opening my own restaurant since I enrolled in culinary school in 2001. At first, I always took roles with greater responsibility as they were available until I held an Executive Chef gig, and then, I backed off and re-tooled by approach.

I took a job as a line cook at a Basque restaurant working under a Eurotoque Master Chef and reset my culinary education. After that I lived, traveled, and studied in Western Europe for the better part of a year. When I returned in 2008, I found a job at Cremant, and while the restaurant was short-lived, the ownership brought me on to be the Executive Chef for the Via Tribunali restaurant group. I learned a great deal about Napolitano food and multi-unit management.

After a year, I felt that I was ready to start my own business. I did pop-ups and catering until I found the restaurant space on Craigslist. I was familiar with Bainbridge through my wife, who's family homesteaded here in the late 1800s.

I OPENED HITCHCOCK IN THE SPRING OF 2010.

We started out very simply with the goal of tapping into the agricultural resources of Bainbridge and the Olympic peninsula and making it available to destination diners from Seattle - an easy walk from the ferry, yet it feels far away.

In 2011, we made several top 10 "best new restaurants" lists for Seattle, followed by a lovely review in the *Seattle Times*. The new attention allowed us to focus on our chef tasting menu, which became the highlight of our menu. As our relationships developed with local farmers, we went from buying as much produce as we could to seed-shopping in the winter for custom crops.

We have since developed
unique relationships with
island oyster farms, hog
farmers, and sheep
rangers, as well as a
half-dozen organic farms.
In 2013, we leased our own
property and began farming,
as well as enjoying the
lovely orchard that was
established on the property.

Our deli company was founded in 2011 next door to the restaurant. We have strived to translate our love for natural, local foods into everyday meals: sandwiches, salads, soup, and coffee/beer/wine. We opened our second deli in Seattle's Georgetown neighborhood in 2014. The atmosphere is fast and casual, yet we cure and smoke all our meats and prepare our own fermentations, preserves, and condiments in-house.

Every year, we are able to push our dedication to local sourcing and preservation further, and it is proudly displayed across our chef tasting menu. Some notable accolades: 2013 People's Best New Chef, *Food & Wine*; 2014 Chef of the Year, *Eater Seattle*; 2014 Semifinalist Best Chef: Northwest, James Beard Foundation; 2015 StarChefs Rising Star Chef/Artisan.

CHEF BRENDAN MCGILL

INSTRUCTIONS

To make the gnocchi dough, simmer potatoes in water gently for about 45 minutes. Remove potatoes from water, peel skin, and push through a ricer or food mill while still warm. Lay your milled potato on a clean, flat surface.

Make a small well in the middle of the potatoes, and crack eggs into it. Using a microplane, grate a "suspicion" of nutmeg over the potatoes, season with a few pinches of salt and a couple turns of your white pepper grinder.

Sprinkle the flour evenly over the top of the potatoes. Using gloves (the potatoes are still quite warm), gently break the egg yolks, and bring the dough together by pushing the potato, flour, and eggs together gently until a kneadable mass forms. Then, gently knead for a few turns so that you have a pliable, slightly tacky, dough.

Using a sharp knife or pastry cutter, cut off a piece about the size of your fist. Roll this dough into a long "snake," about ¾-inches across, and then, dock the snake into uniform pieces.

Using a fork or a gnocchi board, place the gnocchi cut side down on the tines, then "roll" it down the tines, pressing deep grooves into the dough and making a nice gnocchi. Place the gnocchi onto a sheet pan that is dusted generously with flour.

Bring a large pot of salted water to a boil, and then, add the gnocchi in small batches. Boil until they float to the surface, remove one, and bite it to make sure it is cooked through. When they are ready, use a spider to remove from boiling water, and place on a roasting rack. Drizzle extra virgin olive oil over the cooked gnocchi, and allow to cool by an open window.

BAKED GNOCCHI WITH CREAMED NETTLES

Chef Brendan McGill

INGREDIENTS

3 pounds Russet potatoes

2 duck eggs or extra-large chicken eggs

2 cups flour, plus extra for dusting

Salt, nutmeg, and white pepper, to taste

Extra virgin olive oil for drizzling

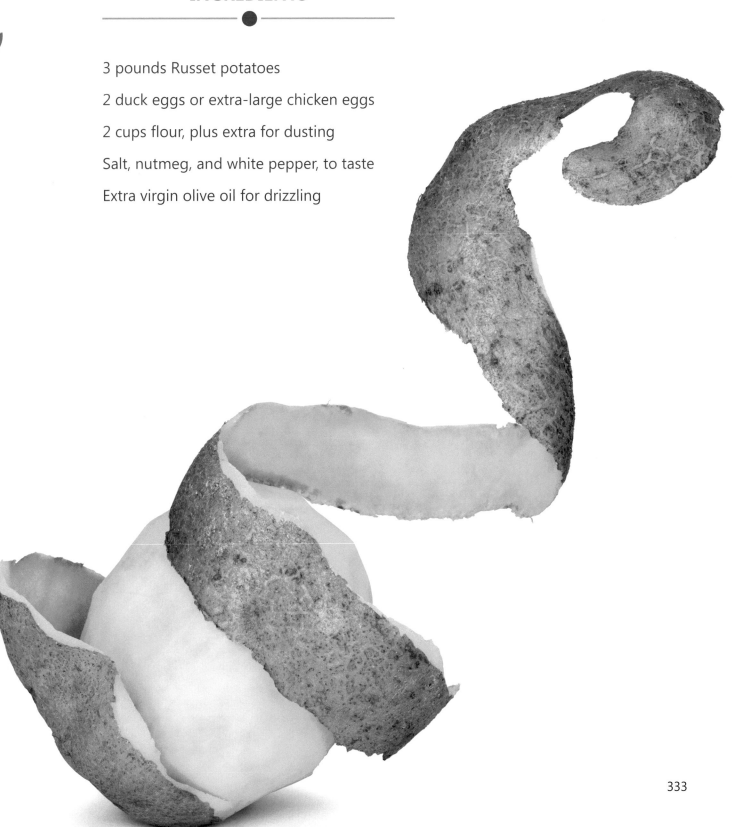

INSTRUCTIONS

It is important to wear gloves when handling the stinging nettles! Pick the leaves and tender shoots off of the stalky stems.

Bring a pot of fresh water to a boil, blanch the nettles for about 30 seconds, and remove. Refresh water, and repeat. Place in a strainer, and press gently to remove excess moisture. (The blanching water can and should be reserved to be enjoyed as a healthful tea, which is also delicious iced.)

In a saucepan, melt butter, and add shallots. Once translucent, add the nettles. Using a wooden spoon, stir to incorporate with the butter and shallots. Finally, add cream, and heat to a low simmer. Add thyme. Reduce by one quarter. Season with salt.

To serve:
Butter
Shallots, fine diced
Grated Parmesan or other hard, cured cheese, to taste
Breadcrumbs, to taste
Lemon zest, to taste
Chives, to taste

Melt and brown butter. Add cooked gnocchi, and quickly sauté for a golden brown exterior. Add a few shallots, and allow to caramelize slightly. Add a ladle of creamed nettles. If needed, adjust consistency with some water, so that your gnocchi are swimming in a nice, tight sauce. Place in a bowl, on top of which you'll shave some cheese, and sprinkle some breadcrumbs. Place under a broiler (or in our case, into a hot wood-fired oven), and allow the top to brown. Remove, and garnish with freshly grated lemon zest and fresh cut chives.

Creamed Nettles

Chef Brendan McGill

INGREDIENTS

1 pound wild nettles *(foraged on the island or Peninsula or purchased at the Bainbridge Farmers' Market)*

2 shallots, fine diced

1 tablespoon butter

1 pint heavy cream

Salt, to taste

1 sprig fresh thyme

Nettle

CHEF ROBERT SPAULDING

EXECUTIVE CHEF, ELLIOTT'S OYSTER HOUSE

In my life, certain people have seen my potential or allowed me the chance to show my potential, and I think that is what FareStart allows people to do. I volunteer my time because if I want things to happen in my community, it is up to me to do my part.

I first became involved with FareStart when I was the Chef De Cuisine here at Elliott's in 2007. I assisted the Executive Chef with Guest Chef Night. Since then, I have done seven more Guest Chef Nights with five as the Executive Chef here at Elliott's and done numerous auction dinners at the restaurant and off-site.

I think FareStart allows people to give themselves the opportunity to have another chance. FareStart helps people see that everything they want to be and can be comes from inside. I am a busy person between my work and family, and I find that FareStart's Guest Chef Night allows me to give back to my community in a very substantial way while sharing my passion for food and people.

EACH GRADUATION EVENT I ATTEND IS PARTICULARLY MOVING FOR ME. THE DIGNITY AND PRIDE THE GRADUATES HAVE IS WONDERFUL TO SEE.

I had a romantic notion of what it is to be a chef when I was young.

Both my grandmothers were excellent cooks with one being from Marseille, France, and the other working as a cook for decades. One of my first jobs was in a bakery, and I found I enjoyed working with food. I went to cooking school at the Seattle Culinary Academy and then, moved to Las Vegas where I spent 10 years before returning to my roots in Seattle.

One of my more memorable experiences sharing food took place in the mountains of Nepal.

I had been walking for a week and a half, eating barley flour mixed with rancid yak butter, tea, potatoes, and Top Ramen™, when I struck up a conversation with a travelling Nepalese school teacher. The teacher had friends at the next hamlet where we both stopped for the night. A friend and I were invited to have dinner with the teacher and his friends. It was a simple meal of rice, curry, and fried eggs, but I still remember how good the eggs tasted after weeks of a mostly vegan diet. I was humbled by the generosity of our hosts in offering us a meal that was by no means modest for them.

In 1975, the Elliott Bay Fish and Oyster Co. opened on Pier 56. Nine years later, it was remodeled and renamed Elliott's on the Pier (now Elliott's Oyster House) and quickly established itself as Seattle's premier waterfront restaurant. **Elliott's has been voted one of the country's top five oyster bars by *Fortune Magazine*.** Elliott's has the largest selection of oysters on the half shell on the West coast and specializes in all seafood from the Pacific coast as well as other specialties from around the Pacific basin.

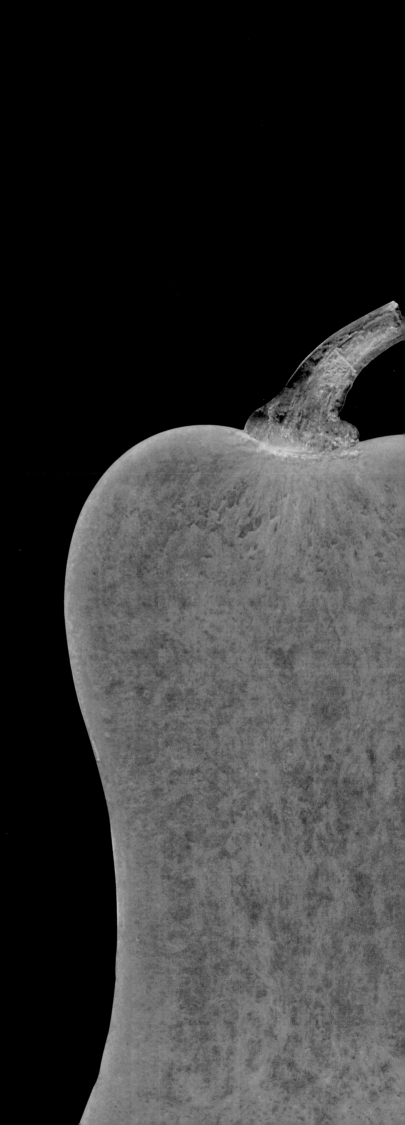

Butternut

Butternut Squash Puree

Chef Robert Spaulding

INGREDIENTS

3 cups cubed butternut squash

1 teaspoon sea salt, plus more, to taste

4 tablespoons butter

¼ teaspoon ground cinnamon

¼ teaspoon ground chipotle pepper, or
use canned chipotle

1 cup hot chicken broth

Ground white pepper, to taste

INSTRUCTIONS

Boil the squash with just enough water to cover and
one teaspoon of salt until tender. Drain, and set
aside.

Melt the butter in a sauté pan over medium heat
until it foams and begins to turn brown. Add the
squash, cinnamon, and chipotle pepper; cook until
the squash becomes golden brown and caramelized.

Place the squash in a blender, and add enough
chicken broth to allow the squash to blend. Season
with sea salt and white pepper.

CHEF AMY MCCRAY

CHEF, TILIKUM PLACE CAFÉ

In the summer of 2000, when I was the chef at Chez Shea, I learned about FareStart and contacted them about hiring a graduate for a position that we had available. It was through this connection that I was asked to do Guest Chef Night.

This was a learning experience for me. I became more aware of the issues that the students faced, of the program's effect on their lives, and of how we can use our resources to help others in need.

I have many memories of my interactions with FareStart: working with the students, listening to their stories, teaching them cooking techniques, and buying a pair of cowboy boots at an auction! The students each have an individuality, but they each are looking to change their lives.

Participating in Guest Chef Nights gives one a chance to see the world from another perspective. It is a joy to interact with the students, to hear their stories, to work together to make a difference in someone's life. The experience always brings me back to the reality of the world around us and gives me a hope that together we can take action to aid others.

A few years ago when I was at FareStart for a Guest Chef event, one of the students came up to me. She told me that she had never really cooked on the line, and she was anxious about how she would perform. I reassured her that I would be there to help. After training her to cook the dish, she took over. She succeeded not only to produce the product, but she trained her classmates as well! The next day, I contacted FareStart and asked her if she would be interested in an internship at the restaurant. One month later, she became a permanent employee. It was great to get to know her and to see how she had turned her life around. I was truly happy to be part of that process.

In regards to how I became a chef, I always tell this story because it is true. When I graduated from college with a major in English literature, my father gave me a present he thought matched my degree - a spatula and forms for employment in the fast food industry. I accepted his challenge and enrolled in cooking school!

After working in the industry for 15 years, my husband, James Hondros, and I decided we were ready to change our roles. We opened Eva Restaurant in the fall of 2000. This gave us the opportunity to create our own space - a place where we could work together and develop our own style.

Food is sustenance; we must eat to survive. Sharing a meal increases the nourishment. When we dine together and share food, we also share ourselves. This gives us the opportunity to make connections that we otherwise might not make. It opens us to others - we give and we receive.

Years ago, my husband and I travelled through India. We had the opportunity to meet many people, and the most bonding experiences came from eating together. We met a young man in Udaipur who took us to his house to have chai with his parents; we ate lunch with an engineer who went to school in my hometown and returned to work in Chennai; we enjoyed snacks with a Sikh family in Mumbai.

These experiences give you an opportunity to connect with others, to see the world from a different perspective. The result is a broadening of our view of the world and the roles we play within it.

I HAVE A FIRM BELIEF THAT WE HAVE THE POWER TO IMPACT THE WORLD AROUND US AND THAT WE HAVE THE RESPONSIBILITY TO WORK TOWARD A GREATER GOOD. IT IS OUR DUTY TO ACT AND INVOLVE OURSELVES IN ACHIEVING THESE GOALS.

Kale, White Bean, and Linguiça Soup

Chef Amy McCray

INGREDIENTS

3 tablespoons butter

1 onion, diced

2 tablespoons garlic, minced

1 pound Linguiça sausage *(Recipe in Book)*

2 cups white beans, cooked

1 pound red potatoes, roughly diced

2 quarts chicken stock

½ pound kale, stems removed and roughly chopped

Salt and pepper, to taste

INSTRUCTIONS

Melt the butter in a heavy, deep soup pot over medium heat. Add the onions, and cook until softened; add the garlic, and cook for one more minute. Turn up the heat, and add the Linguiça, stirring and cooking until the sausage has browned, being careful not to burn the garlic. Pour in the chicken stock, scraping up any of the delicious browned bits crusted on the bottom of the pot. Add the diced potatoes, beans, and kale. Throw in a good bit of salt and pepper to get those flavors moving!

Bring the soup to a simmer, and then, reduce the heat. Cook slowly until the potatoes and kale are tender, around twenty minutes. Taste, and adjust the seasoning.

Kale

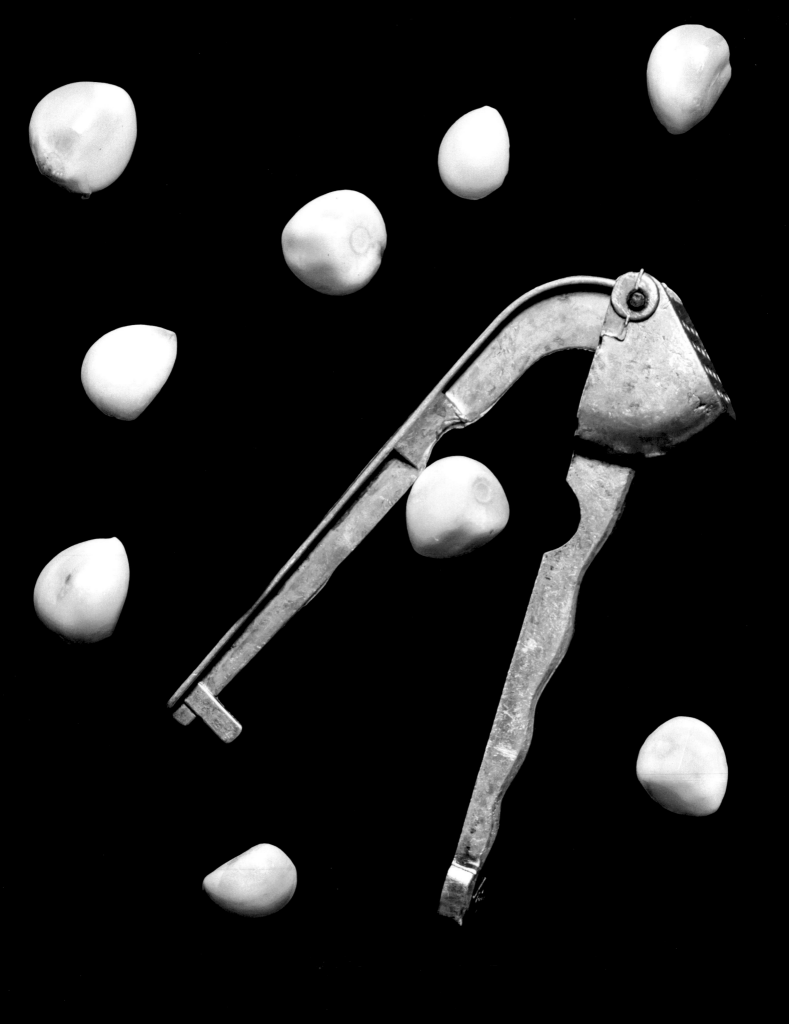

Linguiça Sausage

Chef Amy McCray

INGREDIENTS

1 pound ground pork

3 tablespoons garlic, minced

3 tablespoons hot paprika

Salt and pepper, to taste

INSTRUCTIONS

Mix the garlic, paprika, salt, and pepper into the pork. Make a small patty, approximately one tablespoon, out of the sausage, and cook it in a sauté pan until it is done. Taste, and adjust seasoning as needed.

If not using immediately, refrigerate.

Garlic

KASPARS
SPECIAL EVENTS & CATERING

I BEGAN MY FORMAL TRAINING AS A 16-YEAR-OLD AS CHEF-APPRENTICE AT ZURICH'S HILTON HOTEL.

From there, I continued to grow my talents at various restaurants around the world, eventually landing at the Hilton Worldwide as Chef Gardemanger of The Hotel Vancouver.

While in Vancouver, I met my future wife. She was working in the hotel's accounting office, managing banquets and events. I became Chef Saucier at The Four Seasons Hotel Vancouver, where I quickly moved up the ranks to Sous Chef and then Executive Sous Chef. Eventually, I was offered the position of Executive Chef of the Four Seasons' Inn on the Park in Houston.

Newly wed, we embraced the adventure and moved to Texas.

In Houston, we began fine-tuning a business model for our dream restaurant. When we were ready to open a restaurant of our own, featuring my unique culinary signature and her organizational expertise, we felt that Seattle would be the perfect venue to create a menu that allowed for creativity to showcase epicurean influences of European tradition, fresh Pan Pacific fusion, and continental Texas panache.

Owning a restaurant was always our dream. We both were working long hours on our jobs as employees of other firms, winning awards for them. We decided that if we were going to work that hard, we better do it for ourselves and in the city we wanted to be in! We wanted to come to the Pacific Northwest so decided this was the time to do both!

In 1989, Kaspars Restaurant opened in Seattle to great acclaim, earning awards and accolades that included a top ten ranking for more than a decade in the **"Best Seattle Restaurants"** list.

Eventually, we realized that our true passion was in making a more personal connection with people that leveraged my strengths as a chef and my wife's organization and planning skills. From that realization, Kaspar's Special Events & Catering was born.

We learned to support others from our parents and families who were always involved in donating their time to help the community. We have brought food to food banks on a weekly basis. FareStart is an extension of this, helping to support the training of people who may some day work in Seattle's food community and give them life skills that they will always be able to use.

We still remember when we started with FareStart about 25 years ago. The first event was the Sunday brunch fundraiser at The Painted Table Restaurant, and we have been involved every year since in different events and fundraisers.

We were asked to be a part of a FareStart Brunch Fundraising Auction in the early 1990s. Every chef donated food for the guests and made an art item, usually with a food design, which was auctioned off. We bought a great Chef's jacket with wonderful food artwork on it that Walter Pisano from Tulio's had designed. We still have it!

The FareStart mission is a win-win for us and for the students. We train the future employees in our industry, and they get jobs and regular paychecks. We love to be part of transforming lives.

We enjoy Guest Chef Nights because they allow us to get involved with the community through such a wonderful organization. We love training Seattle's future cooks, seeing how happy they are to be training with us, and seeing our regular customers following us to the FareStart Guest Chef dinners.

FareStart is a great organization and one that we hope will continue to grow and thrive in Seattle. We look forward to helping in any way we can!

KASPAR'S INDIAN DUCK CURRY

Chef Kaspar Donier

INGREDIENTS

¼ cup vegetable oil

2 pounds onions, finely chopped

1½ teaspoons kosher salt, divided

1 ounce fresh ginger, peeled and grated

10 garlic cloves, peeled and chopped

3 tablespoons curry powder

2 beefsteak tomatoes, cut into ½ inch cubes

4 duck legs and thighs, with skin removed

¼ teaspoon ground black pepper

¼ cup fresh cilantro, chopped

INSTRUCTIONS

Put vegetable oil into a heavy saucepan over medium heat. Add onions and 1 teaspoon salt, cover, and simmer over low heat for about 30 minutes, stirring often to avoid burning. Add the ginger, garlic, curry powder, and tomatoes, and keep simmering in a covered pan for another 30 minutes.

Season the duck pieces with remaining ½ teaspoon salt, and then, add to the pan.

Cover, and simmer on very low heat for 1½ hours, until the meat is tender and almost falls off the bone. An induction burner on the lowest setting works best, or cook over the lowest heat possible. If needed, you may add a little chicken stock to prevent it from burning. Just before serving, add the chopped cilantro, and season with salt and pepper, if necessary.

Serve with basmati rice, mango tempura, and steamed vegetables.
Chicken breast and thighs, lamb stewing meat, turkey, or beef may be substituted for the duck.

ck

Kaspar's Apple Cider Vinaigrette

Chef Kaspar Donier

INGREDIENTS

1 Fuji apple

½ teaspoon salt

¼ teaspoon ground black pepper

2 tablespoons honey

½ cup apple cider vinegar

1 cup vegetable oil

INSTRUCTIONS

Quarter and remove seeds from apple. Roughly chop apple, and place into a tall blender cup.

Add salt, pepper, honey, and apple cider vinegar, and blend with an immersion blender until smooth. You may also use a standup blender or food processor. With the blender running, slowly, add the vegetable oil in a thin stream, and blend until creamy.

Dressing may be stored in the refrigerator for up to three weeks in a bottle or jar.

Apple

Catalyst Kitchens has helped
build and grow innovative social
enterprises in 150 communities
around the world.

POWER

With a growing interest in our social enterprise model from other non-profits across North America, we explored ways to share our experiences and expertise in a more sustainable and strategic way.

In 2006, FareStart took the lead in creating a national movement around food service-based social enterprise to benefit individuals with barriers to employment.

FareStart's national leadership initiative, Catalyst Kitchens, was launched in 2011 to help build food service social enterprises that are dedicated to creating jobs and empowering the people facing the greatest barriers to employment across the country.

Using the proven FareStart model, Catalyst Kitchens provides the know-how, resources, networking, and partnerships that organizations need to turn the creative mixture of market-driven business and mission into an effective solution to poverty, joblessness, and hunger.

Catalyst Kitchens' vision is to have a lasting impact

locally and nationally,

breaking the vicious cycle of poverty by providing the

most at-risk populations with a sustainable and

empowering pathway to economic and social

independence and self-sufficiency.

"

"**Our organization,** Community Kitchen Pittsburgh, launched in July 2013, has grown in just 12 months to a $2 million agency with 23 full-time and 7 part-time staff.

Not only are we training individuals with serious barriers to employment, but we are improving the quality and nutrition of meals served to vulnerable populations. Seventy-eight percent of our budget is covered through earned revenues… and although the overall training numbers are still small at this point in our operations, 100% of our graduates have found above-minimum wage employment.

Having Catalyst Kitchens vet our business plan against their proven model helped us gain immediate credibility with key funders and stakeholders, which we were able to then leverage into start-up funds and increase the speed of our launch and growth.

The collective knowledge and experience of the agencies in the CK network is an incredible resource to us… and I consider them instrumental in our continued success."

~ Jennifer Flanagan
Director/Founder, Community Kitchen Pittsburgh

COMMUNITIES ARE CRYING OUT FOR SMART AND
ECONOMICALLY VIABLE SOLUTIONS, AND FARESTART
HAS TAKEN THE LEAD IN FIGHTING POVERTY AND
HUNGER THROUGH FOOD SERVICE SOCIAL ENTERPRISE.

Thousands of lives have been transformed in communities throughout the U.S. and Canada that would not have been if not for Catalyst Kitchens. Without the growth of social enterprise training for those communities who need it, many of our most vulnerable populations and those with multiple barriers to employment would suffer from a lack of viable options and pathways to self-sufficiency.

In addition, we would lose the critical by-product of the food service social enterprises – millions of meals that feed those who would otherwise go hungry. Catalyst Kitchens members provided over 10 million meals in 2014 alone.

Scaling effective social enterprise solutions, such as FareStart, has an extraordinary social return on investment by enabling us to prioritize resources for programs in locations where they are most needed and to leverage the collective knowledge and experience of all the organizations involved. It is a unique and highly effective collaboration whose impact numbers on a national level speak to the power of the model and the efficacy of its replication.

More than ever, as income inequality becomes a glaring, growing problem, our country needs the kind of solutions that FareStart provides – solutions that work to alleviate joblessness, poverty, and hunger.

BLUE CHEESE DRESSING

Chef John Howie

Adapted from Chef Howie's Cookbook - Passion & Palate: Recipes for a Generous Table

INGREDIENTS

2 tablespoons sweet onion, minced very fine

1 teaspoon dry mustard

1 teaspoon black pepper, coarse ground

2 teaspoons onion, granulated

⅛ teaspoon ground white pepper

¼ cup red wine vinegar

1 teaspoon Worcestershire sauce

1½ cups sour cream

1 quart mayonnaise

1 cup buttermilk

12 ounces blue cheese, cut in ¼-inch chunks

INSTRUCTIONS

Place all the wet ingredients, except cheese, into a large mixing bowl with the paddle attachment. Mix on low speed for 1-2 minutes. Add all the remaining ingredients, except cheese, and mix 1 minute.

Add the cheese, and blend for 1-2 minutes. Refrigerate for at least 24 hours to allow flavors to blend.

Cheese

callop

SOUTH OF THE BORDER SURF AND TURF

Chef Robert Spaulding

INGREDIENTS

12 large scallops *(we use U-12 size, meaning they weigh approximately 1⅓ ounces each)*

Sea salt, as needed

Ground black pepper, to taste

½ cup grapeseed oil

1 cup pureed butternut squash, kept warm *(Recipe in Book)*

2 cups mashed potatoes, kept warm *(use your favorite recipe)*

1 teaspoon parsley oil *(Recipe in Book)*

2 cups braised beef chuck, including jus, kept warm *(Recipe in Book)*

½ cup pickled red onion *(Recipe in Book)*

INSTRUCTIONS

Line a rimmed baking pan with a clean kitchen towel. Place the scallops on the towel, and salt liberally; place another towel on top of the scallops, and let sit at room temperature for 10 minutes.

Heat 4 tablespoons grapeseed oil in 12-inch nonstick skillet over high heat until just smoking. Carefully, add half of scallops in one layer, flat side down with space between each scallop, and cook, without moving, until well browned, 1½ to 2 minutes. Using tongs, flip scallops; continue to cook 30 to 90 seconds longer, removing smaller scallops as they finish cooking. Transfer scallops to large plate, and tent loosely with foil. Wipe out skillet with paper towels, and repeat with remaining oil and scallops.

To plate, spoon 2 tablespoons of the squash puree in a 6-inch wide circle in the middle of a plate. Spoon (or use a small squeeze bottle) the parsley oil around the outside of the squash puree. Place ½ cup of the mashed potatoes in the center of the plate with ½ cup of the beef with jus on top of the potatoes. Place the scallops in a triangle on turf squash puree around the potatoes. Garnish the top of the beef with 2 tablespoons of pickled onions, and serve immediately.

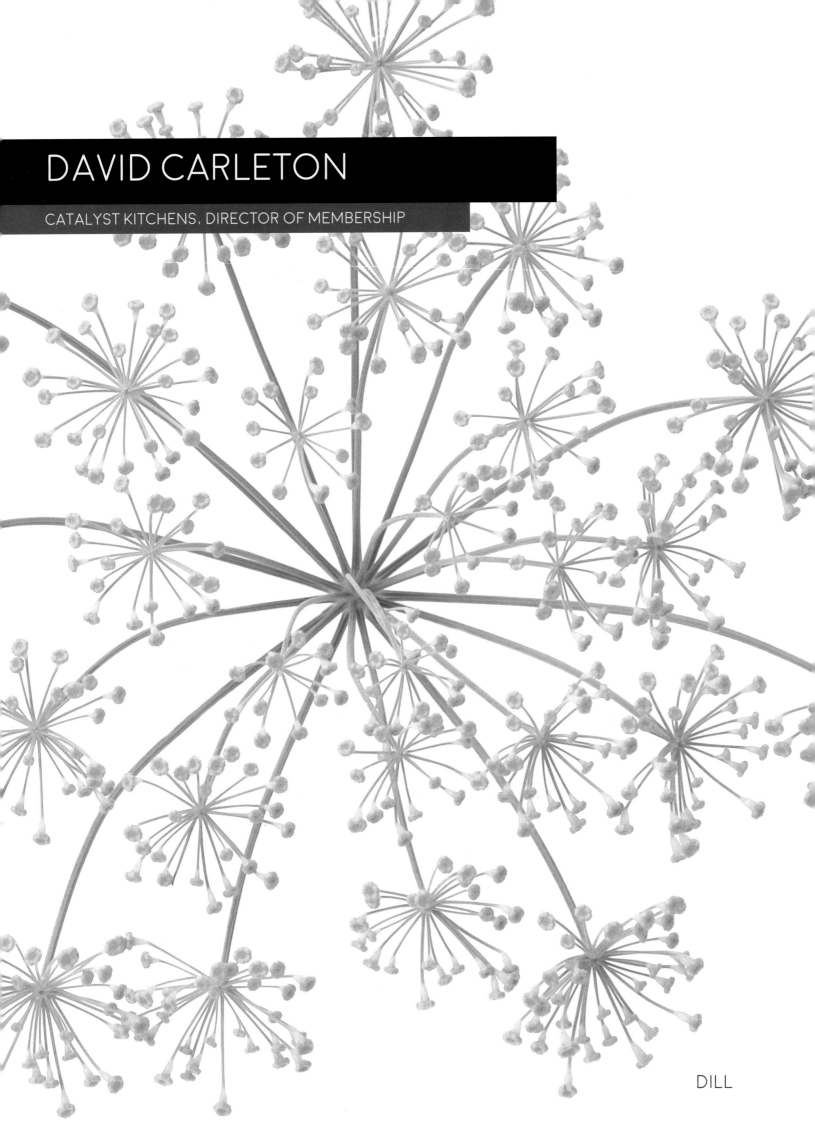

DAVID CARLETON

CATALYST KITCHENS, DIRECTOR OF MEMBERSHIP

DILL

Catalyst Kitchens was a collective thought that I then acted upon.

I volunteered at a fantastic organization in the D.C. area called DC Central Kitchen. After moving to Seattle, I discovered FareStart.

They had a very similar mission but with a more comprehensive model. It spoke to me. Wherever you are on the political spectrum, the **"hand up, not a hand-out"** approach is something you can get behind. I started my association with FareStart as a volunteer. In 2003, after a lot of action and interaction, I joined as a staff member.

For the first 3 years, I handled FareStart's marketing, communications, and PR. It was a blast. I engaged Wongdoody, and their work is still infused in our language and what we do. Tracy Wong came up with our tagline: **"Great Food. Better Lives."**

At that time, the FareStart strategic plan had ten items on it and launching the replication model was seventh. It wasn't that it was a low priority, but the first five on the list were really big things that had to be done, like the capital campaign to purchase the Virginia Street Building.

DC

After three years, I managed to secure funding on my own to create a replication initiative called "Kitchens with Mission." I was excited to learn along the way. Working with these other entities and understanding the problems and barriers they had in implementing our model increased my knowledge.

Success for us was helping organizations succeed by applying our model to their community in a way that had impact.

I learned a lot. For example, in more traditional nonprofits, they think of the kitchen as a cost center. The kitchen just costs the organization money. I would get them to see that they had a functioning kitchen, providing value to their community.

I helped them understand the double-bottom line approach of FareStart, where you separate enterprise revenue and expense from program revenue and expense in order to evaluate them individually and in concert.

When we work with potential organizations, we start with the question, **"What does success look like for the students?"** Then, we ask questions: "Where do the students come from? Who's going to support them? Who are the other stakeholders at the table?"

From this, we define the enterprise and training environment, and then, design the program. Success for us was helping organizations succeed by applying our model to their community in a way that has impact.

DILL

In 2009, Kitchens with Mission merged with FareStart as the Catalyst Kitchens program. The program has really thrived by having the FareStart leadership and resources involved.

I've had my own life experiences along the way, but I've also had the support of family and resources to get me back on track.

I can only imagine people without this and what they've had to face. Part of what creates the environment for transformation is one of no judgment.

It includes our trainees not judging themselves and learning to accept those around them without judgment. Knowing your past informs but does not dictate your future. Overcoming this one obstacle, judgment, is transcending.

When I walk into the FareStart kitchens downstairs, I stop for a minute, hold my breath...working there, all demonstrating a level of ownership, often times, I am unable to tell the difference between a student and a staff member.

The power of that environment, taking it to other organizations, helping them establish programs, and then, walking back into their kitchens later and feeling the same thing - that's what I get through Catalyst Kitchens.

This all started in 2010 when I brought together the partners I'd been involved with, and we had our first summit. We took what we learned from that summit and launched Catalyst Kitchens in January of 2011.

MY CONFIDENCE AND ENERGY TO MAKE THIS HAPPEN ALWAYS CAME FROM MY INTERACTIONS WITH FARESTART.
GREAT PEOPLE!

We've helped more than 150 organizations around the world and have an alliance of more than 65 members, who are transforming lives in their communities. With every new member, I get excited all over again.

When I look at this from a perspective of training and seeing how powerful learning life and technical skills are, I know we've done it.

IT'S A GREAT THING TO BE A PART OF.

DAVID CARLETON

CAULIFLOWER

"When the opportunity to participate in FareStart's program presented itself to me, I enrolled.

I was in a very bad place. I had to make a better life for myself and my children. My two children are my true loves. I would do anything for them."

- Jacob, FareStart 2000 Graduate

$\mathcal{B}$ ay Shrimp

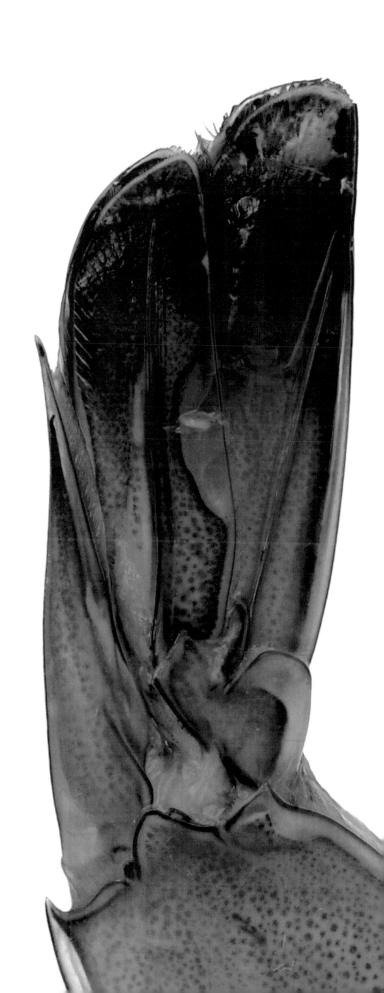

BLUE CHEESE, SHRIMP AND PEAR SALAD

Chef John Howie

Adapted from Chef Howie's Cookbook - Passion & Palate: Recipes for a Generous Table

INGREDIENTS

———————————— ● ————————————

3 cups romaine lettuce, hearts only, ¾-inch julienne

1 cup endive, curly, ½-inch julienne

½ cup grilled Radicchio-Belgian Endive Mix

(Recipe in Book)

1 cup Blue Cheese Dressing *(Recipe in Book)*

4 tablespoons hazelnuts, toasted

½ cup bay shrimp

½ cup sweet "100" tomatoes

¼ cup blue cheese crumbles

1 cup pear, ¼-inch thick, 1 to 2-inches long, julienne

INSTRUCTIONS

———————————— ● ————————————

Toss the romaine, endive, and grilled mix with the dressing until completely coated. Place on plates, and top with hazelnuts, shrimp, tomatoes, and blue cheese crumbles. Top with pear. Serve immediately.

PICKLED ONION

Chef Robert Spaulding

INGREDIENTS

2 tablespoons sugar

2 tablespoons sea salt

1 cup cider vinegar

1 cup red wine vinegar

2 tablespoons pickling spice mix

2 cups red onion, thinly sliced

INSTRUCTIONS

Bring all ingredients, except onion, to a boil.
Pour over the onions, and soak overnight in
the refrigerator.

HOMEWARD BOUND OF MARIN

NOVATO, CALIFORNIA, USA
CATALYST KITCHENS MEMBER SINCE 2012

Homeward Bound of Marin's mission of opening doors to safety, dignity, hope, and independence is coupled with a vision that everyone deserves a place to call home.

Homeward Bound is the chief provider of shelter and support services for homeless families and individuals in Marin County, Calif., serving approximately 1,200 people annually.

Its Fresh Starts Culinary Academy stands at the center of the organization's job training program. Students learn skills designed to help them secure jobs in the culinary industry, including basic food preparation and safety, recipe sizing, and kitchen organization.

GRADUATE SUCCESS STORY: HOMEWARD BOUND

Guests at parties in The Key Room, an event venue in Novato, Calif., may never see **William**, but they taste his handiwork in wraps made with free-range turkey, dried cranberry chutney, baby spinach, and red onions or minestrone soup with cabbage, bacon, and garbanzo beans. William is a central part of the catering production staff for the venue, which hosts everything from wedding receptions to corporate events.

"This is something that I can do well, and it eases my mind," William says.

A U.S. Navy veteran, William arrived at the emergency shelter operated by Homeward Bound of Marin, which offers 450 beds per night for families and adults facing homelessness. It also operates Fresh Starts Culinary Academy and The Key Room, where many residents find new avenues for employment.

"This is the first time I've been homeless. I came in here a wreck, mentally and physically," says William, showing a photo of his bearded, long-haired self. After 20 years as a finish carpenter, William says he lost it all to the recession and "bad decisions" that left him with a prison record. William came to the training kitchen as a volunteer, then enrolled at Fresh Starts Culinary Academy and soon became an intern at Jackson Café in San Rafael, Calif., also operated by Homeward Bound.

"I'll do anything - de-vein prawns, cut meat, chop vegetables. They could see I had decent knife skills," William said. "If you're willing to do things, instead of avoid things, you get ahead."

William has since moved to his own apartment nearby, where he describes his lifestyle as "go to bed early, get up early, stay focused." He's often first in the kitchen before 8 am.

"In the kitchen, I feel like this is home. It's family," William says.
"Homeward Bound does a lot for everyone. They give you a chance."

On his way to work, William passes an engraved list of donors who helped open the center housing, The Key Room, and the training kitchen.

He says, **"It's like a baseball stadium where you see the Hall of Fame.**
People like me have a chance to go to bat. I want to make the best of it."

"FareStart not only gave me the tools to

succeed but the knowledge, the dedication,

and the drive.

Those are things that aren't taught. They are in

you already, but they have to be brought out.

And, FareStart brings that out in everybody."

- Cedric, FareStart 2010 Graduate

OKRA

ARC BROWARD &
ARC BROWARD CULINARY INSTITUTE

SUNRISE, FLORIDA, USA
CATALYST KITCHENS MEMBER SINCE 2011

ARC Broward's mission is to transform the community by providing opportunities for people with disabilities and other life challenges to realize their full potential.

The ARC Broward Culinary Institute uses food as a tool to transform lives and build stronger communities. Students acquire the foundational knowledge and skills of cooking, baking, and teamwork needed to work with competence and professionalism in a commercial kitchen or in a related culinary field.

GRADUATE SUCCESS STORY:
ARC BROWARD

Kyle entered ARC Broward's Entry Level Culinary Arts Certificate program as a referral from the local vocational rehabilitation offices and his high school guidance staff.

Kyle's family and high school counselor were looking for an opportunity where his talents in the kitchen could be groomed.

Though Kyle was capable of standing for long periods and could perform most physical tasks related to his work in the kitchen, **he was very reluctant to work with a knife due to challenges with his eye sight.** He also struggled with a mild learning disability that was exacerbated by challenges with his vision. He arrived on campus one day to meet with staff and to learn a bit more about the program. While very shy, he was clear in his focus and desire to enter the program. He expressed his concern over his sight limitations but felt with the right support he could handle the kitchen activities. His determination gave the team confidence he could make it.

Initially, Kyle struggled with his knife skills. As the weeks progressed, his speed and accuracy in the kitchen improved dramatically. He was often the first student to arrive in the morning and the last to leave for the day. Both the executive and sous chefs marveled at his skill and improvement during his fifteen weeks in the program - ultimately naming him **"most improved student" due to his strong knife skills.**

That went a step further with the selection of Kyle as **"Student of the Year"** thanks to his ongoing commitment to his work, professionalism, and willingness to help with ongoing projects.

After completing his classes, he found a job with a neighborhood pizza shop, working alongside his brother. Everyone who works with Kyle marvels at his passion and commitment to being a great culinarian. His mother recently shared, "We appreciate everything you, the rest of the staff, and many others have done for Kyle.

He has come a long way thanks to the ARC Broward Culinary Arts program. His confidence has improved dramatically, and he has quickly become known by all in our family as 'The Chef.'"

BBQ Base

Chef John Howie

Adapted from Chef Howie's Cookbook - Passion & Palate: Recipes for a Generous Table

INGREDIENTS

1½ teaspoons olive oil

3 tablespoons onion, minced very fine

1½ teaspoons ancho chili powder

⅛ teaspoon chipotle chili powder

¾ teaspoon mild chili powder

1 tablespoon Balsamic vinegar

1½ teaspoons Dijon mustard

2 teaspoons light brown sugar

2 tablespoons molasses

½ teaspoon Worcestershire sauce

½ teaspoon garlic, minced

¼ cup tomato paste

INSTRUCTIONS

Heat olive oil in sauce pan. Sauté onion and chili powders until the onions are soft and translucent.

Deglaze with balsamic vinegar.

Add remaining ingredients, and simmer 3-5 minutes on very low heat.

Cool, and store refrigerated.

Saffron
SAFFRON AND SHRIMP STOCK

Shrimp shells from 10 pounds of shrimp meat
Mirepoix of 2 ounces each of diced
onion, leek, celery, and carrot
6 ounces apple juice
2 ounces tomato paste
2 quarts water
10-12 saffron strands
Standard bouquet garni

Sauté shrimp shells in very hot oil. Add the mirepoix, and continue to sauté.

Deglaze with apple juice. Add tomato paste, water, bouquet garni, and saffron strands, and bring to a simmer. Skim top as needed. Maintain simmering until needed for risotto. Strain.

Saffron Risotto
with Pacific Northwest Fruits De Mar

Chef Jeff O'Brien

INGREDIENTS

●

4 shallots, minced

1 small onion, finely chopped

2 tablespoons butter

3 cups Arborio rice

2 cups chicken stock

8-9 cups saffron shrimp stock, hot

24 sea scallops

16 large shrimp, peeled and deveined

1 pound Halibut fillet, cut into 1-inch pieces

¼ cup sundried tomatoes, not packed in oil, julienned

2 large red bell peppers, diced

1/2 bunch parsley, finely chopped

⅓ bunch basil, chiffonade

7 ounces grated Parmesan cheese

Sea salt and freshly ground pepper, to taste

¼ cup toasted pine nuts

Penn Cove mussels *(optional)*

INSTRUCTIONS

●

Sauté shallots and onions in butter until translucent. Add rice, and mix thoroughly to coat all grains of rice with butter. Sauté until slightly caramelized, and add chicken stock. Simmer until absorbed by rice. Maintain a calm simmer, which will be important throughout the cooking process.

Add hot shrimp stock to the rice 1-2 cups at a time (you want the rice to slowly absorb the stock), stirring and moving pan around after each addition; this will create a creamy texture. Do not over-stir, as it may mash the rice. Continue this process until the rice is cooked through and has a creamy texture coating it.

During the last ten minutes of cooking, add seafood, and cover. Finish with sundried tomatoes, red peppers, parsley, basil, and Parmesan cheese. Season with salt and pepper, if desired. Place in a deep soup plate. Garnish with pine nuts. Place Penn Cove mussels around the perimeter of the plate for a classic Northwest meal.

KASPAR'S NORTHWEST BERRY MERINGUE CAKE

Chef Kaspar Donier

INGREDIENTS

½ cup butter, at room temperature

1½ cups sugar, divided

4 egg yolks, at room temperature

4 tablespoons milk

1½ teaspoons vanilla

¾ cup all purpose flour

½ teaspoon baking powder

4 egg whites

1 cup whipping cream

2 tablespoons powdered sugar, plus more for garnish

½ cup blueberries

½ cup raspberries

½ cup sliced strawberries

8 mint sprigs

Powdered sugar, for sprinkling

INSTRUCTIONS

Preheat oven to 350 degrees F. Grease and flour, or line with parchment, two 8-inch round cake pans.

In the bowl of a mixer fitted with a paddle attachment, cream butter and ½ cup sugar on medium speed until light and fluffy. In a separate bowl, mix together egg yolks, milk, and vanilla. Add to the butter mixture, and beat until combined. Sift flour and baking powder together, and fold gently into the butter mixture until well incorporated. Divide batter between cake pans.

In a clean mixing bowl fitted with the whisk attachment, whip egg whites until stiff, and then, gradually add 1 cup sugar. Keep beating until egg whites form stiff peaks. Spoon the meringue lightly over both pans of cake batter, making sure it covers the entire surface. Bake 25–30 minutes. Remove cakes from oven, and cool on cake racks.

Whip cream and powdered sugar until stiff. Fold in the berries, and gently incorporate. Set aside.

Carefully, remove cakes from cake pans. Place one cake upside-down (meringue-side down) on a serving platter. Spread the berry whipped cream on top of it, and place the second cake on top, meringue-side up. Garnish with mint, and sprinkle with powdered sugar.

This recipe became a Kaspar's standard for 4th of July parties because of the beautiful early summer fruit and red, white, and blue presentation.

BRUCE BURGER

FORMER BOARD MEMBER

EDIBLE FLOUR. CHINESE LANTERN

Back in the 90's, someone told me about this organization that served great meals and trained homeless people. This sounded like a great combination, so I came to one of the dinners to see for myself. It was such a great experience that I began to organize informal groups of friends to come to Guest Chef Night.

THAT WAS THE BEGINNING.

As I talked with people in the food industry and social services arena, I would ask if they'd heard of FareStart. They all had great things to say. Invited by a friend of a Board member, I attended a breakfast meeting at FareStart, and I liked what I saw.

I spoke at length with the Executive Director, Cheryl Sesnon, and every data point was impressive. Following this discussion, I was invited to join the Board, helping with their strategic plan.

The Board did not rest on their laurels. It was self-critical and took time to figure out what was not working and what they could do about it. This was my first Board experience, and I came to see this Board as the model for how a Board should be.

I went on a shelter delivery with a FareStart student once.
She was living in a shelter in Kent, got up at 5 am every
morning, took the bus into town for an AA meeting, and
then, had to get to FareStart to start work on time -
turning her life around and making that magnitude of change.
I've never had to do anything that hard in my life,
and I hope I never will.

All of the students at FareStart make that type commitment. It's pretty amazing. It seems to me that the other real heroes at FareStart are the staff. They're not just doing this on the side; they're devoting their lives to it.

> GIVING SHOULD BE NATURAL.
> BUT, THE TOUGHER QUESTION
> IS HOW MUCH DO YOU GIVE?
>
> DO YOU GIVE UNTIL YOU HAVE
> JUST ENOUGH TO LIVE ON?

One of the things fellow Board member, Bill Adamucci, said was don't think about giving until it hurts; keep giving past that point until it feels good. That helped me give and also helped me ask other people to give.

I realized I'm just giving someone the opportunity to do something they want to do.

I worked on the national growth plan for Catalyst Kitchens. Early on FareStart was getting requests to do something nationally, and we really didn't know how to respond to it. For years, Board member, Gregg Johnson, and I were proponents, but it was a tough issue for the Board to deal with. It took us into a philosophical conversation about what our mission was. We also discussed risk and reputation.

What made Catalyst Kitchens happen is David Carleton.

He had some friends from boarding school, and they were based in New York State where they had a foundation. They were willing to fund a pilot program for 3 years.

At times, the old school tie seems to lead to the rich getting richer, but this was an example of the old school tie leading to great philanthropy.

David was great at taking the high standards of FareStart and adapting them to the needs of the different organizations in Catalyst Kitchens. He was very hands on and spent a lot of time working with each of them as opposed to sitting and writing policies and procedures.

I stayed on the Advisory Board for Catalyst Kitchens five years after I left the FareStart Board.

A lot of what we have, we have through fortune.
There are many areas we can help - *shaping culture, saving the environment, helping the poor.*

Wanting to do something good doesn't seem like it should be thought of as remarkable.
Helping someone is natural.

"FareStart is really supportive. It has made me more accountable with my life. I am really grateful to have the chance to start my life over at my age.

This program is so powerful. You're not judged. They want you to strive to succeed."

- Shanna, 2013 FareStart Graduate

PEPPER

DC CENTRAL KITCHEN

WASHINGTON D.C., USA
CATALYST KITCHENS MEMBER SINCE 2011

DC Central Kitchen offers ground-breaking solutions to poverty, hunger, and poor health.

Since its founding in 1989, DC Central Kitchen has prepared more than 27 million meals for low-income and at-risk individuals in Washington, DC.

The organization also offers a rigorous culinary job training program for unemployed men and women, helping them to replace homelessness, addiction, and incarceration with new careers and changed lives.

Since its inception, the Culinary Job Training program has changed the lives of more than 1,200 men and women.

GRADUATE SUCCESS STORY:
DC CENTRAL KITCHEN

A few years ago, **James** found himself homeless, hungry, and feeling hopeless to change his situation. One morning, he approached a white van serving free breakfasts to people in need. The van was marked "DC Central Kitchen," and the outreach worker handing out sandwiches used that meal to start a conversation with James about the organization's Culinary Job Training program.

"I found much more than breakfast.
I found hope and a new beginning," says James.

James enrolled in the program, and 14 weeks later graduated with a food handlers' license and a new job. "I'm no longer standing in line waiting for a sandwich," he reflects.

From a hot, healthy meal to intensive training and finally, to a steady job, DC Central Kitchen has helped me completely turn my life around.

Recently, DC Central Kitchen offered James another opportunity. There was a job opening in the same street outreach program that offered him a new beginning.

"Today, I'm driving the white van every morning to help people like me get the services and support they need to change their lives."

Veggie Napoleons

FareStart Catering

INGREDIENTS

●

1 eggplant, cut into ¾-inch circular slices

2 red bell peppers, cut into ⅛-inch pieces

2 green bell peppers

2 red onions, cut into ¼-inch rings,

2 zucchinis, bias cut into ¾-inch pieces

1 herb ricotta mix *(Recipe below)*

Herb ricotta mix:

1 pound ricotta cheese

¼ cup grated Parmesan cheese

1 tablespoon dried parsley

2 teaspoons dried basil

2 teaspoon dried oregano

INSTRUCTIONS

●

Preheat oven to 450 degrees F. Preheat grill or grill pan.

Working with one type of vegetable at a time, toss in olive oil, and season with salt and pepper. Keep each vegetable separate, as they will cook at different rates.

Grill the eggplant and onions until marked and soft, 2 to 4 minutes per side. Roast the bell peppers and zucchini on an oiled sheet pan until al dente and slightly blackened on the edges about 7 minutes.

Mix cheese and herbs in a mixing bowl.

Build napoleons by layering eggplant, ricotta, herb mix, bell peppers, onions, and zucchini, topping with another piece of eggplant.

To serve, heat assembled napoleons in a 350 degree F oven until warmed through.

Top with warm red pepper sauce. *(Recipe in book)*

Pepper

LIBERTY'S KITCHEN

NEW ORLEANS, LOUISIANA, USA
CATALYST KITCHENS MEMBER SINCE 2011

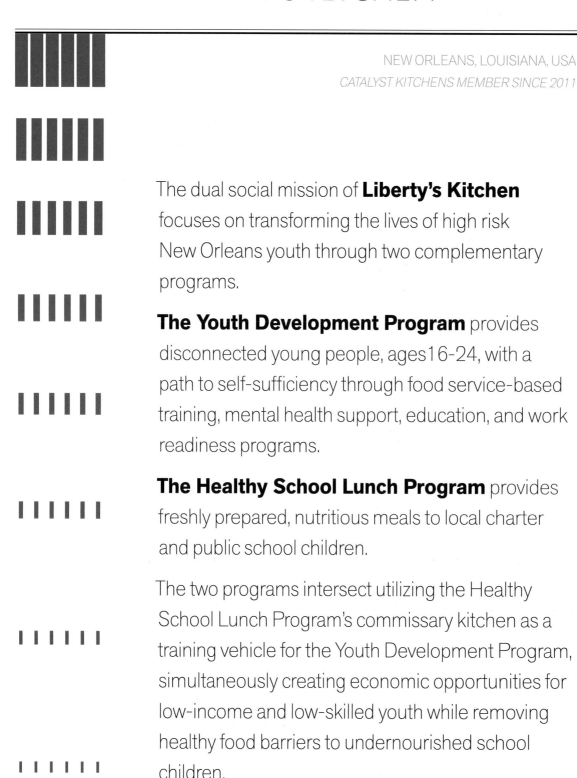

The dual social mission of **Liberty's Kitchen** focuses on transforming the lives of high risk New Orleans youth through two complementary programs.

The Youth Development Program provides disconnected young people, ages 16-24, with a path to self-sufficiency through food service-based training, mental health support, education, and work readiness programs.

The Healthy School Lunch Program provides freshly prepared, nutritious meals to local charter and public school children.

The two programs intersect utilizing the Healthy School Lunch Program's commissary kitchen as a training vehicle for the Youth Development Program, simultaneously creating economic opportunities for low-income and low-skilled youth while removing healthy food barriers to undernourished school children.

GRADUATE SUCCESS STORY:
LIBERTY'S KITCHEN

Syrena was referred to the Youth Development Program by two of her friends who had previously enrolled. Syrena wanted to move beyond the "dead ends" she kept coming up against; she joined Liberty's Kitchen eager to learn and open to the possibilities that lay ahead.

In the organization's **Youth Development Program,** Syrena received both occupational and employability skills training, the primary goal of which is teaching students how to succeed in the workplace. The intensive, attainment-based training program also addresses the myriad of social issues that create barriers to employment - issues ranging from homelessness to criminal records, single motherhood, deficient education, limited social and workplace skills, and various other immense hurdles that hinder youth from becoming productive, employable community members.

During her time at Liberty's Kitchen, Syrena proved to be a **dedicated team player with natural culinary and leadership qualities.** With the support of Liberty's Kitchen, she set goals and strategized for her future. She applied for and **won the John Besh Foundation's Chef's Move! scholarship** for an intensive nine-month course at the French Culinary Institute in New York.

Upon graduation from the culinary institute, **Syrena wanted to give back to Liberty's Kitchen and returned as a team leader, helping to launch the organization's healthy school lunch program.** She served as a role model and sought to inspire the next generation of students.

Motivated to succeed with a strong work ethic,
Syrena now has two jobs to support her mother and herself.

Syrena recently a received a noteworthy promotion in one of the city's finest restaurants, and **she has plans to open her own restaurant in the future!**

"Asking my current coworkers and
employer, I get one common response:

*I am a pleasure to work with,
and there is no doubt that I will
get the job done.*

That was something never
said about me before."

- Jonah, 2014 FareStart graduate

EDIBLE FLOUR. RED CLOVER

> # I founded a nonprofit called "Life's Kitchen," and it is dedicated to the same "transforming lives" mission as FareStart.

At Life's Kitchen, we focus on the young lives, 16–20 years old, and provide a life skills and culinary training program. Additionally, we have internships, placement in the food industry, and continuing education.

I had been in the restaurant business for 35 years and have seen many struggling young people over these years. I sold my restaurant in 2000 and decided to do something in the community. Once you make a decision like that, opportunities present themselves.

My goal in developing the program was to get help to the at-risk youth before they got on the street.

A lot of our trainees come from tough situations. In the first few years, I got to see how broken some of the systems were. I saw students who had been in foster care since the age 10 and had lived in 24 different homes. Learning of their background really helped define the support we needed to provide for them. They had a desperate need for counseling and life skills.

Peer interaction is a critical part of our program. We always have full classes, 10 students at a time, and we add new students 3 weeks into the program. In this way, our older students mentor the newer ones. The new intake gets to see their peer group and visualize their future.

I originally founded Life's Kitchen in 2003, and it
operated in Boise's Lusk District, west of Capitol
Boulevard and the Boise State University campus,
for 11 years. We needed to look elsewhere to
expand and landed on Garden City.

Our future home is blocks from the Greenbelt, the Visual Arts Collective, and Boise River Park. Moving from Boise to Garden City will place Life's Kitchen closer to many of our community partners, including Dawson Taylor Coffee, Cinder Wines, and Payette River Brewing.

We plan to expand our existing social outreach programs, such as making food part of our training for Boise Parks and Recreation afterschool programs, Interfaith Sanctuary, and the Idaho Youth Ranch Hays Shelter Home, and we will increase the number of charitable meals we cook from 105,000 to more than 300,000 each year.

There are some wonderful aspects to being in a smaller community. While we don't have the same population to draw on compared to Seattle, we have intimacy in the community. Home is that place where you have love, family, and support. Boise, being a small town, has some of that natural context.

Megan Karch was an important mentor for me; there was reciprocity because each of us came from such different business backgrounds with a different set of skills, and we were able to share mistakes and solutions. Megan's generosity contributed to the success of a much needed program for youth in our Boise community. **Thank you Megan!**

FareStart is so fortunate to have her as their CEO.

RORY FARROW

CHEVRE CHEESE
WITH TOASTED GARLIC AND CUMIN

Rory Farrow

INGREDIENTS

One 6-ounce log Chevre cheese

2 tablespoons good olive oil

1 tablespoon garlic, finely chopped

1 teaspoon whole cumin seed

Coarse sea salt, to taste

Baguette or crackers

I have been making this recipe for 35 years, and it's still a favorite. Simple and delicious!

INSTRUCTIONS

Place cheese on a serving plate, and split lengthwise.

Heat oil in a small sauté pan over medium-high heat. Add garlic, and fry about 30 seconds shaking the pan until garlic is golden brown. Stir in cumin seeds, and continue frying about 15 seconds; do not over fry, or it will turn bitter.

Drizzle mixture over cheese, sprinkle with sea salt, lightly cover cheese, and let it rest for about 30 minutes at room temperature.

Serve with great bread or crackers.

Baguette

INSPIRATION CORPORATION & INSPIRATION KITCHENS

CHICAGO, ILLINOIS, USA
CATALYST KITCHENS MEMBER SINCE 2011

Inspiration Corporation provides essential social services to individuals in Chicago hardest hit by homelessness and poverty, helping inspire participants to take action to improve their own lives.

At Inspiration Kitchens, individuals in need gain valuable skills and experience that lead to employment in the food service industry.

Once placed into employment, graduates are eligible for indefinite supportive services to ensure job retention and promote career advancement.

GRADUATE SUCCESS STORY:
INSPIRATION CORPORATION

WHEN QUANTRELL WALKED INTO INSPIRATION CORPORATION, HE WAS A CONVICTED FELON, LOOKING TO MAKE A CHANGE IN HIS LIFE.

"They welcomed me into the free culinary training program with open arms," he reflects.

Each day while Quantrell was in training, he worked in the organization's open kitchen and enjoyed watching the faces of the customers as they delighted in the food he prepared. With each passing week, the trainers gave him larger assignments and more responsibility, helping him gain confidence in his work as his skills grew.

Shortly after graduation, Quantrell secured a job at a local restaurant and within two weeks of starting, he was promoted to kitchen manager. He then came back to Inspiration Kitchens, this time as a cook and trainer, helping to teach students in the same program from which he had graduated. Again, he quickly moved up the ranks and was promoted to sous chef and trainer. Not one to settle down, he started working part-time for a local catering program where his skills progressed even further.

Later that same year, Quantrell was awarded a scholarship from Inspiration Corporation to attend Robert Morris College, where he graduated with an Associate's Degree in Culinary Arts.

Today, Quantrell is the chef instructor at the Greater Chicago Food Depository.
"I look forward to helping students in the same ways
Inspiration Corporation helped me," he says.

"Inspiration got me started, and gratitude keeps me going."

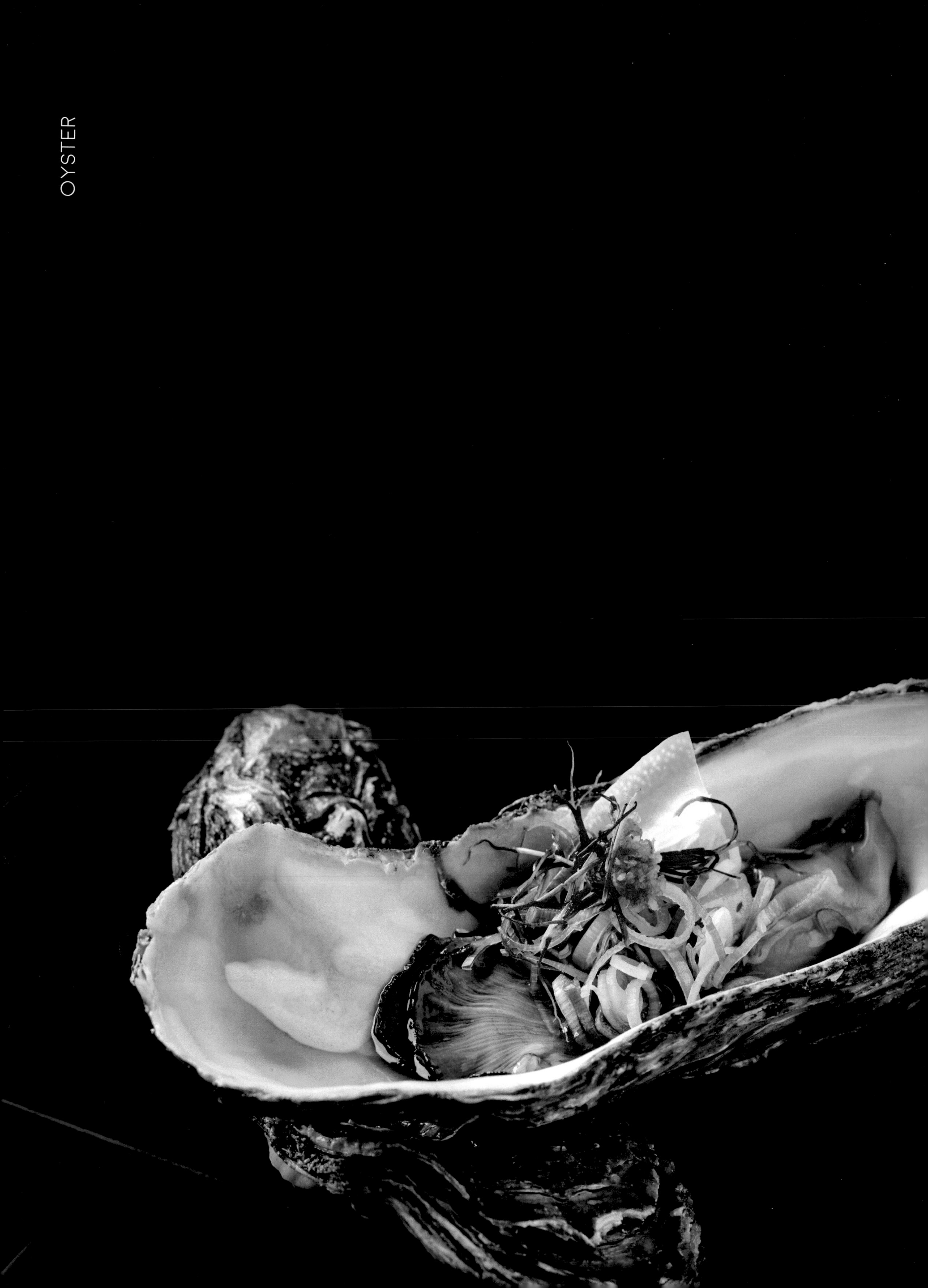

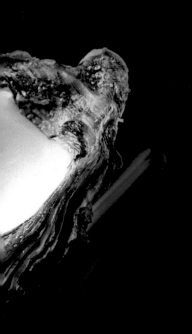

"I've never felt more successful in my life. Thanks to FareStart, I found my voice. During the program, I was knee-deep in the trenches working on my strategy for life.

FareStart gave me a fair start at life - completely inside and out.

I was transformed."

- Diana, 2016 FareStart graduate

LIFE'S KITCHEN

BOISE, IDAHO, USA
CATALYST KITCHENS MEMBER SINCE 2011

Life's Kitchen is dedicated to transforming the lives of at-risk young adults by building self-sufficiency and independence through comprehensive food service and life skills training, placement in the food service industry, and continuing education.

Life's Kitchen provides a 16-week program for young adults, ages 16-20.

During the program, trainees learn the skills needed to become employable in the food service industry. They also spend their time learning the skills required to live independently. These skills include financial literacy, employability skills, such as interviewing and resume building, and experiential activities designed to stimulate their growth as contributing members of society.

GRADUATE SUCCESS STORY:
LIFE'S KITCHEN

When **Candace** came to Life's Kitchen, her goal was to provide a better life for her young son and for herself. As a single teen mom, Candace struggled to find her way. Though she has a supportive family, she lacked confidence in herself and struggled with self-esteem. She knew she had to do something; she did not want her son to have a mom who worked in a fast food restaurant her whole life.

Candace notes that it was tough completing the program as she did not see her son as much as she liked and often came to Life's Kitchen on little sleep. **When she felt she wanted to give up, she had to remind herself of her motivation to succeed. The staff helped Candace stay focused and on track - she felt how much they wanted to help her learn and succeed.**

In addition to the culinary skills she gained, Candace values the life skills she learned, such as good communication and the ability to express her feelings effectively. The staff also helped Candace realize her own worth and build her confidence.

> **"I have so much gratitude for the program, for giving me the chance to learn to be productive, and have a life. [After Life's Kitchen], you can go and do whatever you want."**

Today, Candace is a confident young woman who is pursuing her dream of working in catering as well as in the beauty industry. After completing the Life's Kitchen program and receiving her GED, she enrolled in and completed cosmetology school.

> **"You guys have helped me out more than you'll ever know."**

"One of the things that FareStart is very effective at is breaking down a lot of the barriers and the stigma... Most people know that we come from disadvantaged and criminal backgrounds, but they know that if you made it through FareStart, you are trained to be professional.

I had a job within a week [of graduation]. Within nine days, I had three job offers, and I had to choose!

- 2013 FareStart graduate

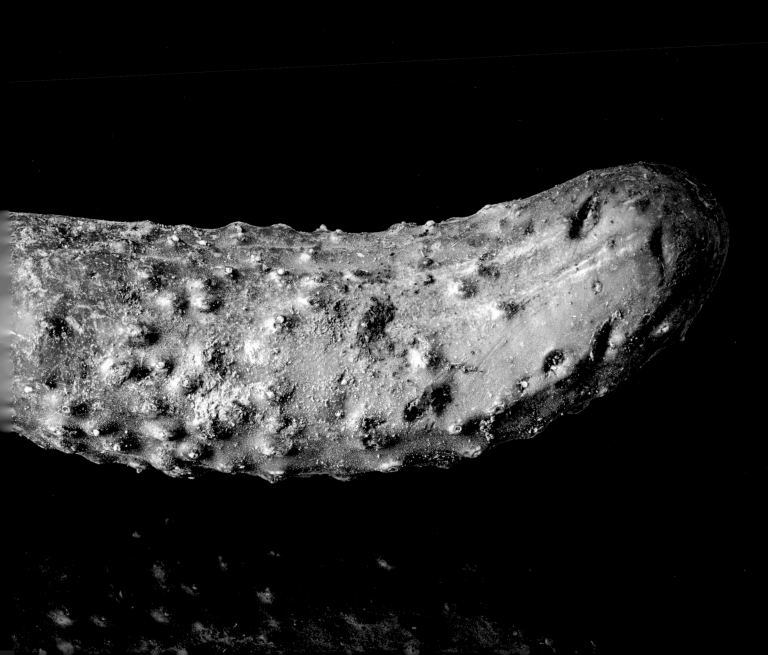

CUCUMBER

Each year, volunteers donate
more than 20,000 hours of
their time to support
the FareStart mission.

TIME

TREAS

&TAL

URE
ENT

WE WOULD LIKE TO **THANK** EACH OF **YOU** WHO HAVE CONTRIBUTED YOUR TIME, TREASURE, & TALENT!

WE ARE HERE TO HELP TRANSFORM LIVES, AND WE ARE *NOT* WILLING TO EVER LET OUR STUDENTS DOWN.

We don't rest on our laurels. Over the past twenty-five years, we have produced success after success, because we know how important our programs are to the people we serve.

Our leadership is unrelenting in feeding the hearts, souls, and careers of the staff and volunteers by giving them new challenges and the resources they need to build momentum.

The longevity and deep commitment of team members is unique to workplaces in general but almost unheard of in the non-profit community.

We generate half of our revenue through mission-focused business combined with our comprehensive training program. This is what makes us stand out in the non-profit community.

Through social enterprise, we not only flood the organization's budget with self-generated revenue but also breed additional support from community members who are drawn to support unique non-profit models that demonstrate self-sufficiency.

It's emotional. And, it's an amazing journey of great people doing great work.

My career as a practicing CPA took me to Japan and then, to Hawaii where I was a controller for a hotel. This path introduced me to the lodging, food, and beverage industry where I found my deep passion.

In Seattle, our accounting firm started a practice in the restaurant industry, and I further developed my expertise in the food and beverage space.

One day, I got a call from a recruiting firm looking for a Board member for FareStart. Back then, it was known as Common Meals. Our firm would shut down the practice for a couple of days each year and do community work as a team. By coincidence, we had painted the walls in the original FareStart building located on 2nd Avenue.

My walks to work each day took me past FareStart. One morning, I saw three chefs in their white cook jackets standing outside on the sidewalk. I stopped and asked them to tell me about the place. One of the cooks told me his story...

He'd come up from Los Angeles looking for work, arrived in Seattle, but ran out of money. **After almost a year on the street, he somehow learned about FareStart. He said it gave him a chance to get on his feet.**

FROM THAT ENCOUNTER, I KNEW THAT THIS WAS MY WORK... IT TOUCHED MY PASSION FOR SERVING IN A WAY THAT WENT MUCH DEEPER AND WAS MUCH MORE IMPORTANT THAN I COULD HAVE IMAGINED.

I followed up on the position and had a meeting with Board member, Bill Adamucci. He said to me, "Gerry, we are interviewing people for Board positions, but I need to tell you this is not an ordinary Board. We will want you to say you're all in. You'll be sitting around a table with people who have made that level of commitment. Time, treasure, and talent."

I let him know I was all in.

It was immediately evident at my first Board meeting: the passion, commitment, and the care. I was able to make contributions to the Board that were very different to contributions I'd made on other Boards. Never before was there an opportunity to be so involved.

I had the joy and the honor of being the Board president in the year we moved into the new facility on Virginia Street. I found myself having the most amazing experiences.

People recognize when your heart's behind something and that opens them up.

As an accountant, I always get asked to do things related to finance. I do finance all day and wanted to be able to contribute in different way. I found that way by helping FareStart's auction committee start fundraising. Over the years, the auction has grown from $250,000 to $1.2 million.

FareStart has an amazing group of people, and I've learned so much from their leadership and their commitment. **What a joy! I get to go hang out with these people who are fully committed and all in.**

I was reminded of my early roots in community service when, ten years ago, I did some work with the Whidbey Institute. A wonderful program. There was an older house on the property, and in the upstairs bathroom, a sign hung on the wall next to the toilet. It looked like an old shingle, but it was actually a piece of wood paneling that my family had cut up in our garage back in 1957. We made them as part of a community service project.

I never thought I'd learned anything from my parents about serving the community, but here was this sign that said:

"All us folks with septic tanks

Give to you our heartfelt thanks

For putting nothing in the pot

That isn't guaranteed to rot.

Kleenex is bad, matchsticks too,

Cigarette butts are taboo.

No hair combings, use the basket,

There's a darn good reason why we ask it!"

My father wrote this poem years back.

St Augustine's in the Woods on Whidbey Island sold these plaques for a dollar. Out in our garage, my parents and I would tear the paper, shellac the poem on a piece of wood paneling, and then, give it to the church to sell.

Years later, I came across one here on this old property. It was one of the signs my parents and I had made.

At that moment, I felt an incredible connection to my parents through this community service project I worked on as a kid.

GA

I've always been an in-service person, from childhood to my current profession. **I'm always trying to work on my human skills: my ability to show gratitude, to be present, to be a good listener.**

I feel it's an honor to be associated with FareStart.

At a FareStart event, tied to the opening of the new building on Virginia Street, a big Samoan gentleman got up to speak.

He talked about his mama cooking pies at a local hotel. He'd grown up in a rough neighborhood in Honolulu and had been in and out of jail.

He said he wanted to try the FareStart program, so he could learn to cook pies like his mama.

He entered the program. ***And, he failed.***
He was readmitted ***and, again, failed.***
And, they brought him back a third time.
Again, he failed.
I think it was his fourth or fifth time of being re-welcomed that he graduated.

He faced the audience in the room
that night and proudly said to us,
"Now, I am a Tom Douglas pastry chef."

I still can't get through telling that story without shedding tears.

It's like I said - *it's emotional.*

And, it's an amazing journey of great people doing great work.

GERRY ADAMS

"Maybe it's just one person's life that has been changed, but that one person could change somebody else's life, too... *a chain reaction.*"

- Kevin, 2013 FareStart graduate

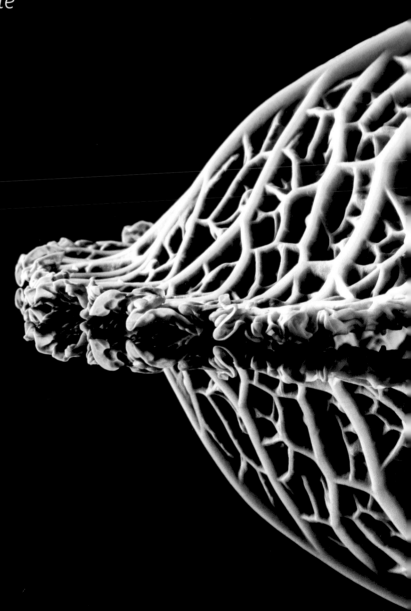

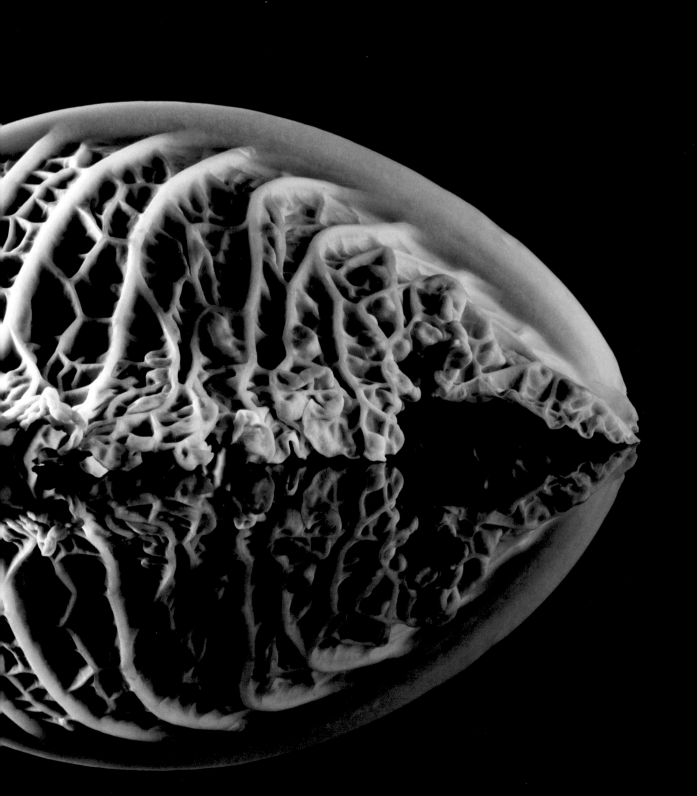

BILL ADAMUCCI

BOARD MEMBER . CAPITAL CAMPAIGN CO-CHAIR FOR 700 VIRGINIA

EDIBLE FLOUR. DANDELION

IT WAS MY MOTHER AND FATHER WHO TAUGHT ME TO BE GENEROUS.

Even though my father didn't have a lot of money, when we went out to dinner, he would always want to pay the bill. He was always helping people, and my mother was always volunteering at our church and welcoming folks to our house for dinner.

I started fundraising in college. There was an athlete in my school in Pennsylvania who had been ill. I started raising money from other students and, by my senior year, was running the campaign.

You don't want to just throw money at a problem.

My spirit of giving continued over my years as an employee at IBM, but it was when I sold my software business that I finally had a financial base to be able to fulfill my passion.

You don't want to just throw money at a problem. I'd been on the Board of United Way in Buffalo, New York, and ran the allocation of who gets what money, so I knew how to evaluate organizations. We started to see the smaller ventures as deserving of an opportunity.

I came of age in the sixties, and we had the mentality of the "great society." We were going to get rid of all the problems. It was a failure.

I STILL DON'T KNOW THE BIG ANSWER AS TO HOW WE ARE GOING TO SOLVE THE HOMELESS PROBLEMS.

The only way to change things is to change one life at a time.

If someone doesn't have a roof over their head, they are homeless, but you need to understand why they got to that position and understand how to get them out of it.

My background gave me the ability to see behind the problems, not just the emotional aspect of homelessness and hunger.

When I understood the FareStart model, I knew it was something that was working. They were changing things one life at a time.

The program FareStart is running today, while more complex, still has the same basic tenants. You're giving someone who is homeless, who is willing to change, the support they need.

And, the change is evident in the graduation stories they tell.

Plaque presented to Bill Adamucci by FareStart for his work done on the FareStart Capital Campaign.

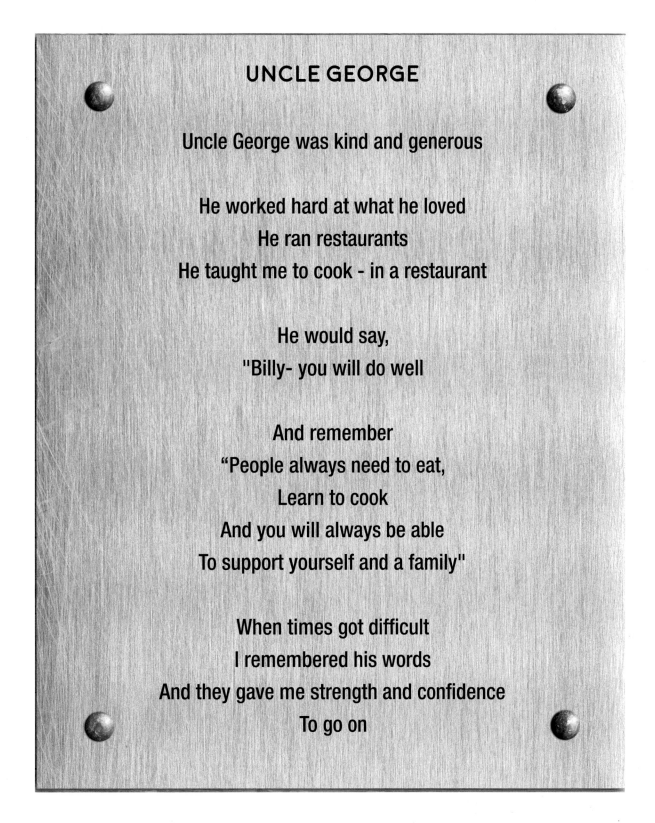

UNCLE GEORGE

Uncle George was kind and generous

He worked hard at what he loved
He ran restaurants
He taught me to cook - in a restaurant

He would say,
"Billy- you will do well

And remember
"People always need to eat,
Learn to cook
And you will always be able
To support yourself and a family"

When times got difficult
I remembered his words
And they gave me strength and confidence
To go on

FROM " UNCLE GEORGE"
BY WILLIAM ADAMUCCI. 2006

I first went to dinner at FareStart as an outing my church organized. There were 10 or so of us that went to the restaurant down on 2ⁿᵈ Avenue. A graduation was taking place, I thought **"Oh my God,"** and I've never left. That was back in 1996.

Whenever I asked myself "why am I doing all of this?",
I would go to dinner, and find the answer.

There was a parking lot next to the FareStart building on 2ⁿᵈ Avenue. I saw a van parked there and a bunch of women got out of the vehicle. One of ladies was dressed a little better than the others.

I was in the restaurant having dinner when the woman I saw in the parking lot got up and told her story. The first thing she did was introduce a woman, Mary, who sat at one of the tables.

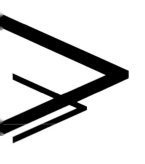

And the woman graduating said...
"A year ago, Mary took
my children away from me,
and today, she gave them back."
...She had transformed her life.

Another graduate, a forty-year-old man, told a story of drugs, alcohol, crime, and family issues. Outside after dinner, I saw him with his mother and father. All three of them were holding hands.

STORIES LIKE THESE HELP ME REMEMBER
WHY I'M DOING ALL OF THIS.

CEO Megan Karch utilizes her Board in providing advice, counsel, and direction. It's like a family. I stayed on the Board for nine years.

I was chairman of the capital campaign, helping raise the money for our Virginia Street location. In October, we got the final estimate for the building. We had planned to start swinging hammers in December or January. We had raised $9.2 million. The estimate for the building came in at $12.5 million.

Around about the same time, I heard about this program called "New Markets Tax Credit." It's a tax credit for low income communities, helping them build infrastructure.

I made the decision to apply, and by December 31st - just in time - we closed on a New Market Tax Credit, raising the $3.5 million we needed.

I am really proud of the building, but I said to Megan...

"This building is a tool.
The building isn't the magic.
The magic is what goes on inside."

BILL ADAMUCCI

LS'03

Peas

SALMON AND PEAS PASTA

Bill Adamucci

INGREDIENTS

12-16 ounces pappardelle *(bow-tie pasta)*

4-8 ounces of frozen garden peas *(amount depending on preference)*

4 tablespoons olive oil, divided

2-3 tablespoons butter

4 cloves garlic, finely chopped

1 small red onion or two shallots, finely chopped

½ teaspoon red pepper flakes

4-6 ounces salmon (blackened, smoked or gravlax), flaked

2 tablespoons capers

Fresh herbs (e.g. tarragon, chives, etc.), chopped

¼ cup grated cheese of your choice

INSTRUCTIONS

Cook pasta al dente. Add peas to pasta about 2 minutes before pasta is cooked. Drain, reserving 1 cup pasta water. Add ½ tablespoon oil and butter to pasta, and toss to coat.

While pasta cooks, heat olive oil. Sauté garlic, onion, and red pepper flakes for 3-4 minutes until soft, but do not brown. Add salmon and capers.

Add pasta to salmon mixture, and add some pasta water to create a sauce. Heat for 1-2 minutes over medium high heat. Add herbs and cheese. Fold everything together.

Serve with a simple green salad, grated cheese, and crusty bread.

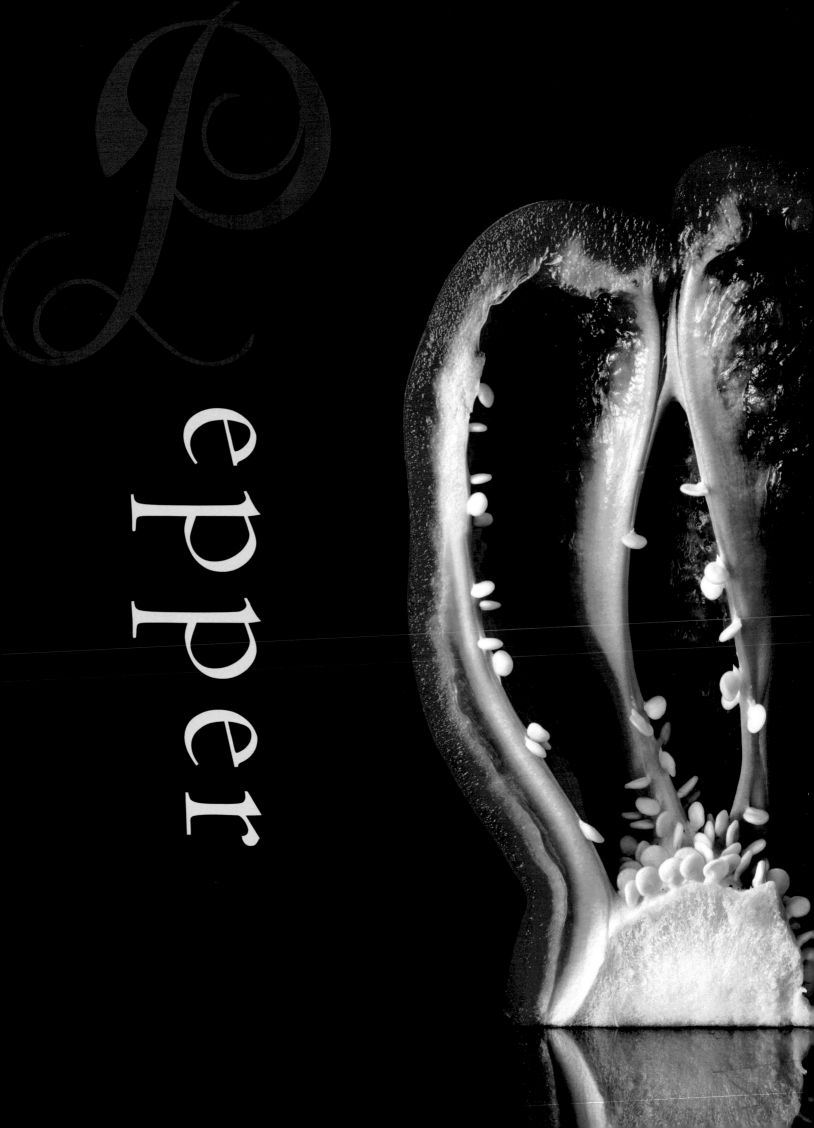

Pepper

ROASTED RED PEPPER SAUCE

FareStart Catering

INGREDIENTS

———————— • ————————

1 28-ounce can roasted red peppers

2 garlic cloves

1 tablespoon balsamic vinegar

1 tablespoon white wine vinegar

1 teaspoon dry oregano

1 teaspoon salt

1 tablespoon smoked paprika

1 tablespoon Dijon mustard

1 cup canola oil

2 tablespoons honey

INSTRUCTIONS

———————— • ————————

Place all ingredients, except canola oil and honey, in blender. Blend briefly, and then, slowly drizzle in canola oil and honey while blender is running. Adjust seasoning as needed.

FareStart Catering drizzles this over our lovely Napoleons. (Recipe in Book)

CONTINENTAL MILLS

Food plays a lead role in so many of the moments that make up our lives. Food engages all of our senses, provides comfort, and works as a vehicle for bringing friends and family together.

Food also plays both a fundamental and heroic role in our society. Fundamental, in that it is as necessary to sustaining life as oxygen. Heroic, in that the food products we offer play a lead role in so many of the moments that make up our lives.

CONTINENTAL MILLS IS A THIRD GENERATION,
FAMILY-OWNED MAKER OF SOME OF
THE BEST-LOVED BREAKFAST, BAKING,
AND SNACK BRANDS.

This includes our flagship brand Krusteaz® pancake and baking mixes, decadent baking products under license from Ghirardelli Chocolate Company, and newer brands, such as WildRoots® Trail Mixes and Buck Wild™ Snacks.

People are at the heart of our success, from founding family members, John Heily, CEO & Chairman, and Andy Heily, President, who are integrally involved in our business, to the hundreds of employees who are part of our broader Continental Mills family.

We know that it's people who have made us successful in the past; they do today, and they will tomorrow. As a family-owned food business, we never lose sight of the honor and responsibility that comes with providing the products that bring friends, families, and communities together.

Our people share a passion for enhancing people's lives with food.

When you buy a box of cookie mix, you're not just buying cookies; you're buying the experience of making those cookies and bringing friends and family together to share the experience. As a family-owned business, we recognize and value those moments and want to enable an experience for people to create favorite memories through sharing good food.

That translates to how we think about our philanthropic activities, too. Any time we can use our skills, talents, and resources to support organizations where we can leverage our expertise in food to bring people together, we want to get involved and make a difference! We focus our involvement in three major areas: food preparation, food distribution, and food delivery.

FareStart is an amazing organization, and we have been proud to partner with them to help transform lives.

IT'S AMAZING WHAT HAPPENS WHEN 'FOODIES' GET TOGETHER!

Our partnership with FareStart began in 2014 as a sponsor of the Gala Auction and through a donation of a beautifully designed cake to be sold in the live auction. The cake, called "Ghirardelli Chocolate Fantasy," was designed and prepared by our Corporate Executive Chef, Dimitri Ponomarchuk. It was in high demand, and the live bidding went up quickly, bringing thousands of dollars to FareStart from just one cake!

> "We have tremendous talent in our R&D Culinary team, and the beautiful cake was not only an impressive showpiece at the event, but it raised money for the FareStart program, which impacts many people's lives."
>
> *– Andy Heily, President.*

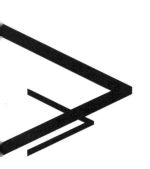

In 2015, Continental Mills Went Big!

In addition to a beautiful and decadent dessert donation for the live auction, Chef Dimitri and several employees from our Research & Development staff also committed to providing the dessert course for the 2015 Gala Auction, serving almost 800 guests! This was a tremendous team bonding experience that gave them the opportunity to volunteer their talents to benefit FareStart.

Continental Mills continues to support FareStart through sponsorships, employee involvement on the auction committee and Catalyst Kitchens national advisory board, and employee volunteers in the kitchen and shelter meal delivery.

Skills and Confidence Transforms Lives

Kelly Duffin-Maxwell is the Senior Vice President of Research & Development/ Quality at Continental Mills and is also on the FareStart Auction Committee and part of Catalyst Kitchens.

"I originally heard about FareStart from an industry colleague. I love the model so much because it provides an experience for the students to learn skills that are sustainable in their life. They learn to respect themselves again, and you see families change for the good...that's amazing!

I'm so impressed with the FareStart staff. They are absolutely passionate about what they do. They truly believe in the program and their mission and keep students at the center of their decisions. This is consistent across the entire staff.

At the first Guest Chef dinner I attended, one of the graduates spoke about her experience with the program and how it transformed her life. She described that the experience and training helped her recognize herself again. That is truly powerful."

"Mission Buck Wild" Benefits Youth Training Program

In 2016, we partnered with FareStart in a new way through the launch of an exciting new brand, Buck Wild™. Buck Wild™ is a unique, all natural snack product line targeted to millennials - the same demographic that FareStart serves through their Youth Training Program.

We wanted to make a community connection to the brand early in the launch and find a way to help others pursue their passions and create their own future. We are excited about the opportunity to leverage this exciting new brand to benefit FareStart's training programs.

NUTS AND BERRIES CHOCOLATE MOUSSE

Chef Dimitri Ponomarchuk

INGREDIENTS

36 ounces heavy cream, separated

1 ounce blackberry extract flavor

1 ounce hazelnut extract flavor

36 ounces milk chocolate chips

INSTRUCTIONS

Combine 24 ounces of cream and extracts. Bring to a boil, and pour over chocolate chips. Whisk to incorporate. Emulsify with a small burr-mixer. Set aside to cool.

When mixture has completely cooled, whip 12 ounces of cream to soft peaks. Gently fold half of whipped cream into chocolate mixture, mixing until combined. Repeat with remaining whipped cream.

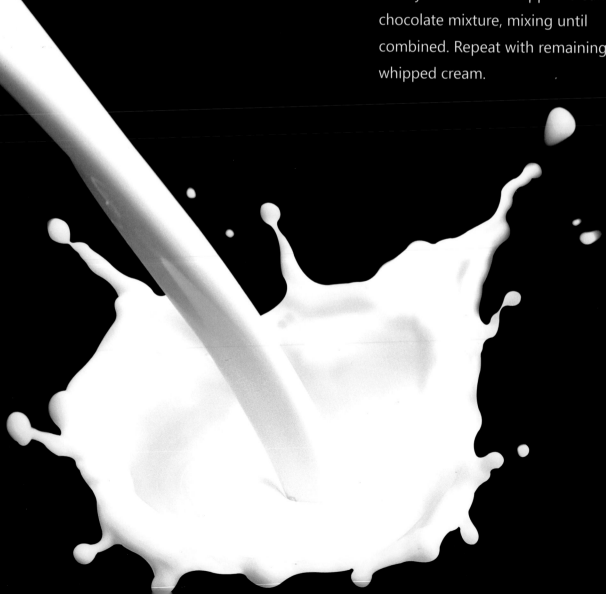

Nuts and Berries Chocolate Martini with Brownie Truffles

Chef Dimitri Ponomarchuk

INGREDIENTS

24 6-ounce martini glasses (or similar), chilled

1¾ pounds Krusteaz® Fudge Brownie Mix

13 ounces hot water

16 ounces ganache topping or coating chocolate, heated

24 decorative picks

4½ pounds **Nuts and Berries Chocolate Mousse**

INSTRUCTIONS

Combine brownie mix and water in a bowl, and whisk thoroughly, scraping the bowl as needed. Place batter into greased half-sheet pan, spread evenly, and bake at 300 degrees F for 30 minutes.

Cool to room temperature. Cut cooled brownies into 24 two-ounce squares. Knead individual brownie squares gently to form soft dough, and roll into a smooth ball. Submerge brownie truffles into heated ganache, and coat the exterior entirely. Drain excess ganache from truffle, and transfer to parchment-lined pan. Chill. Skewer each truffle with a decorative pick. Pipe 3 ounces of mousse into the chilled glasses, and garnish with a truffle.

Cream

Baked Alaska

Chef Dimitri Ponomarchuk

INGREDIENTS

1¾ pounds Krusteaz® Fudge Brownie Mix

13 ounces water

28 ounces dark chocolate ice cream, softened

1 quart meringue

INSTRUCTIONS

Combine brownie mix and water in a bowl, and whisk thoroughly, scraping the bowl as needed. Place the batter into greased or paper-lined 9-inch pan. Bake at 300 degrees F for approximately 20 minutes.

Unmold brownies when cool. Place it in the base of a 9-inch ring mold or spring-form pan, and top with softened ice cream, spreading evenly across the top of the mold. Freeze until set. Pipe meringue around the entire surface of the cake, and lightly caramelize with a torch.

MERINGUE

INGREDIENTS

8 large egg whites

2½ cups granulated sugar

1 teaspoon cream of tartar

INSTRUCTIONS

Beat egg whites until foamy; add cream of tartar and sugar. Continue beating until the egg whites are very stiff.

Egg

JERRY MEYER

FORMER BOARD MEMBER

FareStart is not just about feeding the hungry. It's about "teaching someone to fish," and that's a compelling message.

My journey started a long time ago, growing up in Kansas City. We were a poor family but better off than some. There were 10 of us living in a 1,000 square foot house. We had such a focus on family, culture, and charity.

 MY MOTHER DID SOMETHING THAT WILL RESONATE WITH ME FOREVER.

When my brother and I went to school in the morning, she would pack four lunches for us to take. Two lunches were for us, the other two to be given away anonymously by our teacher to kids who had no lunch.

My mother was empathetic enough to ensure the lunch bags and their contents bore no resemblance to ours.

Her desire was to preserve the dignity of those receiving charity.

When I first got involved with FareStart, I was invited to a presentation around the capital needed to purchase the Virginia Street building. CEO, Megan Karch, and Board member, Bill Adamucci, were at the presentation. During the evening, Bill asked if he could visit me the following week at my office.

When I met with Bill, he said three things I'll never forget.

"I want you to make the biggest gift you've ever given in your life, and I want you to keep giving after that until it feels good. Not until it hurts. Until it feels good. I also want you to give me your time and talent. Even if you write a check today, I want your time and talent, too."

I wrote the check. And, giving my time and talent started an emotional journey that lasts to this day.

I've known people in my life that have had all the gifts, all the opportunities, but have drifted towards homelessness. When you experience this close at hand in your own family, you don't see homelessness in terms of an "us and them" anymore. As hard as these experiences were, they have made me a better and more compassionate person.

I was on the FareStart Board for nine years, contributing to several pivotal milestones. I co-authored the strategic plan in 2005 with Megan Karch and Board member, Gregg Johnson. Balancing the social bottom line with the financial bottom line. I was involved in getting the FareStart Virginia Avenue building financed, designed, and opened.

I took on the role of President of the Board and saw how competent and dedicated the staff at FareStart are. They are professionals of the first order, following their passion and bliss, doing what their hearts guide them to do.

The combination of structure and mission is the alchemy of transformation.

My wife and I were at a recent Guest Chef Night with some friends, and she told these friends that the graduates who speak express their thankfulness and appreciation for the work and commitment of the FareStart staff. She said, "For the graduates, this may be the first time in a long while that they have had an accomplishment they are proud of."

This accomplishment had been enabled by a structured environment that allows someone to succeed. This combination of structure and mission is the alchemy of transformation.

The best friendships I've made here in Seattle have all come through FareStart. I have found a gift that keeps on giving.

I learned to give until it feels good.

JERRY MEYER

Aceitunas Andaluces

(Marinated Olives Andalucia-Style)

Jerry Meyer and Nina Zingale

INGREDIENTS

7-10 ounces green unmarinated olives

or a mix of unmarinated olives *(Arbequinas, Castelveltrano, Picholine, Lugano, Manzanilla, Niçoise, etc.)*

½ teaspoon ground cumin

½ teaspoon oregano

¼ teaspoon rosemary, lightly ground with mortar and pestle to release oils

½ teaspoon fennel seed, lightly ground with mortar and pestle to release oils

2 bay leaves

2 garlic cloves, lightly bruised

4 tablespoons white wine vinegar

Water to fill container

1 2-inch sprig fresh rosemary

INSTRUCTIONS

Pack olives into a clear container filling it close to the brim.

Add the dry ingredients. Pour vinegar into the container, and add enough water to completely cover all of the ingredients. Close the container, and shake vigorously to mix the spices and liquid.

Place the rosemary sprig on the inside of the container as garnish.

Store olives in the refrigerator. They will keep for several months.

Prior to serving, shake vigorously as spices will have settled.

Olives

Someone said, "I believe in you."

FareStart isn't just handing me something but giving me a hand up which I, in turn, can give to other people.

They're not just helping me - they're helping a community that continues to grow and grow and grow.

This started with just one person."

- Paul, 2015 FareStart graduate

Our association to FareStart dates back to the early days when they were on 2nd Avenue. From those beginnings, we helped them raise funds as part of their capital campaign to purchase the building on Virginia. Charlie's contributed significantly in a financial way but also actively told the FareStart story in the community.

FareStart has a great concept of helping individuals down on their luck, giving them the opportunity to train and develop skills, and helping them raise themselves back up. They are the true embodiment of the old proverb:

"Buy a man a fish, and he eats for a day. Teach a man to fish, and you feed him for a lifetime."

> ## The most basic need of humans - besides air and water - is food. Food is our business; it's our life.

Charlie's Produce was started by Charlie, Ray, and Terry in 1978. Originally, they built the business by providing quality, innovative offerings and service to both the retail and food service industries. Today, we are a full-service produce company, supplying restaurants, retailers, healthcare, wholesalers, and the marine industry with a full range of conventional, organic, and specialty produce, floral items, and a huge assortment of fresh-cut produce.

The support of our valued customers over the years has enabled us to grow our business to where it is today. We strive for and value our lasting relationships. Quality and freshness is our goal every day. Our service is second to none. Our core values embody us as an organization. They are uncompromising and endure through time, space, and people. They support our culture, define our character, and guide our decsion-making.

When Charlie and Ray started the business in 1978, they focused on the food service business; restaurants were their clientele. I remember when Charlie and Ray had two trucks. One of them answered the phone, and the other would make deliveries. Charlie's had an early desire to feature the very best quality items with an emphasis on supporting local farms.

Charlie and Ray decided early on that they wanted to be involved in supporting the FareStart mission and cause.

Charlie grew up in a working family environment, and they did not have much. He's always been compelled to help others. He cares deeply about his staff and his employees. He feels like we're a family.

If you look around Seattle, you will see homeless in numbers that we've never seen before. Ten years ago, the homeless were an invisible part of our society. Now, they're visible just about everywhere! I've been with Charlie's for 26 years, and Charlie, Ray, and Terry have always had a deep commitment and obligation to do good within their community. They are humble people, committed to doing their part and doing the right thing.

STUART HOLMES 455

Asparagus

Grilled Asparagus
with Truffle oil and Grana Parmesan

Stuart Holmes

INGREDIENTS

2 pounds asparagus, medium to large size, washed and trimmed

2 to 3 tablespoons extra-virgin olive oil

3 to 4 garlic cloves, finely chopped

Coarse sea salt, to taste

Black pepper, coarsely ground, to taste

¼ cup Parmesan cheese, such as Parmigiano-Reggiano

White or black truffle oil

INSTRUCTIONS

Preheat grill to medium-high heat.

Use a vegetable peeler to produce wide, thin "ribbons" of cheese.

Snap or cut off the tough ends of the asparagus. Place asparagus in a deep-sided square baking pan or sheet. Toss the asparagus with olive oil; add chopped garlic, salt, and pepper.

Place asparagus cross ways to the grill grates, and cook until marked. Turn over, and continue grilling until al dente (approximately 3 minutes total). Remove from grill.

Transfer asparagus to a serving platter, and sprinkle with truffle oil. Top with the parmesan cheese ribbons. Serve immediately.

Jicama, Orange and Avocado Salad

Stuart Holmes

INGREDIENTS

3 oranges

1 teaspoon orange zest

2 tablespoons fresh lime juice

1 tablespoon cider vinegar

2 tablespoons extra-virgin olive oil

Pinch of cayenne pepper

Salt and freshly ground black pepper, to taste

1 pound jicama, peeled, quartered, and thinly sliced

2 Hass avocados, quartered lengthwise and thinly sliced

½ cup crumbled feta cheese

¼ cup chopped cilantro

INSTRUCTIONS

Using a sharp knife, peel the oranges, removing all of the bitter white pith. Working over a small bowl, cut in between the membranes to release the orange sections. Set aside. Squeeze the membranes over a bowl to extract the juice.

Whisk in lime juice, vinegar, oil, cayenne, and all but a pinch of the orange zest; season with salt and pepper. Add jicama, and let stand for 15 minutes. Fold in the orange sections, avocado, feta, and cilantro; top with remaining zest, and serve.

vocado

There's always a tendency, when the tape is running, to exaggerate a story. In my case, the simple truth is that I came into the restaurant business, and my connection with food, by no effort or design of my own.

I really see it as a gift from God.

My first dad was an Air Force pilot who was killed in the Korean War. When I was 8-years-old, my mom moved to Seattle, and I became a Canlis when she met and married widower, Peter Canlis.

Peter had built Canlis Seattle in 1950 and Canlis Hawaii in 1954 and was a dynamic and successful restaurateur. It was fun to be part of a family again. I loved our restaurant: I was proud of it, loved the food, and loved our staff. Like most kids, I wondered what I would "be" when I grew up.

Gradually, I became convinced that restaurant work was not the kind of life I would want. I wanted to do something else, something more exciting.

Right after college, my dad did something wonderful that presaged his love for me and my brother. When my mom decided to divorce him to marry someone else, Peter let her go on the condition she'd let him formally adopt us.

As a kid growing up the way I had in boarding schools, I hadn't seen much of his love and commitment first hand. Now, when I was 21 and was told of the impending divorce, I thought, "Well, here we go again. Who am I? Am I still going to be a Canlis? Do I go back to taking my prior name?" Peter Canlis answered those questions and made his love and commitment clear with my formal adoption.

After college, I joined the Navy and ended up in Pensacola as a Navy pilot. There, I met and married Alice, by far the best decision I ever made.

I also began a journey of discovery about God - who he is and where I fit into his plans. After the military, we lived in the home of Christian missionaries for a year and then, headed off to Stanford Graduate Business School. We eventually settled into a business career in the Bay area.

Then, one day in 1976 when I was 30 years old, everything changed with the news my father had terminal lung cancer.

YOU THINK YOU KNOW WHO YOU ARE AND WHAT YOU WANT TO DO UNTIL SOMEONE YOU LOVE IS FACING DEATH.

Suddenly, we moved to Seattle to join my dad at Canlis.

Before he passed, my dad lived across the street from the restaurant. Alice, our sons, and I moved into the apartment below to be near him and our work. That was a time of really drawing close to him and to Canlis. Before then, he'd been running his restaurants, and we'd been living our life. **Now, we were together every day.**

During those hard months, Dad cooked for Alice and really got to know her and our little boys. He cooked for her because she was pregnant and couldn't be around food due to nausea.

That time forged between us a close bond of connection as we watched him express love to me and my wife in the best way he knew how. After he died in July of 1977, Alice and I, for a period of months, ate the food Dad had cooked and stored in our freezer.

In that way, food and the restaurant became a medium for me finally understanding Dad's love and acceptance.

When my father died, there were four Canlis restaurants, so Alice and I had to decide if restaurants were to be our new way of life. We decided yes, and we became Chris and Alice Canlis of Canlis Restaurants.

Greg Atkinson was the first well known chef we hired, and he had a connection with the city and FareStart. Greg knew our heart and that we would believe in this vision. He suggested that we should put on a Guest Chef dinner at the FareStart restaurant, located in the Josephinum at the time.

Alice and I saw it as "Canlis comes to 'Downtown for a Night.'" We brought in Greg and other Canlis chefs and met with the volunteer staff and talked about service standards. When the time came, Alice and I stood by the front door to greet the guests just like it was Canlis. Gradually, after many such dinners, we drew close to FareStart.

That was around the time when CEO, Megan Karch, and her Board were looking to raise money to move FareStart to a new location. Alice and I were asked to co-chair the capital campaign with Board member, Bill Adamucci.

We had a wonderful experience. It was a flourishing partnership to be around Bill. He was the perfect match for us, and we loved working with this exceptional man.

I think there are three reasons for the success of FareStart.

The first is Megan Karch.

The second is that FareStart's concept is a natural fit for something many people have a heart for but no capacity to engage in. When you live downtown and walk from anywhere to anywhere, you're in contact with people who live on the street all of the time. Some of them are nice people, and some are not - something that's true among everyone, no matter where they live.

I have always had a desire to help the needy - warm them when they're cold, feed them when they're hungry, help them get off the street if they want to. FareStart then came along with an idea of how to accomplish that in a way that's self-sustaining. That's the third reason - how FareStart actually works.

FareStart is well run; they are passionate, and they're sustainably structured.

FareStart and its dedicated staff have almost pioneered the multi-service connection model of an organization that lifts people, literally, from the street.

HUMILITY.

The common trait among people who support FareStart is humility. It's the kind of humility that comes from walking down the street and looking into the eyes of someone destitute and really believing that could be you. It is understanding you were given gifts so that you can give them to others.

FareStart makes it clear to their students that it's a place only for those who commit to being clean and sober. It's a place for individuals willing to take real steps towards showing themselves and the world that they've been given a chance and are willing to make the most of it.

FareStart gives people hope, dignity, and purpose for their lives, letting them see that they have value that they've lost sight.

CHRIS CANLIS

THE CANLIS SALAD

Chris Canlis

INGREDIENTS

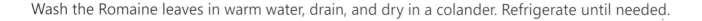

1 large head Romaine hearts, cut into 1-inch squares

½ cup green onion, thinly sliced

¾ cup Romano cheese, freshly grated

¾ cup chopped bacon, cooked

½ cup fresh mint,* thinly sliced

2 tablespoons oregano leaves, thinly sliced

½ cup croutons*

10 cherry tomatoes, halved

Salt and freshly ground black pepper, to taste

Dressing

½ cup olive oil

⅓ cup freshly squeezed lemon juice

¼ teaspoon freshly ground black pepper

1 teaspoon salt

1 coddled egg*

INSTRUCTIONS

Wash the Romaine leaves in warm water, drain, and dry in a colander. Refrigerate until needed.

To make the dressing, put the oil, lemon juice, pepper, salt, and coddled egg in a bowl, and whisk vigorously. Reserve.

In a salad bowl, add the prepared romaine, green onion, cheese, bacon, croutons, oregano, and mint. Pour dressing over salad, and toss thoroughly. Arrange the salad on chilled plates, and finish with cherry tomatoes, and season with salt and pepper, if desired.

Ingredient notes:

*Mint: You can't use too much mint! Experiment for yourself.

*Croutons: It's fun to make your own with cubed baguette, butter, and minced herbs.

*Coddled Egg: Pour boiling water into a cup, and put a whole egg *(in the shell)* into the hot water. Let sit for 1 minute, and then, remove from the water. You may substitute with pasteurized egg mixture *(found in the dairy section in cartons)*.

Tomato

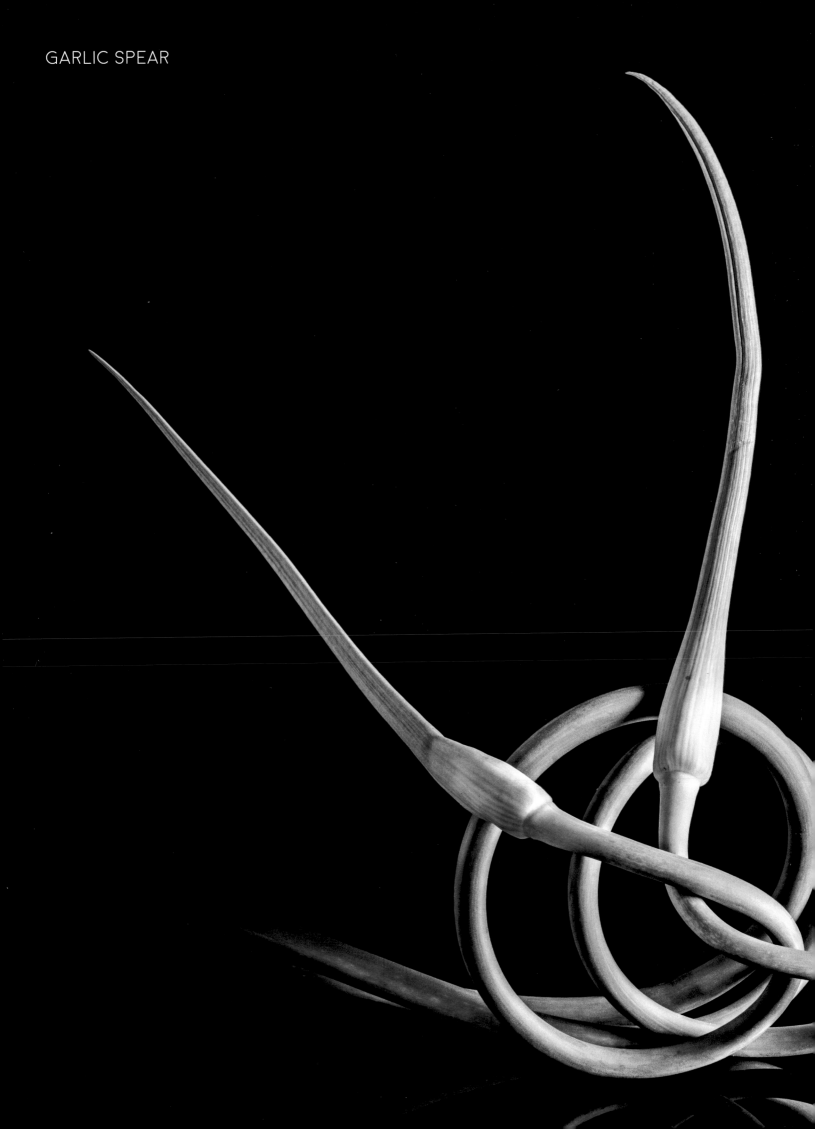

GARLIC SPEAR

"I feel like I am somebody."

- FareStart Barista Student

BONNIE TIBBLES

> ## My mother was raised in New Orleans, born in Kentucky, and my dad came from Broken Bow, Oklahoma. We ate a lot of good food when I was growing up!

My mother and grandmother were my roles models. My son, who is now 62, reminisces about his grandmother and his great grandmother. Those women impressed him so. The things they felt were important they passed on to him.

We had a large number of our family that lived in Spokane Valley for a number of years. Grampa would call around on Friday to let all the families know to meet at Mission Park for a picnic the next day. He didn't have to tell anyone what to bring; we all had our specialties. Mine was au gratin potatoes. My son recently joked with me, **"The only reason I came over for Thanksgiving dinner all those years was for your potatoes."**

Our family came together, ate together, and supported each other.

There was a time in my growing up years when the economy wasn't very good. We ate a lot of red beans and rice or gumbo, but it was good food. Our community life was centered around the church.

I first heard of FareStart through Lillian Hochstein at the Pike Place Market Foundation. I volunteered at the Foundation and came to know her through a family connection who was on the original "Save the Market" group. Lillian was the event manager and had just gotten a job at FareStart as Development Director.

I started volunteering at both the Market and FareStart but soon found I couldn't do both. So, I decided on FareStart.

In those days, we were in the basement of the Josephinum. It was a crummy location with no windows. We ran out of room there, and the development team moved into a tiny apartment space on 2nd Avenue above a whisky bar.

Every day at 4 pm, the cigarette smoke would start to rise through the floorboards. It was something else. But, we got everything done that we needed to do, and we did it well.

The big money drive to get a new building started shortly after. It was to be an epic fundraiser. I heard the Board talking about raising $8 million dollars, and I thought "Good luck guys; that's a lot of money." A few years later, we moved into our new building on Virginia. The person that provided the interior design for the FareStart building was the same person that did this job for Starbucks. He volunteered his time.

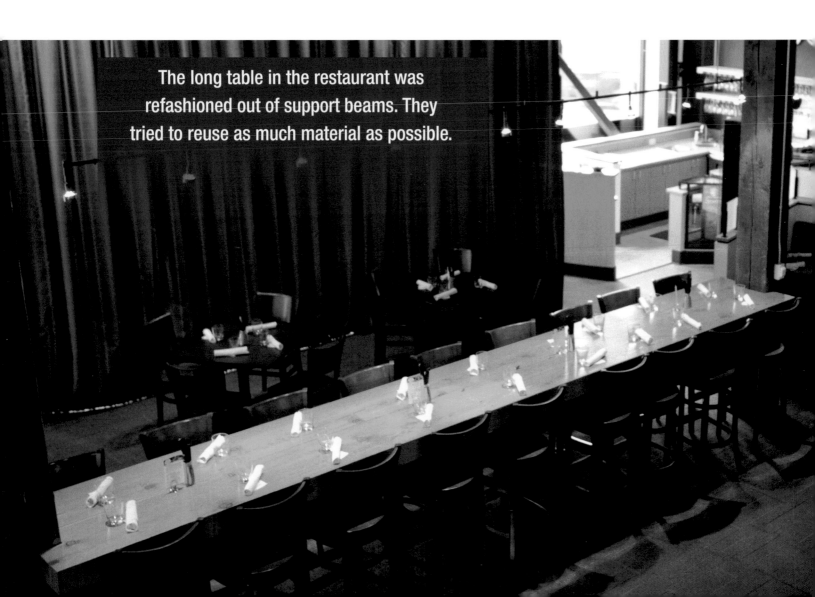

The long table in the restaurant was refashioned out of support beams. They tried to reuse as much material as possible.

At one of the graduation nights, I ran into a student in the elevator. This fellow was going to graduate from the program that night. I asked him how it was going, and he looked at me very seriously and said,

This is one of the best days of my life. Today is my birthday. Tonight, I'm going to graduate. Monday, I have a job to go to. And, I get custody of my little boy back.

The number of people that FareStart has saved...it's unbelievable.

I've been writing handwritten thank you notes to the guest chefs every week for so long now. Many of the chefs would come back a year later, and they remember me. Those that give time and talent - they're good people.

Before my husband passed away, we would come to Guest Chef Night every Thursday, always together. We started that way back when FareStart was on 2nd Avenue. Every morning, he would bring me to work down at FareStart, every evening coming back to collect me.

After all these years, I still really love working here. It's like a family. I am quite a bit older than most of the other staff members. Every once in a while, they forget and call me "Grandma Bonnie."

BONNIE TIBBLES

We got involved with FareStart through Weyerhaeuser. We saw an ad for volunteering at a Guest Chef Night, and this led to volunteering a couple of times a year at special events.

It's a great program, and we love the cause. We haven't stopped volunteering since, and now, we're here almost every week.

FareStart seems to have a different model; they give the homeless everything they need to succeed.

Both of our families are very close knit, and our parents are very active in the community. It's important to us to have a sense of community.

Weyerhaeuser supports employees giving and volunteering, and they have a foundation that supports philanthropy promoting the welfare of human and natural resources. Our senior management team comes into FareStart as volunteers serving tables. It ends up being a humbling experience. The company has a "Making Waves" effort where they match the hours donated.

I had volunteered a lot through my youth group and church. I'd always felt a need to connect with something closer to home, and there's so much need here in Seattle. I'd never known the best way to address homelessness.

It seems just giving money or food doesn't help the individuals get back up on their feet. FareStart seems to have a different model; they give the homeless everything they need to succeed.

Some of my best times have been in the prep kitchen at FareStart, talking to the students and hearing their stories. A lot of times, you don't think you have many commonalities with someone who's been homeless on the street, but when you are cutting vegetables with them, talking about life, you realize you have more in common than you thought. It bridges the gap. The graduations are very memorable.

It's scary how easy it can be to become homeless - all it takes is one small turn.

ANDREW AND ANGELA DODD

Anchovy

Christmas Swedish Meatballs

Andrew and Angela Dodd

INGREDIENTS

1 large or 2 small onions, minced

Butter to cook onions

8 anchovy fillets, minced

⅓ cup breadcrumbs

¾ cup milk

6 twists of white pepper from mill

1 teaspoon ground allspice

½ teaspoon ground cloves

10 ounces ground pork

1½ pounds ground beef

1 tablespoon salt

3 eggs

3 tablespoons corn syrup

Olive oil and butter for frying meatballs

INSTRUCTIONS

Melt butter in saucepan. Add onions and cook until soft but not brown. Add anchovies, letting them "melt" into the onions. Let cool.

Soak the breadcrumbs in milk; when soft, add pepper, allspice, and cloves.

Mix the ground pork, beef, and salt. Add eggs, onion mixture, breadcrumb-milk mixture, and corn syrup.

Make a trial meatball, and fry in a combination of olive oil and butter. Taste, and correct seasoning, if necessary.

Roll small meatballs, and fry carefully, shaking pan to brown evenly on all sides.

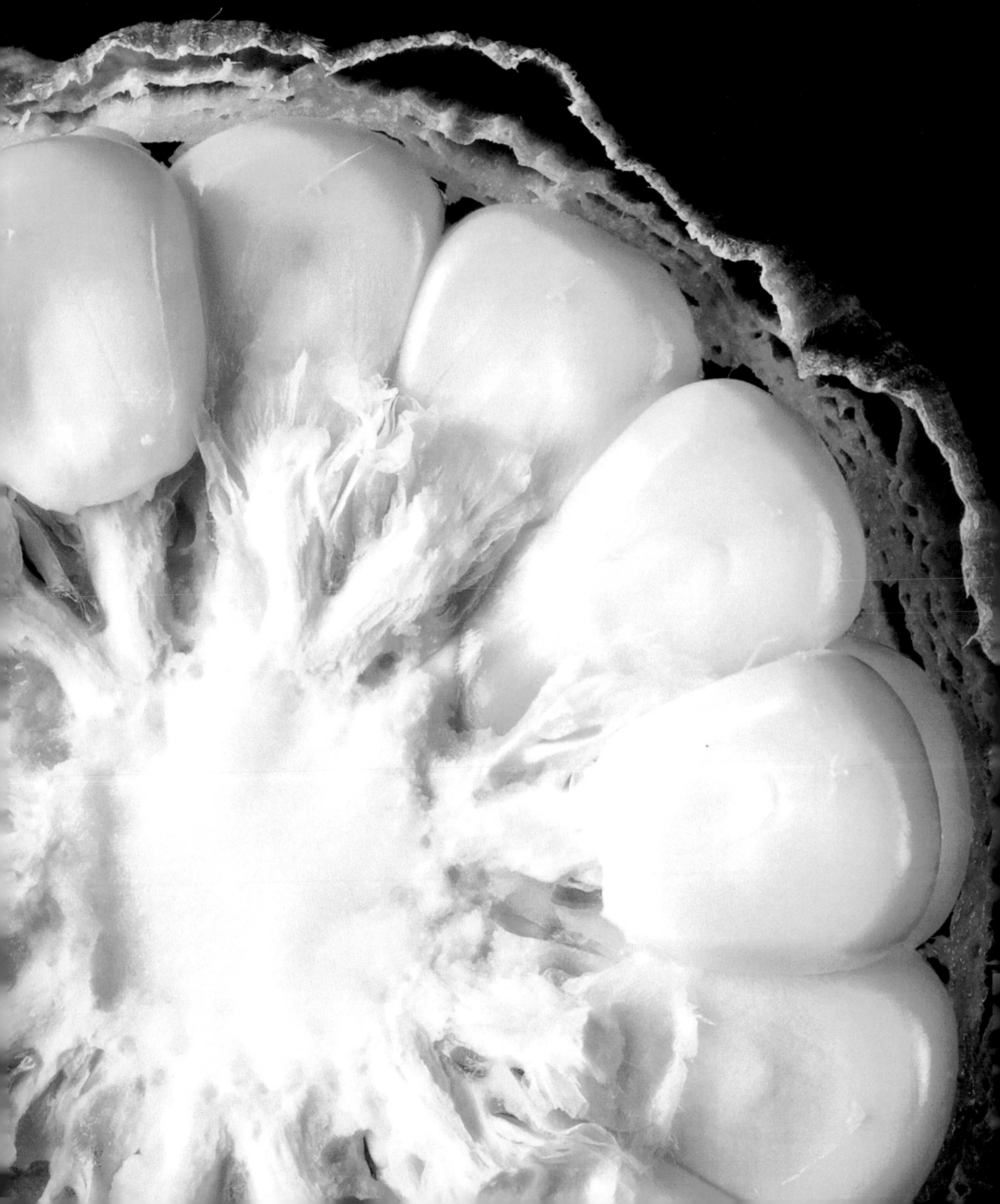

"From the second that I walked through the doors of FareStart, I just felt nothing less than blessed every second that followed.

With an amazing staff and the dedicated chefs...it really has done a lot to put me on that path, which prepared me for the next level of success.

FareStart - *it really lives up to its name.*"

- Tyree, FareStart Graduate

MICROSOFT

Microsoft Philanthropies is a great team, and we're optimistic in our work. I love the whole idea of FareStart because it enables us to take care of immediate needs while at the same time preparing people for employability. Microsoft transforms lives through technology. FareStart transforms lives though culinary and life skills programs. We both enable transformation.

You may only see the one person's life that you changed, but you might also change a thousand others that you don't see.

All you have to do is believe that you can make a difference.

The Microsoft Philanthropies team was created to bring the benefits of technology to those who need it most. By investing the company's strongest assets - technology, money, employee talent, and the company's voice - in partnerships with nonprofits and communities, we can create a lasting, positive impact.

We've challenged ourselves to think holistically about the contribution we can make and ask how we can truly bring to life the promise and potential of technology for everyone. We strive to bridge gaps within and across communities through more widespread access to internet connectivity, technology, and digital skills that enhance the productivity and quality of life for people and organizations who have been underserved.

We're building on the foundation of Microsoft's 30+ years of giving and the insights from our own employees and many of our valued nonprofit partners around the world. Microsoft's total annual giving, including both cash and the fair market value of our software, has now surpassed $1 billion.

I love this job; it is great to be leading Microsoft's Philanthropies team in a company like ours. We can have a such a high level of impact.

Both of my parents were very involved in the community. I grew up in a small town in Kansas, and almost every night my parents were volunteering. My father delivered "meals on wheels" to seniors for decades - even into his eighties! **My desire to help comes from that sensibility.**

My mother was a really good cook, and my grandmother an extraordinary one. Some of their recipes were handed down to me, and one of my favorites is my Grandma Glotzbach's Oatmeal Cake.

I love cooking and scour magazines, newspapers, and online content for new things to try. I have a recipe for jambalaya that I modified towards a healthier lifestyle. It includes sautéed soy tofu, instead of the sausage, and fish, instead of the chicken.

One of the simplest recipes that I make is a rhubarb crisp. My dad always grew rhubarb in a very large vegetable garden, and as kids we made pocket money helping tend the garden and peddling the extra produce to our neighbors. My mother made pies, crisps, and preserves from the rhubarb we grew. Now, I grow my own rhubarb and bake rhubarb crisp for my kids.

Garlic

Jambalaya

Mary Snapp

INGREDIENTS

4 tablespoons olive oil

1 cup soy sausages, diced

1 cup bay scallops

1½ cups onion, chopped

1½ cups celery, chopped

1 red bell pepper, seeded and chopped

1 green bell pepper, seeded and chopped

1½ teaspoons garlic, minced

Seasoning mix

2 cups uncooked rice

3½ cups vegetable broth

1 14-ounce can stewed whole tomatoes

8 ounces cherry tomatoes, halved

12 medium-sized uncooked shrimp, peeled

Seasoning Mix

4 small bay leaves

1 teaspoon salt

1 teaspoon white pepper

1 teaspoon dry mustard

½ teaspoon cayenne pepper *(more if desired)*

½ teaspoon ground cumin

½ teaspoon black pepper

½ teaspoon dried thyme

Combine all ingredients in a small dish.

INSTRUCTIONS

In a large heavy pot or skillet, heat the olive oil over high heat. Add soy sausage and scallops, and cook for 5 minutes, browning slightly. Remove from skillet, and set aside. Add the onions, celery, garlic, bell peppers, and seasoning mix to the skillet. Stir well, and cook until onions are soft and slightly browned, about 10 minutes.

Stir in rice, and cook 5 minutes, stirring and scraping bottom of pan occasionally. Add the broth, canned tomatoes (including liquid), and fresh tomatoes, stir well, and cook for about 20 minutes. The rice will be slightly crunchy. Add more liquid if needed. Return soy sausage and scallops to skillet. Add shrimp, and cook until they turn pink, about 5 minutes.

RHUBARB AND BLUEBERRY CRISP

Mary Snapp

INGREDIENTS

⅔ cup granulated sugar

2-3 teaspoons corn starch

¼ teaspoon ground cinnamon

2½ cups fresh or frozen sliced rhubarb *(if frozen, use unsweetened and thaw)*

1½ cups coarsely chopped fresh or frozen blueberries

2 tablespoons fresh basil leaves, julienned

Topping:

½ cup whole wheat flour

½ cup quick-cooking rolled oats

⅓ cup packed brown sugar

¼ teaspoon salt

5 tablespoons butter, melted

INSTRUCTIONS

Preheat oven to 375 degrees F. In a medium mixing bowl, stir granulated sugar, cornstarch (for fresh rhubarb, use 2 teaspoons; for frozen rhubarb, use 3 teaspoons), and cinnamon together. Stir in rhubarb, blueberries, and basil. Spread fruit mixture evenly in a 10-inch pie plate or an 8-inch square pan. Set aside.

To make the topping, in a medium bowl, stir flour, oats, brown sugar, and salt together. Stir in melted butter. Sprinkle evenly onto fruit mixture.

Bake in preheated oven for 30-35 minutes, or until fruit is tender and bubbling, and topping is golden brown. Serve warm.

Blueberry

Coconut

GRANDMA GLOTZBACH'S OATMEAL CAKE

Mary Snapp

INGREDIENTS

●

1¼ cups boiling water

1 cup quick cooking oatmeal

1 cup brown sugar

½ cup shortening

1 cup white sugar

1 teaspoon vanilla

2 eggs

1½ cups flour

1 teaspoon baking soda

½ teaspoon salt

½ teaspoon nutmeg

½ teaspoon cinnamon

Topping:

6 tablespoons butter, melted

¼ cup cream or half and half

½ cup brown sugar

1 cup coconut

½ cup chopped walnuts or rice krispies

INSTRUCTIONS

●

Preheat oven to 350 degrees F.

Mix boiling water and oats together, and let stand for 30 minutes.

Cream sugars, shortening, and vanilla together. Add eggs, and beat well. Add oatmeal mixture.

Sift together flour, baking soda, salt, nutmeg, and cinnamon. Add to sugar mixture.

Spread evenly in a 9 by 5-inch greased loaf pan, and bake 45 minutes.

Mix all topping ingredients together. Spread topping onto the cake while it's warm.

I started working with FareStart as a volunteer. I knew Barbara Reed Hill, who was Director of Programs at the time, from my days at Starbucks. I originally came in as a volunteer to develop a 5-year strategic plan. This gave me my introduction to the staff, the FareStart Board, and Cheryl, who was Executive Director at the time.

The strategic plan was the first formal long-range planning session ever undertaken. To me, it was everything that I loved, both as a business person and as a social activist.

I USED TO JOKE THAT FARESTART APPEALS TO BOTH SIDES OF THE AISLE - THE DEMOCRATS LOVE THE FACT IT'S HELPING PEOPLE AND THE REPUBLICANS LOVE THAT THERE'S A SELF-SUPPORTING BUSINESS COMPONENT TO IT.

The other thing that happened, simultaneously to my interaction with FareStart, was my wife and I were teaching a class at our local church regarding the story of the Good Samaritan. I was trying to normalize it to the experience in Seattle and the people on the streets downtown.

I asked the kids if they saw a homeless person, would they be the good Samaritan and stop to help? And, the answer we got was,

"Oh no. Those people want to be there. They do drugs. They drink. They're bad. They're dirty. They're less than human."

Both my wife and I were thinking, "This didn't exactly go the way we wanted it to." This was the "us and them" stereotype in action, and these kids simply could not make a connection to the homeless as human. FareStart helps people make that connection.

GJ

I love the fact that FareStart is about food!

As a Board, we've spent a lot of time over the years contemplating alternatives to food being the base of our training experience. Every single time we debate this, we come back to the fact that food, preparing and converting raw material into something nutritious, creates the nurturing environment and provides an experience that allows reconnection.

WE'VE BUILT A COMMUNITY ALLOWING PEOPLE TO COME IN AND RECOGNIZE OPPORTUNITIES IN THEIR LIVES, TO RECOVER FROM CHALLENGES, AND BECOME CONTRIBUTING MEMBERS OF OUR SOCIETY. WE EXPECT THEM TO CONTRIBUTE TO THE PROCESS OF TRANSFORMATION.

But, FareStart in no way transforms anyone's life. We build a community that enables people to *transform their own lives.*

It's not enough for the student to just have one safe place to go. Our job is not done the day they graduate. Graduation is a beginning not an end. The students that graduate make a huge contribution in modeling the behavior required to transform.

I was fortunate to grow up in a family that modeled being a part of the community. In my home life, my folks talked about and acted in accordance with their beliefs. I watch them today still being an active part of their community, still making a difference.

FareStart is a social business, and you always have to think about those two words when you think about the organization.

We have the privilege to be able to measure our success not purely based on business principles, like return on investment. We are constantly challenged with balancing the double bottom line, asking if we are truly creating impact with every decision we make.

GJ

We've had broad range discussion regarding the definition of self-sufficiency. If I'm a person earning $25,000 a year relying on government assistance, and I know how to access and utilize that assistance, am I as self-sufficient as someone earning $200,000 a year and receiving a subsidy from the government in the form of a mortgage tax reduction? **I think so.**

I continue to be amazed by the generosity of the human beings that come in contact with FareStart. We are unbelievably fortunate to receive the trust that people place in us to effectively invest their money in the strategies we believe are the right ones to provide this transformational community.

EVERY TIME I GO TO A GUEST CHEF NIGHT AND HEAR THE STORIES, I CRY. AND, I'VE BEING GOING FOR 20 YEARS.

GREGG JOHNSON

gratitude
Andrew

Tina Koyama, Artist

Egg

Buttermilk Pie

Gregg Johnson

INGREDIENTS

3 eggs

1½ cups sugar

2 tablespoons flour

½ cup butter

½ cup buttermilk

1 pinch salt

1 teaspoon almond extract

1 9-inch unbaked pie shell

INSTRUCTIONS

Melt butter in microwave. Allow to cool.
Beat eggs, sugar, and flour together in a
blender. Add melted butter, buttermilk, salt,
and almond extract. Blend on high speed
for two minutes.

NOTE: You CANNOT overbeat!

Pour into pie shell. Bake at 350 degrees F
for 40 minutes.

Zita's Meat Marinade
(Flank Steak)

Gregg Johnson

INGREDIENTS

½ cup red wine vinegar

½ cup olive oil

1 onion

2 garlic cloves

1 tablespoon oregano

1 tablespoon salt

1 teaspoon thyme

1 teaspoon basil

1 teaspoon sage

1 teaspoon coriander

1 flank steak

INSTRUCTIONS

Blend all ingredients, and pour over flank steak. Marinate 24 hours.

Grill approximately 10 minutes.

Let rest 5 minutes. Slice opposite of grain, and serve.

n

In our hometown of Seattle,
a passion for community is
at the heart of Starbucks
Barista Training Program.

FROM THE BEGINNING, STARBUCKS CHAIRMAN AND CEO HOWARD SCHULTZ, TOGETHER WITH OTHER COMPANY LEADERS CREATED A SET OF VALUES THAT INCLUDED THE INTENT TO INSPIRE AND NURTURE THE HUMAN SPIRIT. THOSE WORDS ARE STILL AT THE HEART OF THE STARBUCKS MISSION STATEMENT.

It's not uncommon to hear Howard talk about the social responsibility of a public, for-profit company and it goes beyond just the business – it's in our DNA. We believe strongly that you can't disconnect the two; **you can't have a healthy business if you're not involved in the community.**

Early on there was a natural fit between Starbucks and FareStart. We saw an organization that not only addressed nutritional needs, but also helped create an environment that allowed transformation of lives. In fact, some of the early FareStart Board members included leaders from Starbucks. Gregg Johnson, a current Board member, was my first boss and he was the one that introduced me to the FareStart mission.

That said, Starbucks connection with FareStart goes much deeper than board involvement and we're proud that our partners (employees) offer time and talent in a number of ways.

Our local field partners participate in volunteer opportunities and work with the youth in the youth barista program. Our teams also attend Farestart's Guest Chef Nights and our Food Service teams have supplied coffee equipment, as well as coffee and tea for more than 15 years.

We're also proud to make in-kind donations, help with interviews, resume writing, and job and life skill training support. **In fact, the restaurant on Virginia Street was designed by a Starbucks partner on their own time.** We also make sure that our partners know about the amazing work at FareStart by hosting educational immersions with Megan Karch, FareStart's CEO at our Seattle headquarters and by offering partners volunteer opportunities to serve at the FareStart restaurant.

The relationship Starbucks has had with FareStart over the course of the last twelve years has also influenced how we think about investing in communities around the world, using our scale for good.

One result from this was creating the connection between YouthCare – an organization that provides life skills coaching, resume and job search support as well as connections to other critical services – with FareStart to establish the Barista Training Program.

By joining the non-profits we were able to grow the impact and while some graduates found jobs with Starbucks, others secured opportunities with retailers, coffee shops and small businesses.

While I feel lucky to be a part of the Board, my relationship to this organization goes even deeper than Starbucks.

Having spent about 20 years of my career in the restaurant business, doing everything from cleaning dishes to bartending to running restaurants, **I feel a personal connection to this work.**

It's incredible to see the Farestart restaurant in action and how they approach the quality of the food, the menu and the care of the staff.

But that is just the beginning. I am most proud of working with this organization when we can help the graduating students turn their lives around.

IT IS AMAZING WHAT PEOPLE ARE CAPABLE OF WHEN THEY ARE GIVEN THE OPPORTUNITY AND I THINK IT IS THE MOST MEANINGFUL PART OF WHAT FARESTART IS ABLE TO DO.

A great example of this came from a young woman who spoke at a Guest Chef Night and described an interaction she had with a boss who wanted to know how she was doing. The question had taken her off guard and she snapped back with a response not realizing his intention had been genuine.

Building simple connections with others wasn't something she was familiar with and for this young woman, who had lived on the streets, establishing interpersonal skills and truly connecting with others in her community was just as important as learning the technical job skills.

That's what's so special about FareStart and their training programs – it provides participants with the tools to develop both.

My personal involvement with FareStart has become an opportunity to serve my community here at home and lend my leadership to an organization I am very passionate about.

Being involved with FareStart is not a corporate mandate.

It's just the right thing to do.

CRAIG RUSSELL

TANGY ASIAN NOODLE SALAD

Craig Russell

INGREDIENTS

1 pound Chinese egg noodles *(if unavailable, you can substitute spaghetti noodles)*

4 medium carrots, grated

2 medium zucchinis, grated

8 ounces mushrooms, sliced

8 ounces sesame oil

8 ounces soy sauce

½ cup rice vinegar

½ cup sugar

1 ounce chili oil

¼ cup sesame seeds

3 green onions *(optional)*

INSTRUCTIONS

Prepare noodles according to package instructions, and simmer until tender. Remove from heat, and rinse immediately in cold water.

Combine sugar, vinegar, and soy sauce in bowl, and stir until sugar dissolves. Drizzle sesame oil and chili oil into mixture, and whisk to emulsify. Add dressing to noodles, stir, and refrigerate at least 3 hours *(overnight is best)*.

Stir in carrots, zucchini, and mushrooms. Garnish with sesame seeds and sliced green onions, if desired.

cchini

GRILLED CHIPOTLE CORN

Craig Russell

INGREDIENTS

4 large ears of corn

1 cup cream

2 chipotles in adobo sauce, seeded and finely chopped

2 teaspoons adobo sauce from can

Zest of 1 lime

¾ cup queso fresco or cotija cheese

½ teaspoons dried oregano

2 scallions, finely chopped

¼ cup cilantro, finely chopped

Lime juice, to taste

INSTRUCTIONS

Preheat the grill or grill pan to medium high. Grill the corn until kernels are evenly charred. Remove from heat, let cool slightly, and cut from cob.

In a small sauce pan over low heat, combine the cream, chipotle peppers, adobo sauce, and lime zest, and gently simmer until thickened and the flavors have come together, about 15 minutes. Reserve, and keep warm.

While cream is reducing, combine cheeses, oregano, scallions, and cilantro in a small bowl. Set aside.

Drizzle the chipotle cream sauce and cheese mixture over the corn, and serve with a squeeze of lime juice.

Consider doubling the batch and using the leftovers in taco salad or tacos.

ime

When you impact one life,
you impact many;
when you impact many lives,
you impact your community.

MEGAN KARCH, FARESTART CEO

ACKNOWLE

DGEMENTS

ERICA & COLIN McCAIG

VOLUNTEERS

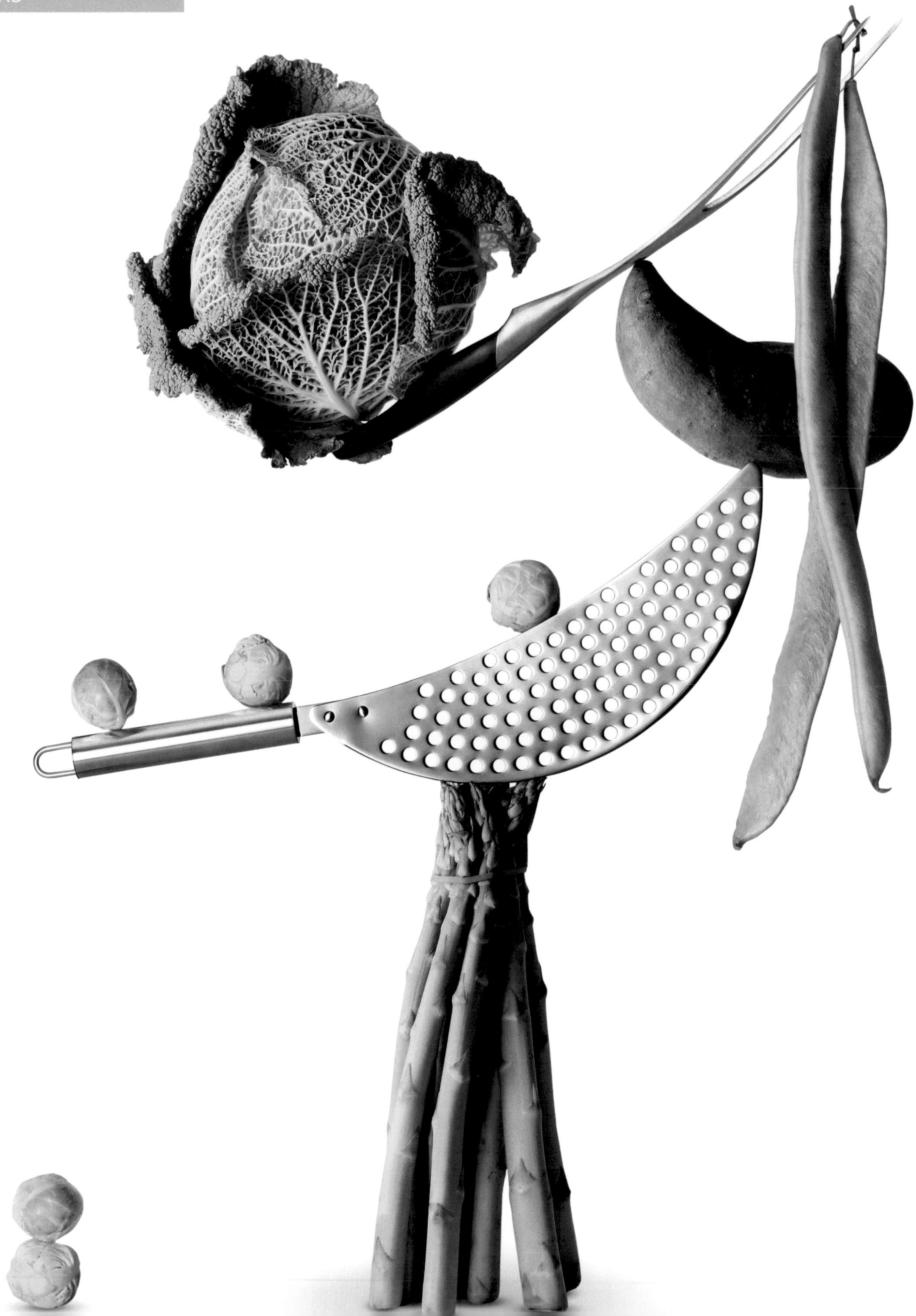

FareStart touched our lives many years ago when we attended a Guest Chef Night. We were looking to find a partner for our philanthropic program, *The Microsoft Cookbook.*

After that evening, we knew we had found the perfect match. Now, several Cookbooks later, we still find ourselves humbled by FareStart's dedication and impact on our community.

As in any journey of passion, building this book has been a transformative experience for both of us, bringing a better understanding of what it takes to make a difference in our community and what it means to be socially responsible. After all of the interviews that we conducted and stories that we heard, we realized we are all more similar than we are different.

We'd like to thank the many individuals that contributed their stories and recipes to this book, bringing together a unique opportunity to tell the FareStart "love story." Thanks also to the team at FareStart, extended team, and book sponsors that made this endeavor a reality. Every page of this book was created through volunteer hours.

Finally, we have a special thanks to the best editor on the planet, our friend and supporter, Liberty Munson.

We hope you enjoy this book as much as we did in creating it.

Erica and Colin McCaig

ACKNOWLEDGEMENTS

THANK YOU...

PROJECT TEAM

Juhee Ahmed

Ilana Bergen

Natasha Doyle

Joyce Halldorson

Megan Hampson

Theresa L. Klaassen

Michelle McDaniel

Liberty Munson

Stephanie Schoo

ARTISTS

Ashley Cecil

Tina Koyama

BOOK SPONSORS

Charlie's Produce

Continental Mills

Microsoft

Starbucks

PHOTOGRAPHERS

Brian Canlis

Clare Barboza

Erica McCaig

Frank Huster

Joe Mabel

Nicholas Prior

Renata Steiner

GUEST CHEFS

Chef Ericka Burke, Volunteer Park Café, Chop Shop Café & Bar

Chef Kim Cosway, FareStart Restaurant

Chef Don Curtiss, Assaggio Ristorante

Chef Kaspar Donier, Kaspar's Special Events

Chef Tom Douglas, Tom Douglas Seattle Kitchen

Chef Lisa Dupar, Lisa Dupar Catering, Pomegranate Bistro

Chef Mauro Golmarvi, Assaggio Ristorante

Chef Gary Haller, FareStart Restaurant

Chef John Howie, John Howie Restaurant Group

Chef Matt Janke, Lecosho

Chef Joseph E. Jimenez de Jimenez, S & J International Gastronomy

Chef Wayne Johnson, FareStart Restaurant

Chef Chris Keff, Argosy Cruises

Chef David Lee, Field Roast Grain Meat Company

Chef Amy McCray, Tilikum Place Café

Chef Brendan McGill, Hitchcock Group

Chef Nikol Nakamura, Tulalip Resort Casino

Chef Jeff O'Brien, Formerly with the Washington State Convention Center

Chef Dimitri Ponomarchuk, Continental Mills

Chef Thierry Rautureau, The Chef In The Hat, Loulay Kitchen & Bar, Luc

Chef Robert Spaulding, Elliott's Oyster House

Chef Ethan Stowell, Ethan Stowell Restaurants